G Covenant Journey

Understanding the Bible story through a historic, covenantal and Kingdom lens

David Duncan

God's Covenant Journey
*Understanding the Bible story
through a historic, covenantal
and Kingdom lens*

By David Duncan

© Copyright 2016

Unless otherwise indicated, all Scripture quotations are from the Holy Bible, New International Version.

Table of Contents:

Endorsements

A reformation is taking place in the church. A tide of New Covenant / Kingdom teaching is reaching the shores of believers across the globe.

In writing *God's Covenant Journey*, David Duncan significantly assists in understanding how the present kingdom works through the New Covenant. I like his title. It is God's journey. It has been God's desire and dream for people on earth to walk with Him as a family and express His love and grace to all creation. It is also our journey.

For those raised by 'Evangelical traditions', our path begins with a change of mind. This book will both challenge your present doctrines and inspire you to begin your new journey. Duncan provides a pleura of Scripture, information and conclusions which will take several readings to comprehend.

This book is not for the lazy ones or for Christians who only want to hear religious stories and be inspired. If you love God's Word, you are holding in your hand a book which goes deep and is vast in its treatment of Scriptural concepts. *God's Covenant Journey* is a book not just to be read, but studied.

I love how Duncan successfully unites two themes - covenant and kingdom eschatology. This book is a rich deposit of truth - truth which will set you free and on a new way of living. I hope this book has a large audience. Its message needs to be heard. Thank you, David Duncan, for this contribution to Better Covenant Theology.

Dr. Stan Newton
President / Kingdom Missions
Missionary to Bulgaria
Author / *Glorious Kingdom* and *Glorious Covenant*

David Duncan's new book is jam-packed with insights and truth. The material in this book will rock you to your foundations and challenge you to a deeper relationship with the beautiful Father God that David presents. Typically you would have to read 1000 pages to get what David will give you in 200!

Dr. Jonathan Welton
Best-Selling Author and President of Welton Academy

A Related Gratitude Statement by the Author

As the author of this book, I'd like to expressly thank Dr. Jonathan Welton in this endorsement section. Having been through 3 years of Welton Academy as a student myself, I have first heard about many of the concepts in this book from the writings and teachings of Dr. Jonathan.

I have added a number of my own concepts as well, of course - things I feel the Lord has shown me personally.

As I do on many occasions within the book itself, I'd like to credit the following specific writings of Dr. Welton: *Understanding the Whole Bible*, *Raptureless*, *The Advancing Kingdom*, and *Understanding the Seven Churches of Revelation*, as well as many Internet Blogs, which I have quoted throughout, as source materials. Thank You, Dr. Welton!

David Duncan

Introduction:

I would hope this book would find its way into the halls of Better Covenant Theology teaching. Better Covenant Theology (BCT) is a term and a hermeneutic for understanding the Bible, from a covenant/Kingdom perspective, which incorporates into its system historical context. Historical context causes one to know the difference in what was spoken to the original audience and what is meant for us to understand and gain wisdom from.

You and I were not the target or original audience for anything that was written by any of the writers of the old or New Testaments. Each author, who ultimately is the Holy Spirit, had as their target a specific group of people living in a specific time in history.

There is certainly application that we gain from the Scriptures, but it is important to understand that we, ourselves, were not the target audience to the things written in the Bible. We have the advantage of living at least 2000 years after it was written, with historical records to connect many things in the Scriptures. Without the advantage of knowing history, the Bible can be a strange book indeed. This is why historical context is key to understanding the Bible.

The information in this book should be used for sermons, teachings, classes and any other use that Christians may grow in Christ and understand the Bible in ways they have never understood before. I do not mind if you teach and expand on this material once you understand it. This is a piece of the New Covenant unfolding to us.

Another key to understanding the Bible is to understand covenant. Covenant has many facets, from the cutting of the covenant, the blood sacrifice used, the benefits, rules or stipulations associated with the covenant, and the goals of each party involved in the covenant. God is a God of covenant, and He seeks to operate with humanity through covenant. In fact, it can be said of the Bible, that is the written record of the covenant journey of God with mankind.

When God set Adam in place that was not necessarily a covenant, but rather, "original mandate". It's the foundational design of God's plan, which is to give man dominion over His works, and then rule with man on the Earth, with Heaven's connection; Heaven and Earth being as one, which is the goal of the Kingdom of God.

Because of sin, God then made a covenant with Noah and his 3 sons. After that, God made a covenant with Abraham, then Moses and Israel, who are the physical seed of Abraham. Within the midst of that journey, God makes a covenant with a shepherd-king named David. David's covenant becomes the foundational covenant for the Kingdom of God.

Abraham's covenant, along with David's, becomes the springboard for the New Covenant and Kingdom of God. Jesus is the New Covenant King, Lord, Savior, Lamb, High Priest, Husband and Almighty God. Jesus is the expression and way to the Father. The Father's heart of love is what God has always wanted to be revealed among humanity.

These are the things we will learn about, within each covenant, and how God was at work to reveal Himself and His plan for the days we experience today. The fullness of the grace message and identity message is that we fully understand the New Covenant, which must be shown against God's previous covenants in the Bible.

According to Dr. Jonathan Welton (President of Welton Academy, Apostle, Teacher, Seer, and Author), the foundational understanding of this system called Better Covenant Theology (BCT) is as follows:

Introducing: Better Covenant Theology (BCT), based on Hebrews 8:6: "But now He has obtained a more excellent ministry, by as much as He is also the mediator of a better covenant, which has been enacted on better promises."

The defining characteristics are:

1. Jesus' birth fulfilled the Abrahamic covenant (and some of the Davidic covenant).

2. Jesus' death created the New Covenant (at the Cross, there was no substitution, no punishment, and no wrath).

3. The New Covenant is between the Father and the Son (We receive the benefits by marriage to Christ. The two become one as we are united with Christ).

4. His ascension/enthronement fulfilled the Davidic Kingdom promises.

5. The destruction of 70 AD removed the Old Covenant finally and fulfilled Hebrews 8:13.

6. Between the Cross and 70 AD, there was a 40-year covenant transition for the Church.

7. The Old Covenant and the New Covenant co-existed for forty years (30-70 AD).

8. The "End of the Age" and the "Last Days" are first century references to the last days of the Old Covenant and the end of the Old Covenant age.

9. There remains no application of the Mosaic Kinship/Vassal Covenants. The feasts, Sabbaths, Civil laws, ceremonial, and moral laws are done away with.

10. The Law of the New Covenant is "Love one another as I have loved you."

Along with this, another topic of importance to understand is "The Finished Work of Jesus", related to His first coming. "Finished Work" is a big phrase used in the Grace Movement. By the way, I love the Grace Movement, but they need to embrace Kingdom eschatology, rather than a dispensational eschatology. The finished work of Jesus is actually, sevenfold, as follows:

1. His birth (The fulfillment of the Seed promises made to Abraham and David).

2. His death on the Cross in 30 AD (establishing the New Covenant in His own blood).

3. His trip to hades to get the keys of death and hades.

4. His Resurrection (bringing about the new creation).

5. His ascension to Heaven and enthronement at the right hand of the Father.

6. His outpouring of the Holy Spirit from the throne of grace (the Kingdom here).

7. His "coming on the clouds of Heaven, in the Spirit, through the events of the destruction of Jerusalem in 70 AD. (This was the key of David at work, to open the New Covenant and close up the Old Covenant).

This is the complete, finished work of Jesus, related to His first coming. It began at His birth and ended at the destruction of Jerusalem in 70 AD.

The Bible is rarely meant to be read as "what does this mean to you?" There are probably some of the proverbs that can be understood in very personal ways, but most of the Bible is written with a covenantal, historical context in mind. It was written, mostly to Hebrew people who had a physical lineage to Abraham. We, as Gentiles, are grafted into the beautiful Messianic promises concerning life and the Kingdom of God.

We shall begin the book with the original mandate of Adam and Eve.

Chapter One
Original mandate

The history of man or of God with man begins in the book of Genesis. Believing that God is eternal, it follows that a lot of time has passed between ages past and the creation story.

Now we arrive at God creating everything, and our history begins. I do not believe there was a creation before Adam, but I could be wrong. I do not find that evidence in the Bible. So, I believe Adam and Eve are the first humans put on Earth, and from them come all people, at least until the flood. After the flood, it was Noah's 3 sons and their wives who began the repopulation of the Earth.

The story of Adam and Eve is the original mandate. A marriage between a man and woman, united to God, and given dominion to rule with God as they are fruitful and multiply. In the case of the Garden, Adam and Eve were the married couple, given dominion together and with God to rule the world. The goal of this original mandate is spelled out at the end of the story, in Revelation:

"Now the dwelling of God is with human beings, and he will live with them. They will be his people, and God himself will be with them and be their God" (Revelation 21:3).

When I read the Genesis story of the Garden, I find something interesting. Actually, we have to go to the book of Ezekiel to learn something extra about the Garden. Eden was actually a mountain!

You were in Eden, the garden of God; every precious stone adorned you: carnelian, chrysolite and emerald, topaz, onyx and jasper, lapis lazuli, turquoise and beryl. Your settings and mountings were made of gold; on the day you were created they were prepared. You were anointed as a guardian cherub, for so I ordained you. You were on the holy mount of God; you walked among the fiery stones. (Ezekiel 28:13-14)

Now lets look at how Genesis frames the words about the Garden:

Now the Lord God had planted a garden in the east, in Eden; and there he put the man he had formed. The Lord God made all kinds of trees grow out of the ground - trees that were pleasing to the eye and good for food. In the middle of the garden were the tree of life and the tree of the knowledge of good and evil. A river watering the garden flowed from Eden; from there it was separated into four headwaters. (Genesis 2:8-10)

The Lord God took the man and put him in the Garden of Eden to work it and take care of it. (Genesis 2:15)

Based on the Scriptures in Ezekiel and Genesis, Eden was a mountain, I suspect, where the throne of God rested. A river went forth from the throne, as in Revelation, and this river went out of Eden's mountain toward the east to water the Garden.

The Garden was located eastward of the mountain, or throne of God. The river flowed from the mountaintop, from the throne, and down the mountain to the Garden. When the river reached the Garden, it split into four heads, to water the whole Earth. Adam's job was to manage all of this.

From a Kingdom perspective, the river from God's throne was to pass through Adam's garden and then water the whole Earth. This is the idea of the Kingdom of God advancing forth from God to cover the whole Earth.

In our case, it's Heaven's Kingdom coming forth from the throne to expand throughout the entire Earth. We even have "rivers of living waters" by the Holy Spirit flowing forth from our inner most being.

Whoever believes in me, as Scripture has said, rivers of living water will flow from within them. (John 7:38)

With that foundation laid, let's now look at an episode in the Garden, before the fall.

Then God said, "Let us make mankind in our image, in our likeness, so that they may rule over the fish in the sea and the birds in the sky, over the livestock and all the wild animals, and over all the creatures that move along the ground." So God created mankind in his own image, in the image of God he created them; male and female he created them. (Genesis 1:26-27)

Now the serpent was more crafty than any of the wild animals the Lord God had made. He said to the woman, "Did God really say, 'You must not eat from any tree in the garden'?" The woman said to the serpent, "We may eat fruit from the trees in the garden, but God did say, 'You must not eat fruit from the tree that is in the middle of the garden, and you must not touch it, or you will die.'" "You will not certainly die," the serpent said to the woman. "For God knows that when you eat from it your eyes will be opened, and you will be like God, knowing good and evil." (Genesis 3:1-5)

Concerning original mandate, Satan also has an original way of tempting and causing one to sin. He challenges our identity, even as he did with Eve. Eve was already made in the likeness and image of God, yet Satan challenged her to eat the fruit so she could be like God. Her response could have been, "I am already like God. I don't have to eat anything to be more like Him." This is an important lesson to learn about our own identity. Who are we in Christ?

We will cover this more in future chapters, but we are children of God, the righteousness of God, made perfect and holy, in love, in His sight. We are perfectly forgiven and redeemed, and awaiting our own bodily resurrection. Yet, we can be challenged to do things in order to remove guilt, and create self-worth, in order to be pleasing to God, rather than just resting in our righteous identity in Christ. We are well pleasing to the Father because of the finished work of Jesus and our faith in Him. This is the "faith of Jesus" that the Bible talks about.

Of course we must learn to live up to our identity in daily life, but the first battle is in what we believe about God's heart and about ourselves concerning our standing in Christ. We must answer the questions, "are we sinners when we sin as Christians or are we always the righteousness of God in Christ?"

Jesus, too, was challenged with His identity, even though He had no sin; Satan's original way of making humanity fall:

As soon as Jesus was baptized, he went up out of the water. At that moment Heaven was opened, and he saw the Spirit of God descending like a dove and alighting on him. And a voice from Heaven said, "This is my Son, whom I love; with him I am well pleased." (Matthew 3:16-17)

The tempter came to him and said, "If you are the Son of God, tell these stones to become bread." Jesus answered, "It is written: 'Man shall not live on bread alone, but on every word that comes from the mouth of God.'"

Then the devil took him to the holy city and had him stand on the highest point of the temple. "If you are the Son of God," he said, "throw yourself down. For it is written: "'He will command his angels concerning you, and they will lift you up in their hands, so that you will not strike your foot against a stone.'"

Jesus answered him, "It is also written: 'Do not put the Lord your God to the test.'" Again, the devil took him to a very high mountain and showed him all the kingdoms of the world and their splendor. "All this I will give you," he said, "if you will bow down and worship me." (Matthew 4:3-9)

Satan went after Jesus, first, challenging Him on His identity. Jesus had just been declared from Heaven to be the Beloved and Well-pleasing Son of God. So Satan challenged Him with "*If You are the Son of God, then do this. Prove it, do some work, do something*", but Jesus could simply say, "I Am the Son of God." Satan then challenged Him to worship him as a final desperate plea.

Original mandate was that God created man and woman in His image and likeness, to be His own children, and to rule and reign on Earth together with their Father. The idea was to take what God had given them, a Garden and rivers, and then spread that throughout the whole Earth. We too have been given a Kingdom, with rivers, to expand throughout the whole Earth. We are in this very process now, of advancing the Kingdom of God throughout the Earth.

The Gospel message in the first 10 Generations of Humanity:

Another interesting thing found in the story of Adam is the 10 generations from Adam to Noah, and the message their names carry when strung together as a sentence:

Hebrew	English
Adam	Man
Seth	Appointed
Enosh	Mortal
Kenan	Sorrow;
Mahalalel	The Blessed God
Jared	Shall come down
Enoch	Teaching
Methuselah	His death shall bring
Lamech	The Despairing
Noah	Rest, or comfort.

"Man (is) appointed mortal sorrow; (but) the Blessed God shall come down teaching (that) His death shall bring (the) despairing rest."

This is the Gospel message hidden within the first ten generations of humanity!

Chapter Two
The three Heaven and Earth systems

This next chapter is going to expose you to something you have probably never heard before. We are also jumping ahead because I am going to explain a few things that Jesus and His countrymen believed and understood. This section takes into account the plan and purpose of God, His love for covenant, His love for Kingdom, His desire to have Heaven and Earth as one, and His desire to make humanity like Him; perfect, righteous, holy, clean and pure.

It seems that we being made from dirt didn't stand a chance. We were made dirty. I am not saying we were made as sin, I am only mentioning a symbol. Dirt is dirty. This is my point: Bodily resurrection, as Jesus has received, is the glory and fullness of Heaven meeting Earth, of Spirit meeting the Physical. Resurrection defeats death. Bodily resurrection is the glory of a humanity made from dirt, but ignited by the Spirit.

I will begin by explaining Paul's experience of "going to Heaven" from a covenantal and Kingdom perspective. In fact, Jesus tells a parable about the Kingdom by beginning it this way:

Jesus spoke to them again in parables, saying: "The kingdom of Heaven is like a king who prepared a wedding banquet for his son. He sent his servants to those who had been invited to the banquet to tell them to come, but they refused to come. (Matthew 22:1-3)

The idea of God desiring a marriage for His Son is the heart of the Kingdom. In the New Covenant, as we will cover later in this book, is a marriage fulfilled, between a perfect Bride (the new Jerusalem, people of God by the faith of Jesus, the circumcised in heart children of Abraham, the sons and daughters of God) and her perfect King Husband, Jesus the Messiah. (The very name Jesus means, "Yahweh is salvation").

So, let's look at what Paul experienced:

I must go on boasting. Although there is nothing to be gained, I will go on to visions and revelations from the Lord. I know a man in Christ who fourteen years ago was caught up to the third Heaven. Whether it was in the body or out of the body I do not know - God knows.

And I know that this man - whether in the body or apart from the body I do not know, but God knows - was caught up to paradise and heard inexpressible things, things that no one is permitted to tell. (2 Corinthians 12:1-4)

I am going to bring forth a covenantal and Kingdom understanding of this "third Heaven" that Paul was caught up to. In order for there to be a third Heaven, there must have been a first and a second Heaven.

What was the first and second Heaven? Many have explained it as being layers from Earth upward. The sky above our head where the birds fly is the first Heaven.

The space where planets are is called the second Heaven. And the place where God dwells is called the third Heaven. I believe other religions take it up higher to 7 Heavens. Who knows?

What I am about to share is something the Holy Spirit revealed to me as I was studying covenant and Kingdom in the Bible. I will share it with you:

There have been three Heaven and Earth systems. Each "system" has a mountain, a marriage, a son and a baptism. Those are 4 interesting constants within each system that I discovered. This term "Heaven and Earth" as a system simply means the way in which God communes and lives with man.

First let me explain what each system basically is, and then I will explain the 4 constants within each Heaven and Earth system.

The three Heaven and systems are as follows:

1. The first Heaven and Earth was God's original creation with Adam and Eve, and it extends until Noah and the flood. The flood brings an end to this system.

2. The second Heaven and Earth was the Tabernacle of Moses, which later became the Temple of Solomon. The destruction of 70 AD brought an end to this system.

3. The third Heaven and Earth is the New Covenant - the new Heaven and new Earth. It's in the Spirit, which is where the Kingdom and God are as well. We, too, are admonished to walk and live in the Spirit, for this reason. There is no end to this system, for it is eternal, but there will be a shift when we receive bodily resurrection.

Therefore, when Paul was caught up to the third Heaven, the paradise of God, He saw the new Heaven and new Earth. He saw the beautiful and pure Bride of the Lord. He saw the New Jerusalem; a city, which has foundations whose Builder and Maker, is God. This is the city that Abraham saw and longed for in his heart. Paul saw the Bride before she came down from Heaven to Earth. Maybe he saw her in Bridal preparation and it was a glorious sight to behold!

Each system has a **mountain**, a **marriage**, a **son** and a **baptism**. Four strange constants are found within each of these Heaven and Earth systems. Heaven and Earth can be understood to be the place where Heaven meets Earth, or God and man connect.

The mountain, marriage, son and baptism are as follows:

1. The **mountain** of the first system is the mountain of Eden. Remember, we covered this in the previous chapter. The **marriage** is between Adam and Eve, the representatives of God in the Earth. The **son** of the first system was Adam. He was made as a type and shadow of the true Son of God, Jesus. The **baptism**, as Peter tells us, is the flood of Noah, which brought an end to this Heaven and Earth as a system. The Earth and Heavens remained, but the system that once existed was gone.

After being made alive, he went and made proclamation to the imprisoned spirits - to those who were disobedient long ago when God waited patiently in the days of Noah while the ark was being built. In it only a few people, eight in all, were saved through water, and this water symbolizes baptism that now saves you also-not the removal of dirt from the body but the pledge of a clear conscience toward God. It saves you by the resurrection of Jesus Christ. (1 Peter 3:19-21)

2. The **mountain** of the second system is Mt. Sinai, where the 10 commandments and design requirements of the Tabernacle were given. The **marriage** is between Yahweh (I Am) and nation Israel (the 12 tribes), the physical and circumcised seed of Abraham. I see Yahweh as the Father, Son & Spirit at work together. The **son** is Israel corporately, a type and shadow of the true Son of God, Jesus. The **baptism** is into Moses through the Red Sea as they escaped Egypt. Paul speaks of this in his first letter to the Corinthians.

The marriage: *For your Maker is your husband - the Lord Almighty is his name - the Holy One of Israel is your Redeemer; he is called the God of all the Earth.* (Isaiah 54:5)

The son: *Then say to Pharaoh, 'This is what the Lord says: Israel is my firstborn son.* (Exodus 4:22)

The baptism: *For I do not want you to be ignorant of the fact, brothers and sisters, that our ancestors were all under the cloud and that they all passed through the sea. They were all baptized into Moses in the cloud and in the sea.* (1 Corinthians 10:1-2)

3. The **mountain** of the third system, which Paul saw in the third Heaven, is Mt. Zion, in Heaven or in the Spirit. This is the mountain of the Kingdom of God. Zion in Jerusalem being a type and a shadow of the reality to be found in the New Covenant. We will study several types and shadows throughout the Bible. Types and shadows are God giving a picture of something before the reality of it arrives. It's

like a prophecy that awaits fulfillment. This is a big part of how God operates within covenant. Paul even mentions the concept of types and shadows:

The spiritual did not come first, but the natural, and after that the spiritual. (1 Corinthians 15:46)

Paul mentions this in relation to Adam being first and then Jesus, the last Adam. Adam was a type and shadow of Jesus, the true Son of God.

The **marriage** of the third system is between Jesus and His Bride, the New Jerusalem, the people of God in Christ. This is the New Covenant, the new Heaven and new Earth relationship. The **son** of the third system is Jesus, of course, but then those who are in Christ are also called sons (and daughters) in Christ. The **baptism** is both the water and the Spirit baptism. Water baptism is ultimately a type and shadow, or picture of the baptism in the Spirit.

I want to focus on the second Heaven and Earth system now, which started out as the Tabernacle of Moses and later became the Temple of Solomon, which Herod later restored and expanded. The fact that the Jews of Jesus' day understood the Temple being Heaven and Earth will help us understand some difficult Scriptures in the Bible. One such Scripture is in Matthew.

"Do not think that I have come to abolish the Law or the Prophets; I have not come to abolish them but to fulfill them. For truly I tell you, until Heaven and Earth disappear, not the smallest letter, not the least stroke of a pen, will by any means disappear from the Law until everything is accomplished." (Matthew 5:17-18)

We have more than likely thought that meant until the Earth is destroyed, the Law is still in force. But, from a historical and covenantal perspective, this Scripture means something very different. One thing we must realize is that the Bible was written in covenantal language. Its not written, though it is interpreted, with our American phrases intact. Certain things simply mean different things.

Concerning the Law, or Law covenant, we must understand this: In order for there to be a law covenant, there must be a Temple in the city of Jerusalem. There must be a Levitical priesthood made up of real Levites. They must wear certain clothing according to the Law. The Temple must have certain furnishings, according to the Law. Animal sacrifice is required, according to the Law. Celebrating the feasts of the Lord is a requirement, which is why some today think God expects you to celebrate the feasts. We will cover what the feasts pointed to later.

When we read Matthew 5:17-18, we have a choice between two options:

1. Heaven and Earth exist = 100% of the Mosaic law is still in force including the Temple system, Levitical priesthood, High Priest, Ark of the Covenant, Temple duties of the Levites, the city of Jerusalem being the location of such Temple, the feasts of the Lord, the 3 annual pilgrimages to Jerusalem, circumcision of the flesh and covenantal wrath (see Romans 4:15). Do Heaven and Earth still exist since none of these things still exist?

2. Heaven and Earth disappear = the Mosaic Law with all its trappings disappears. (Paul and Peter refer to these trappings of Temple Judaism as "elements" in their writings).

So then, if we understand Heaven and Earth to be the literal and physical Earth, then 100% of the Mosaic Old Covenant Law is still in force until the end of this planet. Not one jot or one tittle has passed, and God is still honoring that system of animal sacrifice and Temple worship conducted by Levitical priesthood, until the planet is destroyed.

Or could Jesus be using a Hebraic figure of speech that everyone in the first century understood? Either Jesus was talking about something else or the Law is 100% in effect currently, since the planet is not yet destroyed. We gain another clue the next time Jesus mentions Heaven and Earth in Matthew 24:35

Heaven and Earth will pass away, but my words will never pass away.

22

We will study this later, but Matthew 24 is a prophecy from Jesus about the coming destruction of Jerusalem and the Temple. The Jews of the first century called the Temple system Heaven and Earth, and Jesus referred to it as that twice in Matthew. Peter also mentions it:

By the same word the present Heavens and Earth are reserved for fire, being kept for the day of judgment and destruction of the ungodly. (2 Peter 3:7)

This is the Old Covenant, Temple system that burned to the ground in 70 AD.

But the day of the Lord will come like a thief. The Heavens will disappear with a roar; the elements will be destroyed by fire, and the Earth and everything done in it will be laid bare. (2 Peter 3:10)

The elements mentioned here is the Greek word *stoicheion* and when Paul used it, it always referred to the religion and ritual of the Law (see Galatians 4:3, Galatians 4:9, Colossians 2:8, Colossians 2:20, Hebrews 5:12 for the use of this word *stoicheion*, or elements).

Josephus, a historian during the first century destruction of Jerusalem and the Temple and whose father was a Levite priest, wrote the following:

When Moses distinguished the tabernacle into three parts, and allowed two of them to the priests (the outer courts and the Holy Place), as a place accessible and common, he denoted the land and the seas, these being of general access to all; but he set apart the third division for God (the Holy of Holies), because Heaven is inaccessible to men.

Charles Spurgeon, a Baptist preacher, pastor and theologian of the mid-19th century, said the following:

Did you ever regret the absence of the burnt offering, or red heifer, or any one of the sacrifices and rites of the Jews? Did you ever pine for the feasts of tabernacles, or the dedication? No, because though these were like the old

Heavens and Earth to the Jewish believers, they have passed away, and we now live under new Heavens and a new Earth, so far as the dispensation of the divine teaching is concerned. The substance is come, the shadow has gone, and we do not remember it.

The idea of the Tabernacle being Heaven and Earth goes like this: The holy of holies is as Heaven, where God dwells, and where the High Priest approaches with blood of the lamb once yearly. This is where the Ark of the Covenant rested. The holy place was as the land, even having a dirt floor, and the bronze laver was as the sea. Thus you have Heaven and Earth. They really called the bronze laver the sea:

He then made ten basins for washing and placed five on the south side and five on the north. In them the things to be used for the burnt offerings were rinsed, but the Sea was to be used by the priests for washing. (2 Chronicles 4:6)

In Hebrews, we can see a contrast between the holy of holies being Heaven and the real Heaven where Jesus took His blood:

For Christ did not enter a sanctuary made with human hands that was only a copy of the true one; he entered Heaven itself, now to appear for us in God's presence. Nor did he enter Heaven to offer himself again and again, the way the high priest enters the Most Holy Place every year with blood that is not his own. (Hebrews 9:24-25)

The Roman armies (the wrath of God) destroyed this second Heaven and Earth system in 70 AD. This is a big theme in the New Testament, as well as in prophecies throughout the Old Testament. We will study this in depth in later chapters.

New Covenant is the new Heaven and Earth, with a new Mt. Zion, a New Jerusalem, a new marriage, a new baptism, and a new King, the Lord Jesus Christ. The writer of Hebrews shows us this in beautiful, covenantal language:

But you have come to Mount Zion, to the city of the living God, the Heavenly Jerusalem. You have come to thousands upon thousands of angels in joyful assembly, to the Church of the firstborn, whose names are written in Heaven. You have come to God, the Judge of all, to the spirits of the righteous made perfect, to Jesus the mediator of a New Covenant, and to the sprinkled blood that speaks a better word than the blood of Abel. (Hebrews 12:22-24)

We can also see the writer of Hebrews mention the destruction and shaking of Heaven and Earth, which was the Temple system, and which happened in 70 AD.

See to it that you do not refuse him who speaks. If they did not escape when they refused him who warned them on Earth, how much less will we, if we turn away from him who warns us from Heaven? At that time his voice shook the Earth, but now he has promised, "Once more I will shake not only the Earth but also the Heavens." The words "once more" indicate the removing of what can be shaken - that is, created things - so that what cannot be shaken may remain. Therefore, since we are receiving a kingdom that cannot be shaken, let us be thankful, and so worship God acceptably with reverence and awe, for our "God is a consuming fire." (Hebrews 12:25-29)

The fire of God, by His wrath, according to the Law, is what ultimately brought down the system of the Old Covenant. He used Roman armies to accomplish His purpose of removing the old and revealing the Kingdom in power.

I would like to add that I believe the entire New Testament was written prior to the destruction of Jerusalem in 70 AD. Hebrews would have been one of the last letters written before the destruction, and we can see a lot of the mentioning and warning of this coming destruction, the removal of that Heaven and Earth system so that the new Kingdom can be brought forth in power.

Chapter Three
Noah and his 3 sons

After sin, which entered the world (Greek, cosmos) through Adam's disobedience, the Earth was corrupted. The corruption, in my opinion, seems to be unique in all of history. Many believe angelic corruption, through sexual interaction, was the reason for the flood. If one believes that angels having sex with women can produce a race of giants, then this is the view to hold.

I tend to lean in that direction, because of historical findings and writings, such as the book of Enoch. The book of Enoch is not canonical or considered to be inspired by the Spirit, yet Jude quotes it in our Bible. Enoch seemed to be prophesying about the end of a group of people through a judgment, with a righteousness coming forth from it. Those people that Enoch prophesied about were the unbelieving Jews of the first century who rejected Jesus as Messiah.

As I mentioned previously, the flood ended the first Heaven and Earth system, which began with Adam. Noah was the man God chose to facilitate the survival of a remnant and establishing a covenant of blessing in the Earth. Baptism is a picture of death and new life, which is why Peter describes the flood as a type of baptism.

Noah lived in a very wicked time. Humanity had no covenant with God. Few probably knew Him, and they only had their generational stories to understand anything about Him. It's possible that Noah lived during a time when angels and mankind mingled together. This would mean understanding that it was the angels who were called sons of God, or sons of Heaven, during this time. Jude describes it as a time when some of the angels had fornication with some of the human females, and some believe that this is what produced the race of giants, or a hybrid of human and angel. If this were true, then this would have been the cause of the flood, which is what I believe to be true.

And the angels who did not keep their positions of authority but abandoned their proper dwelling - these he has kept in darkness, bound with everlasting chains for judgment on the great Day. In a similar way, Sodom and Gomorrah and the surrounding towns gave themselves up to sexual immorality and perversion. They serve as an example of those who suffer the punishment of eternal fire. (Jude 1:6-7)

But during this time, Noah stood out. He was a man that found favor in the eyes of the Lord.

But Noah found favor in the eyes of the Lord. (Genesis 6:8)

After the flood, something shifted that was once part of the first Heaven and Earth system. Man having dominion over all the Earth. God told Noah to be fruitful and multiply but He did not tell him to take dominion over all the Earth like He did Adam. Even the diet changed, from only herbs, to include eating the animals that you were once told to reign over.)

Then God blessed Noah and his sons, saying to them, "Be fruitful and increase in number and fill the Earth. The fear and dread of you will fall on all the beasts of the Earth, and on all the birds in the sky, on every creature that moves along the ground, and on all the fish in the sea; they are given into your hands. Everything that lives and moves about will be food for you. Just as I gave you the green plants, I now give you everything. (Genesis 9:1-3)

If Noah's covenant with God had a symbol, it would be the rainbow. The rainbow was a sign that God would not destroy everything again. This is also a type and a shadow of the promise of Heaven's Kingdom coming into the Earth. The rainbow is seen surrounding the throne in Heaven, so this symbol becomes important within the context of the bigger, Kingdom picture.

The Lord smelled the pleasing aroma and said in his heart: "Never again will I curse the ground because of humans, even though every inclination of the human heart is evil from childhood. And never again will I destroy all living creatures, as I have done." (Genesis 8:21)

This is the covenant promise:

"I have set my rainbow in the clouds, and it will be the sign of the covenant between me and the Earth. Whenever I bring clouds over the Earth and the rainbow appears in the clouds, I will remember my covenant between me and you and all living creatures of every kind. Never again will the waters become a flood to destroy all life. Whenever the rainbow appears in the clouds, I will see it and remember the everlasting covenant between God and all living creatures of every kind on the Earth." (Genesis 9:13-16)

The rainbow is something we can still see today, usually after a rain. We should use that symbol as a moment to worship and thank God for His enduring love, allowing our hearts to remember the kindness of God, and not His judgment. The rainbow speaks that one day the Kingdom of God will cover the Earth, and sin will be no more.

One huge thing the Cross did was forever forgive and remove sin from between God and mankind. The only thing left for humanity to do is embrace the Resurrected Lord Jesus Christ as King, God and Son of God for the New Covenant. He is our High Priest, our Shepherd, even Everlasting Father is a name given to Him through Isaiah. Jesus is salvation for the world. Faith is the only right response to His salvation.

Noah had 3 sons who helped him with the ark, and who received the imparted blessing from God to the men of that family (Genesis 9:1-3). Under that dispensation of time, the men of the family were considered to be the priests of their immediate family of wife and kids. The oldest male member of the family at large was the high priest of the family lineage. So, one older man, the oldest male member of his extended family, would be the priest for the entire family.

Noah's 3 sons were Shem, Ham, and Japheth. I don't know if they were triplets, or just born close together. Regardless, Shem is the father of the Abrahamic family, and Shem was alive when Abraham was on Earth. In fact, Shem, outlived Abraham by about 35 years. So, this mysterious Melchizedek person in Genesis 14 is actually the king of Salem, an early name for Jerusalem, and priest of the Most High God, for his family lineage, which included Abraham. He was a real person, and it was Noah's son Shem, the father of the Abrahamic family, the Hebrews. This Shem was Melchizedek, the king of Salem, king of righteousness. He brought the body and blood of our Lord when he met Abram.

Melchizedek was Shem:

At the time of Abraham, the cultural dictate was that the oldest male member of a family was the priest. Therefore, Abraham's priest would have been his still living great grandfather, Shem. Ten Generations older, Shem outlived Abraham by 35 years!

The name "Melchizedek" is a title, it means Righteous King, and Shem was a righteous king over Salem, the earlier name for Jerusalem.

In Hebrews, there is a debate over if Jesus could really be our high priest, since He was from the tribe of Judah and Not from Levi. The author answers that Jesus is greater than the Levitical priesthood because He is in the order of the Melchizedek priesthood. But Hebrews says that Melchizedek was without father or mother, without beginning of days or end of days.

The answer to that is, Levite priests were required to carry papers proving their heritage at all times (who was their father and mother), as well as their birth certificate because they were only able to be a priest from 30-50 years old. Whereas Jesus in the order of Melchizedek, didn't need to prove His genealogy, and his priesthood didn't end at 50, it is eternal. (Abraham would have given tithe only to his oldest male ancestor as the priest.)

So, now let's look at this blessing that God gave Noah and his 3 sons, and who the blessing landed on.

Melchizedek blessed Abraham with the blessing of God. Shem, being Melchizedek, was blessed by God, along with Noah and the other 2 brothers. Shem gave this blessing, which included the body and blood of the Lord, to Abram. Now Abram is blessed, and this blessing is transferred to Jesus.

So those who rely on faith are blessed along with Abraham, the man of faith. (Galatians 3:9)

Abraham was blessed. He was blessed because Melchizedek, Shem, blessed him with the blessing of God, which was given to him after the flood. We, then, in Christ, become partakers of that Noahic blessing and covenant, yet, unlike Noah, we have the mandate to reign with Christ in this new Heaven and new Earth.

Genesis 9:1-3 tells us that God blessed Noah and his sons. His sons were Shem, Ham and Japheth. It was the mandate of the 3 sons to promote this blessing into all the Earth. I suspect they 3 became kings over regions in order to accomplish this. It's common, ancient Jewish thought, that Shem was Melchizedek. He was the priest of his family line, which included Abraham, and it was his responsibility to bless his own family and those under his reign as King of Salem (an early name for Jerusalem).

Beginning at Genesis 14:18, we see this Melchizedek (his title, not his name) bringing out a prophetic emblem of the body of Christ, bread and wine, to Abraham, by which he immediately pronounced a blessing over Abraham. It was through the seed of Abraham that all the nations of the Earth would be blessed, so this mandate to be fruitful and multiply finds its resting place in the blessing pronounced over Abraham, the father of faith.

We will look more at the blessing of Abraham in the next chapter, but I wanted to show how this blessing passed from God to Noah to Abraham and to Jesus, and those who have faith in Him.

The next event after the blessing given to Noah and his 3 sons is the tower of Babel incident. The ancient word "Bab-El" literally meant "the gate of God". In contrast, the word Beth-El means "the house of God." Babel becomes the place where man is in rebellion to God, not willing to spread out and populate the Earth.

Now the whole world had one language and a common speech. As people moved eastward, they found a plain in Shinar and settled there. They said to each other, "Come, let's make bricks and bake them thoroughly." They used brick instead of stone, and tar for mortar.

Then they said, "Come, let us build ourselves a city, with a tower that reaches to the Heavens, so that we may make a name for ourselves; otherwise we will be scattered over the face of the whole Earth." But the Lord came down to see the city and the tower the people were building.

The Lord said, "If as one people speaking the same language they have begun to do this, then nothing they plan to do will be impossible for them. Come, let us go down and confuse their language so they will not understand each other."

So the Lord scattered them from there over all the Earth, and they stopped building the city. That is why it was called Babel - because there the Lord confused the language of the whole world. From there the Lord scattered them over the face of the whole Earth. (Genesis 11:1-9)

The name Babel later came to mean confusion, but it originally meant "the gate of God", and it seems they were building a ziggurat tower to worship the stars and planets. If there was angelic corruption before the flood, Enoch's writings explain that it was these fallen angels that taught mankind to worship the stars and planets and gave them knowledge about it.

It's possible that what was happening at Babel was a carryover from that previous sin, which caused the flood, angelic (fallen angels) knowledge and interaction corrupting mankind.

The people of Babel wanted to remain in one place and be one people of one language and one speech, but God wanted diversity, and different cultures and expanding over all the Earth. This is where God confused their languages so they could no longer understand one another, and then went to various places such as Africa, India, China, Russia, Spain, Germany, England, although those names did not exist then.

Sometime after that, the Asian people migrated across Alaska and into North America. This created races of people throughout North and South America.

We do know that the landmasses divided at a certain time in history:

Two sons were born to Eber: One was named Peleg, because in his time the Earth was divided; his brother was named Joktan. (Genesis 10:25)

The Noahic story covers from the time of Adam up until the Tower of Babel (Genesis, chapters 1 -11). Chapter 12 of Genesis begins a new story, and a New Covenant, through a man named Abram, who later became Abraham.

Chapter Four
Abraham

Before we start with Abraham, we have to first call him Abram. Abram was his name when he met God, and God later changed his name to Abraham. Also, Abraham lived during a time, after the flood, where God was known as God Almighty, or El-Shaddai.

I believe Job lived before the flood, and he also acknowledged God by the name El-Shaddai, or God Almighty. This is how they knew Him. We know Him as Father in the New Covenant.

God meets Abraham

The Lord had said to Abram, "Go from your country, your people and your father's household to the land I will show you. "I will make you into a great nation, and I will bless you; I will make your name great, and you will be a blessing. I will bless those who bless you, and whoever curses you I will curse; and all peoples on Earth will be blessed through you." (Genesis 12:1-3)

That is a power-packed set of verses that many false doctrines have sprang from. Many Christians have made it their goal to always bless and support a nation called Israel because of this, so that God will not curse them. It breeds fear and confusion when you do not understand what this section of Scripture was speaking about.

God first begins telling Abraham to get out of that country. We learn later, in Joshua, that Abraham lived in a pagan environment with the worship of many false gods and demons.

Joshua said to all the people, "This is what the Lord, the God of Israel, says: 'Long ago your ancestors, including Terah the father of Abraham and Nahor, lived beyond the Euphrates River and worshiped other gods... (Joshua 24:2)

Next we see that it was God's desire to make of him a great nation and make Abram's name great. It's interesting to compare that it seemed Eve wanted to be great, and the people of Babel building the tower wanted to make a great name for themselves, but God gives this to Abraham as a free gift, a grant covenant.

One of the things we will discover throughout the teaching of this book is that there are 3 types of covenants represented in our Bible - a Grant covenant, a Kinship covenant, and a Vassal covenant. A grant covenant is what God gave to Noah and to Abraham. When we get to Moses, we will see that God first made a grant offer to them, which they later rejected.

He then gave them a kinship covenant, which required a mediator, meaning, Moses, and then after 40 years of grumbling in the wilderness, God downgraded the kinship covenant with an addendum called a vassal covenant, which they were told to place on the side of the Ark of the Covenant. I will not go any deeper than that for now, concerning the 3 types of covenants in the Bible.

After blessing Him, God promised to "*bless them that bless you, and curse him that curses you.*" He then adds, "*and in you shall all the families of the Earth be blessed*". This all began with the blessing pronounced on Noah and his 3 sons.

Shem, one of Noah's sons, who they knew as the king of righteousness (Melchizedek), then later transferred that blessing to Abram, and now we see God using this Melchizedek to transfer the blessing which He promised to Abram. Yet, the blessing given to Abraham was but for an even greater purpose. Paul teaches us something very important in Galatians 3:

The promises were spoken to Abraham and to his seed. Scripture does not say "and to seeds," meaning many people, but "and to your seed," meaning one person, who is Christ. (Galatians 3:16)

It was to Abraham and his Seed, Jesus, not national Israel that the promises were made. This is very important to understand. Jesus is where the blessing is. Not in modern Israel, or any other false teaching.

We are blessed in Christ alone, and not by blessing Israel. The promise was for Abraham and Jesus. National Israel was simply a type and shadow between Abraham and Jesus. This is incredibly important to grasp, with all the Israel worship and bad teaching concerning such things.

The blessing first comes to Abraham (Abram)

Then Melchizedek king of Salem brought out bread and wine. He was priest of God Most High, and he blessed Abram, saying, "Blessed be Abram by God Most High, Creator of Heaven and Earth. And praise be to God Most High, who delivered your enemies into your hand." Then Abram gave him a tenth of everything. (Genesis 14:18-20)

This is the vehicle God used to give this blessing to Abram. Shem, king of Salem, who is also Melchizedek, king of righteousness, brings to Abraham the body and blood of the Lord Jesus, the foundation of the New Covenant.

He brings out the ultimate source of all blessing to Abram, which is important for us to understand where blessings flow for humanity today - through the New Covenant made in the body and blood of Jesus, the Lamb of God. We also see another person involved seeking to put himself in covenant with Abram:

The king of Sodom said to Abram, "Give me the people and keep the goods for yourself." But Abram said to the king of Sodom, "With raised hand I have sworn an oath to the Lord, God Most High, Creator of Heaven and Earth, that I will accept nothing belonging to you, not even a thread or the strap of a sandal, so that you will never be able to say, 'I made Abram rich.' I will accept nothing but what my men have eaten and the share that belongs to the men who went with me - to Aner, Eshkol and Mamre. Let them have their share." (Genesis 14:21-24)

We shall learn later in this study that Old Covenant, first century Jerusalem became known as 3 different names: Babylon, Sodom and Egypt.

We see here a type and a shadow for Abraham, that the king of Sodom (a future derogatory name for Old Covenant Jerusalem, the harlot) offered to be in covenant with Abram, but Abram boldly refused, knowing that God had already blessed him through Melchizedek. Abram turned down a bad covenant with the king of Sodom for a better covenant with Melchizedek the kingly priest of God.

The intent of this book is not to go into too many details concerning this covenant journey of God with mankind. I want to give you the foundation so that you can do your own study and teaching. This book is meant to be a foundation that you can build upon. With that said, I am not going to go into detail with Isaac and Jacob, although those are worthy for study.

We know that the blessing of the covenant that God made with Abraham then passes on to Isaac and then to Jacob, the father of the 12 tribes of Israel. It's during the days of Jacob that the 12 tribes ended up in Egypt under good circumstances, which later turned out to be bad, as they found themselves in slavery in Egypt many generations later.

I do want to look at the actual covenant that God made with Abram and the few instances later where God "confirmed" or "expanded" the covenant that He made with Abram.

After this, the word of the Lord came to Abram in a vision: "Do not be afraid, Abram. I am your shield, your very great reward." But Abram said, "Sovereign Lord, what can you give me since I remain childless and the one who will inherit my estate is Eliezer of Damascus?" And Abram said, "You have given me no children; so a servant in my household will be my heir."

Then the word of the Lord came to him: "This man will not be your heir, but a son who is your own flesh and blood will be your heir." He took him outside and said, "Look up at the sky and count the stars - if indeed you can count them." Then he said to him, "So shall your offspring be." Abram believed the Lord, and he credited it to him as righteousness. (Genesis 15:1-6)

God makes covenant promises to Abram, and we can see a few things here. First of all, the Kingdom operates through a Father and Son relationship. Abram offered his servant Eliezer to become his heir, but God said it had to be his own son. Abram became the father of faith, by believing God and it being accounted to him as righteousness.

This is part of the grant type of covenant. Simply believe. Often times there can be a few requirements involved in a grant covenant, but it's always the best type of covenant. We have a grant covenant in the New Covenant Kingdom of God. We believe and receive the love and promises of God, which come in Christ.

Abram asks God a question:

But Abram said, "Sovereign Lord, how can I know that I will gain possession of it?" So the Lord said to him, "Bring me a heifer, a goat and a ram, each three years old, along with a dove and a young pigeon." (Genesis 15:8-9)

He asks God, *"How shall I know that I will receive the inheritance?"* God then begins to tell him what to get to make a covenant with Him. The answer to inheritance is covenant, with God. We have the inheritance in Christ because of the New Covenant. Many things happening in the life of Abram become a type and shadow of the reality and substance of the New Covenant.

When the sun had set and darkness had fallen, a smoking firepot with a blazing torch appeared and passed between the pieces. On that day the Lord made a covenant with Abram and said, "To your descendants I give this land, from the Wadi of Egypt to the great river, the Euphrates - the land of the Kenites, Kenizzites, Kadmonites, Hittites, Perizzites, Rephaites, Amorites, Canaanites, Girgashites and Jebusites." (Genesis 15:17-21)

The initial promise of the covenant, so far, includes a seed and a large area of land, which we will see later how David obtained the land through wars and gave it to Solomon for his kingdom to enjoy.

God cuts covenant with Abraham. It becomes a type and shadow of the Cross in Christ. When God made covenant with Abram, He had him gather 5 animals, cut them in half, and lay them on each side of a ravine so the blood would flow to the middle. God then walked through the middle of the ravine, splashing the blood with His feet. This was a common way of cutting covenant during that time.

Fast forward to the Cross. Jesus' arms were spread wide, blood running down His body from every wound, which penetrated Him. We have thought that God was punishing Him on our behalf, but that is not what was happening on the Cross.

God was cutting covenant again, a New Covenant, in the body of His Son, the best sacrifice. God was not far off, but Paul tells us that God was in the midst of what was going on, reconciling the world to Himself, not considering sin.

> *… that God was reconciling the world to himself in Christ, not counting people's sins against them. And he has committed to us the message of reconciliation.* (2 Corinthians 5:19)

God was walking through the blood again, cutting covenant, forgiving the sins of the world through the act of the Cross. The New Covenant was not about satisfying the wrath of an angry God. It was actually love on display.

Sin is either judged or forgiven. God forgave sin on the Cross, all sin, for everybody, past, present and future. The connection to what He did is our faith, when we believe and are saved.

God's love on display at the Cross

> *This is how God showed his love among us: He sent his one and only Son into the world that we might live through him. This is love: not that we loved God, but that he loved us and sent his Son as an atoning sacrifice for our sins.* (1 John 4:9-10)

40

The Cross was God cutting a New Covenant, in the body of His Son, an eternal covenant that brought redemption for mankind, for those who believe in Jesus. The Cross forgave everyone, making Christ the propitiation, atoning sacrifice, for the sins of the world, but everyone does not receive the forgiveness until they "embrace Jesus" as their Savior and Lord. God's covenant with Abraham was a picture of Jesus and the Cross. God then begins to confirm and expand the covenant with Abraham.

> *When Abram was ninety-nine years old, the Lord appeared to him and said, "I am God Almighty; walk before me faithfully and be blameless. Then I will make my covenant between me and you and will greatly increase your numbers."*

> *Abram fell facedown, and God said to him, "As for me, this is my covenant with you: You will be the father of many nations. No longer will you be called Abram; your name will be Abraham, for I have made you a father of many nations. I will make you very fruitful; I will make nations of you, and kings will come from you. I will establish my covenant as an everlasting covenant between me and you and your descendants after you for the generations to come, to be your God and the God of your descendants after you. The whole land of Canaan, where you now reside as a foreigner, I will give as an everlasting possession to you and your descendants after you; and I will be their God."* (Genesis 17:1-8)

God then confirms or expands the covenant by changing Abram's and Sarai's name to Abraham and Sarah. It's important to understand that Sarah is just as important as Abraham in this covenant. It's only the seed that comes from the union of Abraham and Sarah that carries the covenant blessing. The Kingdom is connected to marriage and family.

Another area of contention to understand is when we see the term "everlasting", such as the everlasting covenant God made with Abraham, and later certain things that God told Moses was to be everlasting. The term everlasting actually means "age-during", meaning, "as long as this age endures."

This is one of those translation issues with most Bibles. Therefore, Abraham's covenant finds its continuance in Christ, but Moses' covenant, as we will cover in the next chapter, finds its fulfillment and end in Christ. The New Covenant is a new age, though it receives the promises given to Abraham originally. The New Covenant turns the land promises given to Abraham to those of the Kingdom in the Spirit.

God continues on and expands the covenant to include fleshly circumcision. Circumcision becomes a big type and shadow in the New Covenant, as it becomes the circumcision of the heart, in the Spirit, the new birth, into a new nation in Christ. If Abraham's covenant had a symbol, it would be circumcision, even as the symbol of Noah's covenant is the rainbow.

The expanding of the covenant to include circumcision

"This is my covenant with you and your descendants after you, the covenant you are to keep: Every male among you shall be circumcised. You are to undergo circumcision, and it will be the sign of the covenant between me and you.

For the generations to come every male among you who is eight days old must be circumcised, including those born in your household or bought with money from a foreigner - those who are not your offspring". (Genesis 17:10-12)

God continues on and expands the covenant to include the actual child, which is Isaac.

"But my covenant I will establish with Isaac, whom Sarah will bear to you by this time next year. " (Genesis 17:21)

God then gives them strength to make a baby together, in their old age. Abraham was about 100 and Sarah was about 90 when Isaac was conceived. God blessed their union. This is all the same covenant that God made with Abraham. God keeps expanding it to include more as He journeys with Abraham.

42

The story then takes a very different turn, right after the conversation of the birth of Isaac. It goes into judgment against Sodom and Gomorrah. Remember, I mentioned earlier that Old Covenant Jerusalem became known as 3 names: Babylon, Sodom and Egypt.

All three of those cities or nations required the covenant people of God to escape and leave. So, we see that with the promise of the seed to be born the following year, God then proceeds to deal with the sin of "wicked" Sodom. This is a picture of the birth of the New Covenant at the Cross, and the subsequent destruction of Jerusalem in 70 AD. The Bible is full of these connections, and it's important to see it because it's a theme woven throughout the story of the Bible. We will cover more of the 70 AD judgment in later chapters.

Then the Lord said to Abraham, "Why did Sarah laugh and say, 'Will I really have a child, now that I am old?' Is anything too hard for the Lord? I will return to you at the appointed time next year, and Sarah will have a son." Sarah was afraid, so she lied and said, "I did not laugh." But he said, "Yes, you did laugh."

When the men got up to leave, they looked down toward Sodom, and Abraham walked along with them to see them on their way. Then the Lord said, "Shall I hide from Abraham what I am about to do? Abraham will surely become a great and powerful nation, and all nations on Earth will be blessed through him. For I have chosen him, so that he will direct his children and his household after him to keep the way of the Lord by doing what is right and just, so that the Lord will bring about for Abraham what he has promised him."

Then the Lord said, "The outcry against Sodom and Gomorrah is so great and their sin so grievous that I will go down and see if what they have done is as bad as the outcry that has reached me. If not, I will know." (Genesis 18:13-21)

God then gets Lot and his family, because of their connection to Abraham, out of the cities so that He can destroy them. This is a picture of God's covenant people of first century Israel escaping the destruction of Jerusalem while the unbelievers were consumed in the city.

Once again, I have wondered if angelic corruption was involved in these cities as well. Also, the fruit of the angelic corruption seems to be sexual immorality and giants. We see giants appear later in Israel's history, and David even kills a giant named Goliath.

The next episode in the story of Abraham is a picture of the Cross, again.

Some time later God tested Abraham. He said to him, "Abraham!" "Here I am," he replied. Then God said, "Take your son, your only son, whom you love – Isaac - and go to the region of Moriah. Sacrifice him there as a burnt offering on a mountain I will show you."

Early the next morning Abraham got up and loaded his donkey. He took with him two of his servants and his son Isaac. When he had cut enough wood for the burnt offering, he set out for the place God had told him about.

On the third day Abraham looked up and saw the place in the distance. He said to his servants, "Stay here with the donkey while I and the boy go over there. We will worship and then we will come back to you." Abraham took the wood for the burnt offering and placed it on his son Isaac, and he himself carried the fire and the knife.

As the two of them went on together, Isaac spoke up and said to his father Abraham, "Father?" "Yes, my son?" Abraham replied. "The fire and wood are here," Isaac said, "but where is the lamb for the burnt offering?" Abraham answered, "God himself will provide the lamb for the burnt offering, my son." And the two of them went on together.

When they reached the place God had told him about, Abraham built an altar there and arranged the wood on it. He bound his son Isaac and laid him on the altar, on top of the wood. Then he reached out his hand and took the knife to slay his son. But the angel of the Lord called out to him from Heaven, "Abraham! Abraham!" "Here I am," he replied. "Do not lay a hand on the boy," he said. "Do not do anything to him. Now I know that you fear God, because you have not withheld from me your son, your only son."

Abraham looked up and there in a thicket he saw a ram caught by its horns. He went over and took the ram and sacrificed it as a burnt offering instead of his son. So Abraham called that place The Lord Will Provide. And to this day it is said, "On the mountain of the Lord it will be provided." (Genesis 22:1-14)

This was a very big moment in the life of Abraham and humanity. This was another type and shadow of the Cross, where Isaac is a type of Christ, but in this case, it's also a test, where God is testing Abraham. In Abraham's culture, it was common to sacrifice a child to your god, but in the case with God, He would never actually require that, so He stopped the killing of Isaac and gave them a Ram, another type of Christ, to be sacrificed as an act of worship to God. At this point, Abraham also came to know another aspect of God - The Provider. Abraham called that place "The Lord is my Provider".

Chapter Five
Moses and Israel

The idea of Israel being a covenant people of God comes from them being the physical seed of Abraham. Also, every male, on the eighth day of their life, was circumcised according to the Abrahamic covenant, when they became a part of the Law Covenant with God.

Though Abraham knew God as El-Shaddai, God Almighty, the children of Israel knew Him by a more personal name derived from "I Am". The name: Yahweh, or Jehova. A name, which means: "Self-existent One".

After Israel had been in Egypt for 400 years, God began His plan to rescue them. Through the 10 plagues, God showed His power and might to deliver Israel. Then when they were allowed to leave, Pharaoh and his army chased after them to enslave them again, but God delivered them by baptizing them into Moses in the Red Sea.

For I do not want you to be ignorant of the fact, brothers and sisters, that our ancestors were all under the cloud and that they all passed through the sea. They were all baptized into Moses in the cloud and in the sea. They all ate the same spiritual food and drank the same spiritual drink; for they drank from the spiritual rock that accompanied them, and that rock was Christ. (1 Corinthians 10:1-4)

Prior to their escape from Egypt, God had them all celebrate their first Passover, where the blood of a lamb was applied to the doorposts. This was when the death angel "passed over" the homes with doors anointed with blood. The death angel then killed the first born of man and animal throughout the land of Egypt, sparing the people of Israel because of the blood. This became a type and shadow of the Cross as the blood of Jesus delivers us from death into life.

This first Passover was when God put Himself into covenant with Israel, the physical seed of Abraham. This Passover was a grant type covenant. They were receivers of the provision and protection of God, and He was going to deliver them out of bondage.

We can see that the Trinity was at work throughout the covenant God had with Israel and His journey with them. After God brought them through the Red Sea, and drowned the Egyptian army in the Red Sea, He brought them to the base of Mt. Sinai where He offered them something wonderful:

God seeks to expand the grant covenant:

"Now if you obey me fully and keep my covenant, then out of all nations you will be my treasured possession. Although the whole Earth is mine, you will be for me a kingdom of priests and a holy nation. These are the words you are to speak to the Israelites." (Exodus 19:5-6)

The basic requirements to keeping this covenant with God, at this point, were to keep the Passover every year, and honor the Sabbath weekly. It was at this point that Israel made a big mistake. As we will see, they stepped back in fear, and sent Moses to be the mediator of a different type of covenant.

God was offering a grant covenant to the whole group, a personal relationship with each person, and for them to be His Kingdom of priests, yet they ended up with the kinship covenant, with its Tabernacle, ten commandments, Ark of the Covenant, and Levitical priesthood.

And the Lord said to Moses, "Go to the people and consecrate them today and tomorrow. Have them wash their clothes and be ready by the third day, because on that day the Lord will come down on Mount Sinai in the sight of all the people. Put limits for the people around the mountain and tell them, 'Be careful that you do not approach the mountain or touch the foot of it. Whoever touches the mountain is to be put to death. They are to be stoned or shot with arrows; not a hand is to be laid on them.

No person or animal shall be permitted to live.' Only when the ram's horn sounds a long blast may they approach the mountain." After Moses had gone down the mountain to the people, he consecrated them, and they washed their clothes.

Then he said to the people, "Prepare yourselves for the third day. Abstain from sexual relations." On the morning of the third day there was thunder and lightning, with a thick cloud over the mountain, and a very loud trumpet blast. Everyone in the camp trembled. Then Moses led the people out of the camp to meet with God, and they stood at the foot of the mountain.

Mount Sinai was covered with smoke, because the Lord descended on it in fire. The smoke billowed up from it like smoke from a furnace, and the whole mountain trembled violently. As the sound of the trumpet grew louder and louder, Moses spoke and the voice of God answered him. (Exodus 19:10-19)

This became a big mistake in Israel's history, and it was also a test from God. He was testing them with the scary mountain appearance to see if they would press through. You have to include another part of the story found in Deuteronomy chapter 5 in order to get the big picture of what was going on:

When you heard the voice out of the darkness, while the mountain was ablaze with fire, all the leaders of your tribes and your elders came to me. And you said, "The Lord our God has shown us his glory and his majesty, and we have heard his voice from the fire.

Today we have seen that a person can live even if God speaks with them. But now, why should we die? This great fire will consume us, and we will die if we hear the voice of the Lord our God any longer. For what mortal has ever heard the voice of the living God speaking out of fire, as we have, and survived? Go near and listen to all that the Lord our God says. Then tell us whatever the Lord our God tells you. We will listen and obey."

The Lord heard you when you spoke to me, and the Lord said to me, "I have heard what this people said to you. Everything they said was good. Oh, that their hearts would be inclined to fear me and keep all my commands always, so that it might go well with them and their children forever!"

Go, tell them to return to their tents. But you stay here with me so that I may give you all the commands, decrees and laws you are to teach them to follow in the land I am giving them to possess." (Deuteronomy 5:23-30)

What we see is that the people, who were drawing near the mountain, stepped back in fear, and sent the elders, the heads of their tribes, to talk to Moses. The elders then expressed the fears of the people, and how they thought they would die if they continued. Remember, these were slaves in Egypt, and I can assume they have a slave mindset, and not a mindset of royalty to be His Kingdom of priests.

The Lord heard their words, fears, and concerns, and accepted what they said, and He then changed His covenantal plan to that of the kinship covenant. He tells them "Get to your tents", as a command to get out of His face.

In Dr. Jonathan Welton's book, "Understanding the Whole Bible", he does a perfect job of explaining the kinship and vassal covenants that God made with Israel. I will try to cover the high points and suggest that you read His book, as well as Dr. Stan Newton's books, "Glorious Kingdom" and "Glorious Covenant", along with this book for a fuller understanding of the Bible and Better Covenant Theology.

The kinship type of covenant becomes the covenant of the 10 commandments, the Ark of the Covenant, the Tabernacle, the Levitical priesthood, all the furnishings and the feasts, as well as the sacrificial system for forgiveness. It's a covenant that brings wrath, based on Romans 4:15. Wrath becomes a topic to be understood. I will share this:

I have noticed 3 schools of thought concerning wrath:

1. Wrath is an aspect of God's character and He is still wrathful at sin in the New Covenant.

2. Jesus took "all" God's wrath so we have no wrath now, but there is a coming wrath in the future. (How does that work if Jesus took "all" the wrath?)

3. God has never had wrath, He has always been like Jesus, and the wrath was coming from another source, such as the devil.

All three of those popular views are wrong. The fivefold ministry needs to know where wrath fits into the Kingdom of God, and our Bible. The correct view, in brief, is as follows:

Wrath is not an aspect of God's character. Wrath is an aspect of the Law. Prior to the Law, God became angered and grieved at sin, but not wrathful, and His anger and grief was the result of sin not yet being atoned for. Wrath breaks out because of covenant violation. There has to be a covenant which has wrath in it for there to be wrath between God and people. Wrath did not come until the Law covenant. There was no wrath at the Cross because God was cutting a New Covenant in the body of His Son, and walking through the blood, as He did with Abraham, and not pouring out wrath.

The wrath of God was completely poured out on the destruction of Jerusalem in 70 AD, and there remains no more wrath at all. God is love, and He has always been love, but the presence of sin, and the Old Covenant, veiled His love. People still sin today, even Christians, but Jesus has taken sin out of the way in relation to God's dealings with humanity. God is no longer holding people's sins against them, whether they are lost or saved.

God sees humanity as either Christian or pre-Christian. He sees humanity as either His child or as a lost child who needs to come home. Wrath was tied to the Law, and with the Law covenant gone, wrath is gone. The Law covenant never reflected the heart of God; it veiled His heart. He magnified the covenant above His own heart (see Psalm 138:2).

The New Covenant has revealed Jesus Christ as the perfect representation of God. God is love. The New Covenant unites God's word with His name (see Psalm 138:2).

When we think of "the Law", which began with this kinship covenant at Mt. Sinai, we must realize that it was specifically for the Hebrew people, and no one else. It's now a system that is done and over with, and it's not something for Jewish people today, or for anyone else. The Law covenant was a temporary covenant, until Jesus came.

Why, then, was the law given at all? It was added because of transgressions until the Seed to whom the promise referred had come. (Galatians 3:19)

Apostle Paul teaches us that the Law covenant, given to Israel, was given because of transgression. Many times we may think it's because of our Gentile sinfulness, but that is not really what he was talking about. In fact, the Law covenant was never for any Gentile, but only for the physical seed of Abraham, the people of national Israel. So, for what transgression was the Law given?

1. Their rejection of God to be a Kingdom of priests in Exodus 19 brought the kinship covenant of Exodus 20, with its 10 commandments, Ark of the Covenant, priesthood, Tabernacle, and many other items. This was their initial sin.

2. Their rejection of the good report from Joshua and Caleb when they spied out the land, and the acceptance of the bad report from the other 10 spies, and their 40 years of grumbling in the wilderness brought the downgrade to the Law covenant, the vassal covenant of Deuteronomy.

That was the transgression, which brought the Law covenant. God used it to conceal Christ, through types and shadows, able to be realized in substance within the New Covenant. These were the final sins, which brought about the Law-based, vassal covenant, with its blessings and curses.

Another area that we must understand "wrath" is in the activity that went on between God and Israel before the Law Covenant at Mt. Sinai and then after the Law Covenant at Mt. Sinai. Here are a few examples:

Before the Law, no wrath:

- Before the Law was given, in Exodus 15:22-26, the Israelites' grumble at the start of their journey which led to no punishment from God.
- Before the Law was given, in Exodus 16:1-15, the Israelites' grumble about the manna and quail which led to no punishment from God.
- Before the Law was given, in Exodus 16:27-30, a Sabbath violation resulted in only a reprimand from God, but no punishment.
- Before the Law was given, in Exodus 17:1-7, the Israelites' grumble over the water which led to no punishment from God.

After the Law, wrath comes:

- After the Law was given, in Numbers 11:1-3, the Israelites' grumble led to a destroying fire.
- After the Law was given, in Numbers 11:33-34, the Israelites' grumble about the manna and quail led to a killing plague.
- After the Law was given, in Numbers 15:32-36, a Sabbath violation resulted in death by stoning.
- After the Law was given, in Numbers 21:4-6, the Israelites' grumble over food and water led to the Lord sending deadly serpents among the people.

Something radically changed at Mt. Sinai with the giving of the Law covenant. What changed is that the Law covenant brought with it wrath, administered by angels as representatives of God.

The book of Leviticus contains the Tabernacle duties for the Levitical priesthood. It also contains blessings and curses, along with future judgment, based on the obedience of the priests.

Next, we move on to the book of Numbers, where things got worse for Israel.

God told Moses to send 12 spies into the land to see what God was about to give them. Ten spies returned with a negative report. Only Joshua and Caleb believed God.

For each day the spies spent in the land, the people would wander one year in the wilderness (see Numbers 14:34). Only the ten spies who gave the negative report were killed instantly. Yet, the forty years in the wilderness were actually a "death sentence", as God revealed in Numbers 14:29-30.

"In this wilderness your bodies will fall - every one of you twenty years old or more who was counted in the census and who has grumbled against me. Not one of you will enter the land I swore with uplifted hand to make your home, except Caleb son of Jephunneh and Joshua son of Nun. As for your children that you said would be taken as plunder, I will bring them in to enjoy the land you have rejected. But as for you, your bodies will fall in this wilderness. Your children will be shepherds here for forty years, suffering for your unfaithfulness, until the last of your bodies lies in the wilderness. For forty years - one year for each of the forty days you explored the land - you will suffer for your sins and know what it is like to have me against you". (Numbers 14:29-34)

By the end of the forty years in the wilderness, the twenty year olds would be sixty, and all the slave minded people of the older generation would be dead, except for Joshua and Caleb.

This marks another significant shift in Israel's history and mindset. Before, when they had rebelled against God, even under the kinship covenant, He had primarily responded with mercy, only punishing the people directly responsible for the rebellion. Now an entire generation had to pay, and they learned the meaning of God's words in Numbers 14:34, having God be against them rather than for them. After pardoning them over and over, God was done with that generation.

A similar scenario to this played out when Old Covenant Israel rejected the Cross. For the next 40 years, God gave them a chance to transition from the Old to the New Covenant. It was a death sentence for those who did not come into the New Covenant and embrace the Lamb of God, Jesus. The 9th of Av, 70 AD, was the destruction of Jerusalem and the Temple, and the evidence that God was done with that generation.

Numbers 15-36 contains the story of their forty-year journey. During this time, the Canaanites actually began to come out into the wilderness and attack Israel, which meant God had to defend them as Israel's covenant partner. In Exodus 23:23-33, God had promised to drive the Canaanites out through His own means, and this is what He would have done if the spies had not spread the negative report. But the Israelites were now stuck wandering in the wilderness for forty years, and during that time, the Canaanites actually became aggressors against them. This set up an enemy scenario between the Israelites and Canaanites that would ultimately be walked out in the conquest of Canaan years later under Joshua's leadership.

However, it was not God's original intention for Israel to make enemies and for God to have to fight their enemies. When the Israelites reached the end of the forty years, they experienced another shift, a change in covenant from kinship to vassal.

Let me reiterate some of what I have already discussed:

God initiated a grant covenant with Israel at the Passover, and led them across the Red Sea in victory, but at Mt. Sinai something radically changed when the Law Covenant was given. To understand what happened, we need to start at the beginning.

Then Moses went up to God, and the Lord called to him from the mountain and said, "This is what you are to say to the descendants of Jacob and what you are to tell the people of Israel: 'You yourselves have seen what I did to Egypt, and how I carried you on eagles' wings and brought you to myself. Now if you obey me fully and keep my covenant, then out of all nations you will be my treasured possession. Although the whole Earth is mine, you will be for me a kingdom of priests and a holy nation.' These are the words you are to speak to the Israelites." (Exodus 19:3-6)

As part of this grant covenant, which began at the first Passover, here we have another element of God's offer to them. He promised divine protection and the privilege of being a nation of priests unto Him. In other words, everyone would have direct access to God as a priest. This was an incredible offer. In verse 8, the people wisely accepted His offer, saying, "We will do everything the Lord has said."

The Lord said to Moses, "I am going to come to you in a dense cloud, so that the people will hear me speaking with you and will always put their trust in you." Then Moses told the Lord what the people had said. And the Lord said to Moses, "Go to the people and consecrate them today and tomorrow. Have them wash their clothes and be ready by the third day, because on that day the Lord will come down on Mount Sinai in the sight of all the people. Put limits for the people around the mountain and tell them, 'Be careful that you do not approach the mountain or touch the foot of it. Whoever touches the mountain is to be put to death. They are to be stoned or shot with arrows; not a hand is to be laid on them. No person or animal shall be permitted to live.' Only when the ram's horn sounds a long blast may they approach the mountain." (Exodus 19:9-13)

In the above verses, God gave Moses instructions for how the people should prepare themselves for the covenant ceremony (this was the test for them similar to how God tested Abraham). He told them to consecrate and wash themselves over three days, and on the third day God would come down on the mountain in a dense cloud. He told them they must not touch the mountain or come near it until they heard the blast of the ram's horn. After that blast, they could come. They were invited to approach, but only after three days. So the people did as God said. In verses 16-17, on the morning of the third day, a thick cloud came down over the mountain, with lightning, thunder, and a loud trumpet blast. Everyone in the camp trembled, and Moses led them out to meet with God at the foot of the mountain. The story continues -

Mount Sinai was covered with smoke, because the Lord descended on it in fire. The smoke billowed up from it like smoke from a furnace, and the whole mountain trembled violently. As the sound of the trumpet grew louder and louder, Moses spoke and the voice of God answered him. (Exodus 19:18-19)

It is at this point in the story that we need some missing information. In Deuteronomy 5 we see the behind the scenes story of what happened when the people heard God speaking in Exodus 19:19

"When you heard the voice out of the darkness, while the mountain was ablaze with fire, all the leaders of your tribes and your elders came to me. And you said, "The Lord our God has shown us his glory and his majesty, and we have heard his voice from the fire. Today we have seen that a person can live even if God speaks with them. But now, why should we die? This great fire will consume us, and we will die if we hear the voice of the Lord our God any longer. For what mortal has ever heard the voice of the living God speaking out of fire, as we have, and survived? Go near and listen to all that the Lord our God says. Then tell us whatever the Lord our God tells you. We will listen and obey." (Deuteronomy 5:23-27)

The people then got scared and told Moses they didn't want to hear God anymore and that Moses should go on their behalf (as a mediator) and simply get the rules and they would obey. Because of their slave-minded fear, they sacrificed relationship and asked for rules instead. Now we can understand the rest of the story in Exodus 19

The Lord descended to the top of Mount Sinai and called Moses to the top of the mountain. So Moses went up and the Lord said to him, "Go down and warn the people so they do not force their way through to see the Lord and many of them perish. Even the priests, who approach the Lord, must consecrate themselves, or the Lord will break out against them." Moses said to the Lord, "The people cannot come up Mount Sinai, because you yourself warned us, 'Put limits around the mountain and set it apart as holy.'" The Lord replied, "Go down and bring Aaron up with you. But the priests and the people must not force their way through to come up to the Lord, or he will break out against them." So Moses went down to the people and told them. (Exodus 19:20-25)

We can see from this that the Lord "adjusted" to the Israelites request, and rather than the whole nation coming up to have relationship, only Moses and Aaron (mediator and high priest) were allowed to come up to get the rules. In the New Covenant Jesus is both Mediator and High Priest of the covenant with His Father.

This was Israel's most tragic moment, because when God came down and talked to the whole nation audibly in Exodus 19:19, they decided, even though they realized they could hear His voice and live, they did not want to hear Him anymore. Instead they chose Moses as a mediator because of their slave-minded fear. Today, we could call that an orphan heart, when we fail to know God as Father, and we are afraid of Him as an angry God who is always pointing out our sin. Thank God in the New Covenant, love has come to drive out fear, and we can know that we are the children of God by faith in Jesus Christ.

From Grant to Kinship Covenant

This is how, in Israel's worst moment, they shifted their covenant with God from a grant covenant to a kinship covenant. In Exodus 19:3-6, God proposed extending their grant covenant, which they received at Passover to make them all a nation or a Kingdom of priests. Yet, in Exodus 19:19 and the parallel passage in Deuteronomy 5:23-27, the Israelites responded in fear to God and asked Moses to be the mediator (this is reiterated in Exodus 20:18-19).

Immediately following this is the giving of the Ten Commandments, which is actually a kinship ceremony according to ancient near-east customs. Rather than Exodus 20 being the record of God making every person a priest, a holy nation, and a treasured possession (see 1 Peter 2:9), as He had proposed to do with them, it is the record of a kinship ceremony, which Paul says brought the ministry of death written and engraven on stones (see 2 Corinthians 3:7).

Now we move on to the vassal covenant section. The vassal covenant came because of their rebellion for 40 years in the wilderness. It was added as an addendum to the previous covenant to witness against them for their rebellion.

The vassal covenant becomes the downfall of national Israel. Deuteronomy contains the prophetic judgment against a future, apostate Israel, mainly, the Song of Moses found in Deuteronomy 32.

The book of Deuteronomy is the end of Moses' life, and transference of leadership is necessary. God used this opportunity to downgrade the Kinship covenant to a Vassal covenant, as an addendum to be placed on the side of the Ark of the Covenant:

"Take this Book of the Law and place it beside the ark of the covenant of the Lord your God. There it will remain as a witness against you." (Deuteronomy 31:26)

Deuteronomy also contains the Song of Moses, which becomes the song sang in the book of Revelation by the Jewish saints in Christ who wanted deliverance from the harlot, Old Covenant system:

Then the Lord appeared at the tent in a pillar of cloud, and the cloud stood over the entrance to the tent. And the Lord said to Moses: "You are going to rest with your ancestors, and these people will soon prostitute themselves to the foreign gods of the land they are entering. They will forsake me and break the covenant I made with them. And in that day I will become angry with them and forsake them; I will hide my face from them, and they will be destroyed. Many disasters and calamities will come on them, and in that day they will ask, 'Have not these disasters come on us because our God is not with us?' And I will certainly hide my face in that day because of all their wickedness in turning to other gods.

"Now write down this song and teach it to the Israelites and have them sing it, so that it may be a witness for me against them. When I have brought them into the land flowing with milk and honey, the land I promised on oath to their ancestors, and when they eat their fill and thrive, they will turn to other gods and worship them, rejecting me and breaking my covenant. And when many disasters and calamities come on them, this song will testify against them, because it will not be forgotten by their descendants. I know what they are disposed to do, even before I bring them into the land I promised them on oath." So Moses wrote down this song that day and taught it to the Israelites. (Deuteronomy 31:15-22)

Now we can briefly look at the connection between Deuteronomy and Revelation:

Deuteronomy and Revelation - A change in covenant and leadership

Deuteronomy – a change from kinship to vassal covenant; change in leadership from Moses to Joshua

Revelation – a change from Old Covenant to New Covenant; change from Temple rulership to Jesus and the Kingdom of God

Similarities:

Deuteronomy - Israel rejected the offer to enter the Promised Land when they believed the negative report of the 10 spies. This led to the vassal covenant, which was a witness against them of their eventual downfall. The testimony of Joshua and Caleb witnessed against them that they should have believed God. A 40-year death march began in which an entire generation died in the wilderness.

Revelation - The generation, which rejected the Cross, began a 40-year death march, which ended in the destruction of the Temple and Jerusalem in 70 AD. The Law and the prophets, who spoke of Jesus, witnessed against Old Covenant Israel that He was their Messiah.

The vassal covenant structure of Deuteronomy:

Deuteronomy Covenant Structure

1. Preamble (1:1-5)
2. Historical Prologue (1:6 – 4:49)
3. Ethical Stipulations (5:1 – 26:19)
4. Sanctions (27:1 – 30:20)
5. Succession Arrangements (31:1 – 34:12)

The vassal covenant structure of Revelation:

Revelation Covenant Structure

1. Preamble: Vision of the Son of Man (1)
2. Historical Prologue: The Seven Churches (2-3)
3. Ethical Stipulations: The Seven Seals (4-7)
4. Sanctions: The Seven Trumpets (8-14)
5. Succession Arrangements: The Seven Vials (15-22)

Deuteronomy warned of what would happen to them. The judgments played out in the book of Revelation.

Four series of Seven judgments

Four times in chapter 26 of Leviticus God says, "I will punish you seven times for your sins" (Lev. 26:18,21,24,28)

Seven is a Heavenly number, while four is an Earthly number (4 rivers flowed out of Eden to water the Earth, 4 corners of the Earth, 4 horns on the altar) – It's a Heavenly judgment poured out on the Earth (the land of Israel)

If a vassal kingdom violated the terms of the covenant, the king would send messengers to the vassal, warning the offenders of coming judgment, in which the curse-sanctions of the covenant would be enforced. This turns out to be the function of the Biblical prophets in the Old Covenant; they were prosecuting attorneys, covenant lawyers, bringing God's message of Covenant Lawsuit to the offending nations of Israel and Judah.

Like other biblical prophecies, the book of Revelation is a prophecy of Covenant wrath against apostate Israel, which irrevocably turned away from the Covenant in her rejection of the Cross. Like Deuteronomy, and other Biblical prophecies, the book of Revelation is written in the form of the Covenant Lawsuit.

The Old Covenant did not reflect God's heart. It was not His first idea for Israel. We can see that in the words of Jeremiah, the prophet:

"This is what the Lord Almighty, the God of Israel, says: Go ahead, add your burnt offerings to your other sacrifices and eat the meat yourselves! For when I brought your ancestors out of Egypt and spoke to them, I did not just give them commands about burnt offerings and sacrifices, but I gave them this command:

Obey me, and I will be your God and you will be my people. Walk in obedience to all I command you that it may go well with you. But they did not listen or pay attention; instead, they followed the stubborn inclinations of their evil hearts. They went backward and not forward. From the time your ancestors left Egypt until now, day after day, again and again I sent you my servants the prophets.

But they did not listen to me or pay attention. They were stiff-necked and did more evil than their ancestors". (Jeremiah 7:21-26)

So, what was it He first spoke to Israel? What was the offer He wanted to give them? It was the grant covenant at Passover and then the offer to be His Kingdom of priests. This was His heart, that they would be His Kingdom of priests, each person in personal relationship with Him.

Then Moses went up to God, and the Lord called to him from the mountain and said, "This is what you are to say to the descendants of Jacob and what you are to tell the people of Israel: 'You yourselves have seen what I did to Egypt, and how I carried you on eagles' wings and brought you to myself.

Now if you obey me fully and keep my covenant, then out of all nations you will be my treasured possession. Although the whole Earth is mine, you will be for me a kingdom of priests and a holy nation.' These are the words you are to speak to the Israelites." (Exodus 19:3-6)

God had already put Himself in covenant with Moses and Israel through the Passover and deliverance from Egypt. He then met with them to expand that covenant, by offering them to be His Kingdom of priests. When they rejected that offer, the Law covenant came, with Moses as the mediator. The Law covenant did not reflect the heart of God. It veiled His heart. The offer to them to be His Kingdom of priests, which is what we have in the New Covenant, did reveal His heart. All the judgments of apostate Israel, which are mentioned in Deuteronomy, were played out in the Revelation of Jesus Christ. There is no more wrath. We have God's heart now in the New Covenant. We must learn to live up to this high calling in Christ Jesus as His Kingdom ambassadors.

When we understand the covenant journey that God had with Israel through Moses and the Law covenant, we can then realize that we do not live under such a covenant. The New Covenant is between the Father and the Son. It was first given to the remnant of believers in Israel according to grace, and they became the new and true Israel of God in Christ. It was this new Israel, organized around 12 apostles and not 12 tribes that carried the message of the Kingdom to the Gentile world. If you are in Christ, you are a part of the Commonwealth of Israel, the arm of the Kingdom of God on the Earth.

Chapter Six
The prophetic life of
Phinehas and Samson

As I discovered the eschatological significance of these two stories in the Bible, I wonder how many more there are in the Old Testament.

Phinehas and the covenant transition of the First century

God certainly likes to paint a prophetic picture for us to see something that relates to the Kingdom of God breaking in through a story in the Old Testament. The story of Phinehas is one such story, obscure, as it may seem.

During the First century, from the Cross of 30AD until the destruction of Jerusalem and the Temple in 70 AD, it was like the 40 years' wilderness experience all over again, like in the days of Moses. Those of Israel who believed in Jesus and embraced the New Covenant would eventually come through this wilderness and inherit the Promised Land, the New Jerusalem, but those of Israel who did not believe in Jesus would die in this wilderness, being destroyed in the city of Jerusalem when the Roman armies broke through.

There is a story in the Old Testament about a man of the priestly line named Phinehas. Paul uses the story of Phinehas as an example for those in the First century to not play the harlot by stubbornly remaining in the Old Covenant, but to come on across in the New Covenant in Christ.

The story involving Phinehas in Numbers goes like this:

Then an Israelite man brought into the camp a Midianite woman right before the eyes of Moses and the whole assembly of Israel while they were weeping at the entrance to the tent of meeting.

When Phinehas son of Eleazar, the son of Aaron, the priest, saw this, he left the assembly, took a spear in his hand and followed the Israelite into the tent. He drove the spear into both of them, right through the Israelite man and into the woman's stomach. Then the plague against the Israelites was stopped; but those who died in the plague numbered 24,000. (Numbers 25:6-9)

Interestingly, Paul referred to this story, along with a few others, and compared it to what the First century Jewish believers in Christ were also going through:

Now these things occurred as examples to keep us from setting our hearts on evil things as they did. Do not be idolaters, as some of them were; as it is written: "The people sat down to eat and drink and got up to indulge in revelry." We should not commit sexual immorality, as some of them did - and in one day twenty-three thousand of them died. We should not test Christ, as some of them did - and were killed by snakes. And do not grumble, as some of them did - and were killed by the destroying angel. These things happened to them as examples and were written down as warnings for us, on whom the culmination of the ages has come. So, if you think you are standing firm, be careful that you don't fall! (1 Corinthians 10:6-12)

In context, the warning of 1 Corinthian 10 was to them of the First century and not us today, yet I am sure there is some application we can draw from it for ourselves today.

It's important to understand that 2 ages were at hand, beginning from the birth of Jesus until the destruction of 70 AD. The age of Moses, of the Old Covenant, was fading away, and the age of the Kingdom, of the New Covenant in Christ, was rising upon them. The warning to them was to enter and then remain inside the New Covenant. Get away from the Temple and from the city of Jerusalem, as Jesus had warned them, and fully enter into the New Covenant, which is in the Spirit.

The warning was to heed the words of Jesus and survive alive through the great tribulation.

"When you see Jerusalem being surrounded by armies, you will know that its desolation is near. Then let those who are in Judea flee to the mountains, let those in the city get out, and let those in the country not enter the city. For this is the time of punishment in fulfillment of all that has been written. How dreadful it will be in those days for pregnant women and nursing mothers! There will be great distress in the land and wrath against this people. They will fall by the sword and will be taken as prisoners to all the nations. Jerusalem will be trampled on by the Gentiles until the times of the Gentiles are fulfilled". (Luke 21:20-24)

Eventually, the city and Temple would fall, and a wonderful liberation would come to the people of God, one of the Spirit. Paul said, *"these things happened to them as an example and were written down as warnings for us, on whom the culmination of the ages has come."* The culmination of the ages was the colliding of the 2 ages of the old and New Covenants. It was a period where 2 ages overlapped, as one ended and a new one began.

Another aspect of this is that God honored Phinehas and his generations with a "covenant of peace" (like the New Covenant), and declared him to be righteous (like Abraham or like we are by faith in Christ).

The Lord said to Moses, "Phinehas son of Eleazar, the son of Aaron, the priest, has turned my anger away from the Israelites. Since he was as zealous for my honor among them as I am, I did not put an end to them in my zeal. Therefore tell him I am making my covenant of peace with him. He and his descendants will have a covenant of a lasting priesthood, because he was zealous for the honor of his God and made atonement for the Israelites." (Numbers 25:10-13)

They yoked themselves to the Baal of Peor and ate sacrifices offered to lifeless gods; they aroused the Lord's anger by their wicked deeds, and a plague broke out among them. But Phinehas stood up and intervened, and the plague was checked. This was credited to him as righteousness for endless generations to come. (Psalm 106:28-31)

God used the "act of righteousness" that Phinehas did as a sign to the generation of Israel who would be leaving the Old Covenant and entering into the true "covenant of peace" and the true "declaration of being righteous" by entering in to the New Covenant of grace. This took courage and boldness, like Phinehas displayed.

God made a memorial of that event, by making a promise and covenant of peace to Phinehas and his generations within that Old Covenant system, or within that age. Many times, when the term forever, eternal, everlasting, and words such as these are used, the real meaning is "age enduring", meaning, to endure until the end of that age.

It all pointed to a greater reality to be realized in Christ. It was a warning to that First century Jewish generation to not play the harlot by remaining in the Old Covenant, but to act as Phinehas, and enter in to the true "covenant of peace" where righteousness truly dwells!

Samson and First Century Israel

There is eschatological significance within the life of Samson. His name means "Sunlight", and he was a Nazarite from birth. His life was a prophetic warning to First century Israel.

1. He was a picture of what Israel was supposed to be to the world: Light and strength, because of their relationship with God.

2. His Nazarite vows pointed to the fact that Israel were supposed to be believers, but by him breaking all 3 of the Nazarite vows, he became like First century, unbelieving Israel who rejected Jesus and the Cross, becoming unbelievers.

3. Within a marriage to God, the Old Covenant in the First century was a harlot in the eyes of God. Those who rejected Jesus in the First century clung to the harlot system of the Old Covenant.

4. Samson, a married man, embraced a harlot, and ended up with Delilah who was also a harlot, and he fell in love with her.

5. First century, unbelieving Israel were blinded and enslaved by the Old Covenant.

6. Samson became blinded and enslaved by the Philistines.

7. The house (Temple) of Israel fell upon them because of their own doing in the destruction of 70 AD, and destroyed a generation who did not believe.

8. A house fell on Samson because of his own doing, and killed him, because of his disobedience.

I would never teach that the things that happened to Samson could happen to us, in the Spirit, in the New Covenant. We are always in Christ, in the place of redemption. God will never turn His back on us, because we are His children, adopted with the blood of His Son.

Samson's life and end become a picture of Old Covenant Israel who embraced the harlot, became blinded, and was brought into bondage until their house collapsed on them.

Chapter Seven
David

The covenant/promises that God made with David loom large in the minds of Jewish people, both then and now. The Davidic Covenant is foundational to the Kingdom of God in the New Covenant. The State of Israel today has the Star of David on its flag, signifying the expectation of the Davidic/Messianic kingdom.

What they miss is that their Messiah has already come, and the Kingdom God promised to David is in the Spirit, and accessed by faith in Jesus Christ. We are not waiting for Israel as a nation to come to Christ through a Jewish revival so that we can enter into a fuller expression of the Kingdom. It would be great if that happened, but it's not necessarily going to happen.

I believe, eventually, the Kingdom of God and the religion of Christ will capture the world, and every nation in this world. Israel without Jesus is just another nation. Without Jesus, the King, you have no Kingdom.

Jesus fulfills the Seed promises made to both Abraham and David. Jesus is the Son God promised. Israel should have believed about their Messiah, that God Himself would be His Father, and He would be God's Son.

The Kingdom and throne are eternal which places its location "in the Spirit". We need not get confused about what it means to be in the Spirit. For us now, it means a faith relationship empowered by the indwelling Holy Spirit, and learning to live out of that reality. But in the future, it will be us living in the glory of Heaven and Earth, which is in bodily resurrection, the fullness of both physical and spirit, Heaven and Earth, humanity and Spirit.

I want to share with you Eight Major Aspects to Understanding the Davidic Covenant:

1. It's foundational to the Kingdom of God.

2. The operation of the key of David.

3. David fought for and obtained the land, which was promised to Abraham.

4. The New Jerusalem fulfills the types and shadows of David and Solomon's kingdom.

5. Dominion restored to humanity in Christ.

6. The restored Tabernacle of David.

7. The writings of David and Solomon prophesy many things concerning the covenant transition period of the First century.

8. David speaks of the Melchizedek priesthood concerning the Messiah.

As I mentioned before, Jesus is the fulfillment of the Seed promises made to Abraham and David. Let's look at the teaching of the Apostles concerning David:

This is the genealogy of Jesus the Messiah the son of David, the son of Abraham. (Matthew 1:1)

...regarding his Son, who as to his Earthly life was a descendant of David. (Romans 1:3)

Remember Jesus Christ, raised from the dead, descended from David. This is my gospel. (2 Timothy 2:8)

Matthew points out that Jesus is the fulfillment of the Seed promises made to both Abraham and David. This is the point of contention with the Jewish people today who are not Christian. If they claim to be people of faith, then they are waiting for the Messiah to come. He has come! And He is coming again, which we will discuss later in this book. Paul focuses on how Jesus is the fulfillment of the Seed promise made to David, which is tied to the Kingdom. This is a part of preaching the gospel of the Kingdom. We must include the significance of these previous covenants and how they pertain to the New Covenant today, so that we may be people of faith with understanding of the things we believe.

The gospel is simple, but growing in Christ requires knowledge. Understanding covenant and the Kingdom requires knowledge.

The Davidic covenant goes like this:

"Now then, tell my servant David, 'This is what the Lord Almighty says: I took you from the pasture, from tending the flock, and appointed you ruler over my people Israel. I have been with you wherever you have gone, and I have cut off all your enemies from before you. Now I will make your name like the names of the greatest men on Earth. And I will provide a place for my people Israel and will plant them so that they can have a home of their own and no longer be disturbed.

Wicked people will not oppress them anymore, as they did at the beginning and have done ever since the time I appointed leaders over my people Israel. I will also subdue all your enemies. 'I declare to you that the Lord will build a house for you: When your days are over and you go to be with your ancestors, I will raise up your offspring to succeed you, one of your own sons, and I will establish his kingdom.

He is the one who will build a house for me, and I will establish his throne forever. I will be his father, and he will be my son. I will never take my love away from him, as I took it away from your predecessor. I will set him over my house and my kingdom forever; his throne will be established forever.'" Nathan reported to David all the words of this entire revelation. (1 Chronicles 17:7-15)

First Point: It's foundational to the Kingdom of God

The first point I want to make is that the Davidic covenant is foundational to the Kingdom of God in the New Covenant, where Jesus is King. According to verses 12 and 14, this throne and this Kingdom are forever. There exists today contention in the Body of Christ as to when this Kingdom started, or if it has started at all. The book of Acts, with Peter preaching, clears up this timing issue:

"Fellow Israelites, I can tell you confidently that the patriarch David died and was buried, and his tomb is here to this day. But he was a prophet and knew that God had promised him on oath that he would place one of his descendants on his throne. Seeing what was to come, he spoke of the resurrection of the Messiah, that he was not abandoned to the realm of the dead, nor did his body see decay.

God has raised this Jesus to life, and we are all witnesses of it. Exalted to the right hand of God, he has received from the Father the promised Holy Spirit and has poured out what you now see and hear. For David did not ascend to Heaven, and yet he said, "'The Lord said to my Lord: "Sit at my right hand..."'" "Therefore let all Israel be assured of this: God has made this Jesus, whom you crucified, both Lord and Messiah." (Acts 2:29-36)

Peter stated that it was at the Resurrection of Jesus that He obtained this throne and this Kingdom. He even gives us the span of this Kingdom reign of Jesus: From the Resurrection *"until I make your enemies a footstool for your feet"*. We see the picture of this in a prophetic vision that Daniel saw:

As I looked, thrones were set in place, and the Ancient of Days took his seat. His clothing was as white as snow; the hair of his head was white like wool. His throne was flaming with fire, and its wheels were all ablaze. A river of fire was flowing, coming out from before him.

Thousands upon thousands attended him; ten thousand times ten thousand stood before him. The court was seated, and the books were opened. Then I continued to watch because of the boastful words the horn was speaking. I kept looking until the beast was slain and its body destroyed and thrown into the blazing fire.

(The other beasts had been stripped of their authority, but were allowed to live for a period of time.) In my vision at night I looked, and there before me was one like a son of man, coming with the clouds of Heaven.

He approached the Ancient of Days and was led into his presence. He was given authority, glory and sovereign power; all nations and peoples of every language worshiped him. His dominion is an everlasting dominion that will not pass away, and his kingdom is one that will never be destroyed. (Daniel 7:9-14)

The Jewish people of the First century who awaited the kingdom of David and who received the gospel message with joy and were saved, these became the new Israel of God. Those Jewish people who missed the Resurrection of Jesus, and did not believe in Jesus, these became the wicked and adulterous generation who rejected Christ, the tares thrown into the fires of the destruction of Jerusalem, also referred to as Gehenna in the gospels.

Today, we live in the power of the Resurrection of Jesus through the born again experience. We live in the Spirit and are ambassadors of the Kingdom of God, which is covering the Earth. God is raising up many ministries to bring His Kingdom into the Earth, and to reverse the effects of curses which bring wars, poverty, rape, darkness.

We live inside the New Covenant, inside the new Heaven and new Earth of the Kingdom. We are pillars in the New Jerusalem, and we walk in dominion, on streets of gold, as we reign in life with Christ. We are seated with Him and in Him, and we are equal sons and daughters of God, equal with Christ in all things. These are the things we must learn to believe about ourselves so that the Kingdom can come fully and the Earth and humanity may be restored.

Second Point: The operation of the key of David

The second aspect of the Davidic covenant is the key of David. Isaiah mentions this for the first time, and he prophesied a few hundred years after David.

I will clothe him with your robe and fasten your sash around him and hand your authority over to him. He will be a father to those who live in Jerusalem and to the people of Judah. I will place on his shoulder the key to the house of David;

what he opens no one can shut, and what he shuts no one can open. I will drive him like a peg into a firm place; he will become a seat of honor for the house of his father. All the glory of his family will hang on him: its offspring and offshoots - all its lesser vessels, from the bowls to all the jars. "In that day," declares the Lord Almighty, "the peg driven into the firm place will give way; it will be sheared off and will fall, and the load hanging on it will be cut down." The Lord has spoken. (Isaiah 22:21-25)

The main point to draw from this is the *"what he opens no one can shut, and what he shuts no one can open"*. What Jesus opened was the New Covenant Kingdom of God. He did this as He established the New Covenant with His Father at the Cross. His death forgave sin, but His Resurrection brought the new creation.

Jesus opened the New Covenant, and He shut or closed up the Old Covenant forever. None shall open it again. It cannot be reopened, because a Muslim mosque sits on the very place where a Jewish Temple would have to be built. Also, there are no more records of who is a Levitical priest. Also, there is no Ark of the Covenant, no tablets or manna or Aaron's rod that budded. That system was meant to be temporary *"until the Seed should come"*, which Paul speaks about in Galatians chapter 3.

The Isaiah 22 section also speaks the language of a new Temple, based on a new throne, and the vessels of the Temple becoming a born again humanity. This is echoed in Matthew 5 where Jesus speaks of the salt and light of the Temple now being people who are salt and light in the world.

Third Point: David fought for and obtained the land, which was promised to Abraham

The third aspect to the Davidic covenant is that David won the land, which was promised, to Abraham. David won it through war, subduing the surrounding kingdoms to Israel, where they brought tribute to him and his kingdom. Solomon enjoyed this for 40 years of peace:

The people of Judah and Israel were as numerous as the sand on the seashore; they ate, they drank and they were happy. And Solomon ruled over all the kingdoms from the Euphrates River to the land of the Philistines, as far as the border of Egypt. These countries brought tribute and were Solomon's subjects all his life. (1 Kings 4:20-21)

The land, which David won and Solomon enjoyed, was the land promise that God gave to Abraham:

On that day the Lord made a covenant with Abram and said, "To your descendants I give this land, from the Wadi of Egypt to the great river, the Euphrates". (Genesis 15:18)

Yet, the book of Hebrews gives us a clue as to what Abraham knew his true inheritance to be. He knew it had to be more than just land:

By faith he made his home in the Promised Land like a stranger in a foreign country; he lived in tents, as did Isaac and Jacob, who were heirs with him of the same promise. For he was looking forward to the city with foundations, whose architect and builder is God. (Hebrews 11:9-10)

The reign of David:

David's reign and Tabernacle is related to the 40 yr. covenant transition period, from 30AD to 70 AD, where the New Covenant was in its infancy and the Kingdom was being restored to the true Israel in Christ. Solomon's reign and the "permanency" of His Temple is related to 70 AD and beyond, to us today. These are types and shadows pointing to a greater reality in Christ.

David's kingdom was a time of warfare and transition, as he and Israel's armies were taking the land promised to Abraham. This is similar to the covenant transition period the apostles and first Church lived in. There was great persecution from every side (warfare), for the Church, and the Tabernacle of David was being restored (Acts 15:15-18).

In David's day, he won the greater land promises made to Abraham through warfare, and, in like manner, the early Church was gaining their inheritance in Christ in the midst of great persecution, with David's Tabernacle being restored.

Solomon's kingdom was a time of peace. He enjoyed the inheritance that David won, and expanded on that kingdom through marriages to the daughters of other kings and kingdoms, creating peace and trade between the kingdoms, which were subdued under him. After 70 AD, the marriage of Jesus and His spouse occurred (a picture of Solomon and his many wives, as in the Song of Solomon), and the Kingdom became present with power after 70 AD, able to advance its agenda of peace, love and forgiveness throughout the Earth.

We live in the marriage to Jesus, the New Covenant, as His spouse, co-heirs with Him. Paul knew it, even saw it, being called up to the "third" Heaven to see the New Jerusalem before she came down to Earth, and he wrote about it, but it was fully released and realized after the Old Covenant harlot system fell out of the way after the events of 70 AD. Our inheritance in Christ comes by understanding Him and ourselves (our identity in Christ), and releasing that into the world we live in through faith and love. The New Covenant is far more glorious than we realize thus far. Let's dig in deeper to all God has for us to find in Him, for we have inherited Jesus Himself.

Lets go to the next point in this series, point 4.

Fourth Point: The New Jerusalem fulfills the types and shadows of David and Solomon's kingdom

The fourth point to understand concerning the Davidic covenant is the New Jerusalem being the reality of the types and shadows of the Old Testament.

The city spoken that Abraham looked for would be the ultimate city, the New Jerusalem, which is made up of the people of God who were the Bride but are now Wife of Jesus the King. This changes everything, and causes us to look at the things of the Old Testament as types and shadows pointing toward a greater reality in Christ. Having the mindset and understanding of Hebraic types and shadows is important if we are going to understand the Bible and the covenant journey of God with man.

The New Jerusalem:

God made a promise to Abraham concerning a large piece of land, which stretched from the River in Egypt to the Great Euphrates River to the east. There were actually 2 aspects to this promise. Within this large piece of land, there was the promise of tribal inheritance for Israel's 12 tribes, which Joshua obtained for Israel through wars. It wasn't until David came that the greater land promise was obtained, with him and Israel's armies fighting and winning battles, causing all surrounding nations and kingdoms to serve him and Israel with tribute. Solomon then got to enjoy this greater land promise for 40 years without any wars, only tribute and service from the surrounding kingdoms and nations. After Solomon's reign, the kingdom divided, and things went into disarray, with eventual capture by the Assyrian and Babylonian armies. See the chapter on Bible Chronology for a better understanding of where various people and events fit into the history of Israel.

The kingdom history of Israel mentioned thus far were types and shadows of a greater reality to be realized in Christ and the New Covenant Kingdom of God. You see, though Abraham was Promised Land, he was looking for something else, a city:

> *By faith he made his home in the Promised Land like a stranger in a foreign country; he lived in tents, as did Isaac and Jacob, who were heirs with him of the same promise. For he was looking forward to the city with foundations, whose architect and builder is God.* (Hebrews 11:9-10)

Abraham looked for the New City of Jerusalem. He had previously met Melchizedek (Shem), who was king of Salem, an early name for Jerusalem, but later he looked for the substance of what those things stood for, a New Jerusalem, a city which has foundations, whose builder and maker is God, with a King and High Priest named Jesus.

So how does the land promises made to Abraham, the tribal inheritance promises made to Moses and Joshua and then the New Jerusalem with Jesus and the New Covenant all tie together?

Abraham's promise begins with this command:

"Go, walk through the length and breadth of the land, for I am giving it to you." (Genesis 13:17)

And then Paul expands on that for us in the New Covenant:

...may have power, together with all the Lord's holy people, to grasp how wide and long and high and deep is the love of Christ. (Ephesians 3:18)

Paul took a two-dimensional land promise and translated it into a 3 dimensional experience. No longer a flat piece of land, but a spiritual "cube", indicating fullness, which is also the shape of the New Jerusalem, as well as the Holy of Holies of the Tabernacle and Temple.

The holy of holies in the Tabernacle and Temple was a cube. It was equally wide as it was deep and tall. In the Tabernacle, it was 10 cubits cubed, and in Solomon's Temple, it was 20 cubits cubed.

How does the tribal land inheritance of the 12 tribes fit into the New Jerusalem scenario? There are 12 gates in the New Jerusalem, the entry into the Kingdom. These 12 gates contain the names of the 12 tribes of Israel, thus reflecting the tribal land inheritance promise given to Moses and Joshua, fully realized in Christ.

It had a great, high wall with twelve gates, and with twelve angels at the gates. On the gates were written the names of the twelve tribes of Israel. (Revelation 21:12)

The Old Covenant was built on the Law and the prophets, but the New Covenant is built upon the prophets and the apostles. God takes the New Covenant prophecies, spoken in the Old Testament by the various prophets, and joins them with the teachings of the Lord's 12 apostles to created the foundational operation of the New Jerusalem:

Consequently, you are no longer foreigners and strangers, but fellow citizens with God's people and also members of his household, built on the foundation of the apostles and prophets, with Christ Jesus himself as the chief cornerstone. In him the whole building is joined together and rises to become a holy temple in the Lord. (Ephesians 2:19-21)

The wall of the city had twelve foundations, and on them were the names of the twelve apostles of the Lamb. (Revelation 21:14)

With all of this said, anytime we read things in the Old Testament, about a glory and goodness being revealed and placed upon Jerusalem or Zion, we are to understand this within the context of the New Covenant.

But you have come to Mount Zion, to the city of the living God, the Heavenly Jerusalem. You have come to thousands upon thousands of angels in joyful assembly. (Hebrews 12:22)

Zion was the place where David built his palace, and was the location of his throne, the seat of authority for the kingdom. Jesus sits, now, upon the throne of David, in Heaven, a Heavenly Zion and a Heavenly Jerusalem, even a Heavenly Israel, that we, in Christ, are all a part of. The types and shadows and physical things find their fulfillment and substance in the New Covenant.

It's in the Spirit! The New Jerusalem is the Kingdom of God! It's now!

Fifth Point: Dominion restored to humanity in Christ

The fifth point to realize about the Davidic covenant is that it brings back the idea of man having dominion. Adam was given dominion, but he lost it. When God made covenant with Noah, there was no promise of Noah and his descendants having dominion. But, in Psalm 8, we see David writing about this:

When I consider your Heavens, the work of your fingers, the moon and the stars, which you have set in place, what is mankind that you are mindful of them, human beings that you care for them? You have made them a little lower than the angels and crowned them with glory and honor. You made them rulers over the works of your hands; you put everything under their feet: (Psalm 8:3-6)

The writer of Hebrews tells us that David was speaking about Jesus in those verses:

But there is a place where someone has testified: "What is mankind that you are mindful of them, a son of man that you care for him? You made them a little lower than the angels; you crowned them with glory and honor and put everything under their feet."

In putting everything under them, God left nothing that is not subject to them. Yet at present we do not see everything subject to them. But we do see Jesus, who was made lower than the angels for a little while, now crowned with glory and honor because he suffered death, so that by the grace of God he might taste death for everyone. (Hebrews 2:6-9)

Jesus declares that this dominion now reaches beyond the realm of Earth, but also includes the realm of Heaven. It's the union of Heaven and Earth that God is after for His Kingdom purpose.

Then Jesus came to them and said, "All authority in Heaven and on Earth has been given to me. (Matthew 28:18)

The goal of the Kingdom, of dominion, of salvation, of relationship with God is the unity of Heaven and Earth in its fullness. This is also the glory of bodily resurrection. It's the fullness of purpose, the fullness of humanity, the fullness of God, the fullness of intimacy with Him.

...as a plan for the fullness of time, to bring all things in Heaven and on Earth together in Christ. (Ephesians 1:10, Berean Study Bible).

We also see that when the Kingdom came in power, after the events of 70 AD, that Jesus said He was "making all things new". This speaks of the continuance of growth as the Kingdom of God spreads through the Earth like leaven working its way through the dough.

He who was seated on the throne said, "I am making everything new!" Then he said, "Write this down, for these words are trustworthy and true." (Revelation 21:5)

What we see at work with the Kingdom of God flowing from Heaven into the Earth is a dominion restored to the redeemed of the Lord for the purpose of restoring the Earth. This is a big part of the New Covenant. For so long, the Church has believed the Earth is unredeemable and that God's plan is to burn it up and make a new one. The burning of Heaven and Earth that Peter spoke of in 2 Peter 3 was in reference to the Old Covenant Temple, not the literal Heavens and Earth. The Jews saw the Temple as a figure of Heaven and Earth itself, and they called it such. We will cover this in later chapters in this book. Much of this may be a paradigm shift in thinking for you, but this is the historical, covenantal, Kingdom, and scholarly view of the Scriptures. It's Better Covenant Theology, a system of interpreting the Bible and living out the Kingdom coined by Dr. Jonathan Welton.

Sixth Point: The restored Tabernacle of David

The sixth area to understanding the Davidic covenant is the restored Tabernacle of David. Historically, the Tabernacle of David was a time in Israel's history, under the reign of David, when the Ark of the Covenant was retrieved from the Philistines, and brought back to Jerusalem where no Temple yet existed. David put up a temporary Tabernacle and tent to cover the ark, and every person in the city of Jerusalem had access to the presence of God. This was a picture of the New Covenant where there is no veil. In the book of Acts, when the apostles saw that Gentiles were being filled with the Holy Spirit too, James, the half-brother of Jesus and Apostle of the Church in Jerusalem, quoted from the prophet Amos:

"In that day I will restore David's fallen shelter - I will repair its broken walls and restore its ruins - and will rebuild it as it used to be, so that they may possess the remnant of Edom and all the nations that bear my name," declares the Lord, who will do these things. (Amos 9:11-12)

When they finished, James spoke up. "Brothers," he said, "listen to me. Simon has described to us how God first intervened to choose a people for his name from the Gentiles. The words of the prophets are in agreement with this, as it is written: "After this I will return and rebuild David's fallen tent. Its ruins I will rebuild, and I will restore it, that the rest of mankind may seek the Lord, even all the Gentiles who bear my name", says the Lord, who does these things - things known from long ago". (Acts 15:13-18)

The Restored Tabernacle of David

Throughout the time period of the Judges, approx. 400 years, the Tabernacle of Moses fell into disarray. Most of the furnishings were probably lost, but they held on to the Ark of the Covenant.

The ark was captured and traveled from here to there for many years, and even landed in the house of Abinadab for 20 years. Saul finally got it back and put it in the battle camp of Israel, thinking he would use it to fight battles.

When David became King, he decided to move the ark to Jerusalem and make Jerusalem the place of worship for Israel. After a mishap of him trying to transport it on a new ox cart, and Uzza touching it and dying, the ark landed in the house of Obed-Edom for several months, where God greatly blessed his home.

David eventually got the ark to Jerusalem where he pitched a tent for it, the Tabernacle of David. This was a place of open worship for all of Israel to stand in the presence of God, where 24/7 worship went on conducted by the Levites. It was a beautiful time in Israel's history.

During the First century, after the Resurrection of Jesus, when the Spirit was poured out, and the gospel began to make in-roads to the Gentiles, the apostles realized a promise being fulfilled, that God would rebuild the Tabernacle of David. God's presence and power was available to everyone who would believe.

This rebuilding of the Tabernacle of David, as prophesied in Amos and fulfilled in Acts 15, was part of the covenant transition period where the Old Covenant was fading away and the New Covenant was emerging.

Historically, the Tabernacle of David lasted for a period of time, until Solomon built a permanent Temple, a house for God, which was David's desire all along. In like manner, this rebuilding of the Tabernacle of David was for a period of time, until 70 AD, when the true Temple, New City of Jerusalem, and where God Himself is the Temple, emerged forth on the Earth.

I did not see a temple in the city, because the Lord God Almighty and the Lamb are its temple. (Revelation 21:22)

Seventh Point: The writings of David and Solomon prophesy many things concerning the covenant transition period of the First century

The seventh point that I want to make about the Davidic covenant is that David, in the Psalms, and even Solomon, in the Proverbs, prophesied in various ways such topics as the Cross, the new birth, the downfall of harlot Jerusalem, the first coming of Jesus to redeem Israel, the ending of the Old Covenant system, and a generation of unbelieving Old Covenant people being destroyed, which we know happened in 70 AD.

I will give one example from Psalms and one example from Proverbs:

All of Psalm 2 is about God using the heathen or Gentile armies to destroy the wicked of His people, but in verse 12, something profound is stated, that is Messianic:

Kiss his son, or he will be angry and your way will lead to your destruction, for his wrath can flare up in a moment. Blessed are all who take refuge in him. (Psalm 2:12)

The exhortation to Israel was to kiss or embrace the Son (the Messiah, Son of David and Son of God according to the Davidic covenant) when He comes. It then speaks of His wrath, the wrath of the Lamb, which was poured out on Jerusalem and the Temple in 70 AD, the great tribulation. But, blessed are all they that put their trust (faith) in Him (Jesus). That is very straightforward.

In Proverbs 7, Solomon writes about the wiles of a seducing harlot, and the eventual death of the man who embraces her. We all know that a man can be with a harlot and not die, but this is actually speaking covenantally to Israel. The Old Testament prophets began to call Israel, Jerusalem and Judah a harlot, an adulterous woman, committing whoredoms and spiritual adultery with her Husband, Yahweh. When you read what Solomon wrote in Proverbs 7, it becomes a prophecy to Israel to avoid this harlot when the day approaches. The New Covenant is about a pure Bride marrying her King Husband, Jesus. Since Jerusalem had become this harlot, the harlot of Babylon, then the book of Revelation becomes a sentence of judgment against this harlot for her unfaithfulness. This is the divorce of a harlot played out with judgments according to the Law she boasted of. We will cover more of this in later chapters.

Eighth Point: David speaks of the Melchizedek priesthood concerning the Messiah

The eighth and final point I want to make about understanding the Davidic covenant is that David mentions Melchizedek, the priest of God who met Abraham. As we discussed, this Melchizedek is Shem, Noah's son, who was the king of Salem, an early name for Jerusalem. The types and shadows of that are amazing!

Psalm 110, written by David, is a prophetic message for the destruction of the old system and the coming of the New Covenant: (Are you noticing this as being a theme throughout the Bible?)

The Lord says to my Lord: "Sit at my right hand until I make your enemies a footstool for your feet." The Lord will extend your mighty scepter from Zion, saying, "Rule in the midst of your enemies!" Your troops will be willing on your day of battle. Arrayed in holy splendor, your young men will come to you like dew from the morning's womb.

The Lord has sworn and will not change his mind: "You are a priest forever, in the order of Melchizedek." The Lord is at your right hand; he will crush kings on the day of his wrath. He will judge the nations, heaping up the dead and crushing the rulers of the whole Earth. He will drink from a brook along the way, and so he will lift his head high. (Psalm 110:1-7)

Jesus one day questioned the Pharisees about this Psalm.

While the Pharisees were gathered together, Jesus asked them, "What do you think about the Messiah? Whose son is he?" "The son of David," they replied. He said to them, "How is it then that David, speaking by the Spirit, calls him 'Lord'? For he says, "'The Lord said to my Lord: "Sit at my right hand until I put your enemies under your feet."'' If then David calls him 'Lord,' how can he be his son?" No one could say a word in reply, and from that day on no one dared to ask him any more questions. (Matthew 22:41-46)

Jesus quoted from the first line of the Psalm, which was the Hebraic way of drawing your audience to the entire Psalm. He basically asked them, "What does this Psalm mean?" They did not know. The connection to Melchizedek, to David's covenant, and to the New Covenant was more than they could comprehend.

It would be good for us if we had a better understanding than the First century Pharisees had. The Pharisees admitted that the Christ is the Son of David but they failed to admit that He is also the Son of God, according to the Davidic Covenant. It was their refusal to believe that Jesus was the Son of God, which lead to His crucifixion.

The Davidic Covenant

The Davidic Covenant (a Grant Covenant) - "A House for God"

2 Samuel 7:5-17, 2 Samuel 7:28-29

(1 Chronicles 17:11-14, 2 Chronicles 6:16, Psalm 89:3-4, Psalm 110, Matthew 1:1, Matthew 22:42, Jeremiah 23:5, Jeremiah 30:9, Isaiah 9:7, Isaiah 11:1, John 7:42, Acts 2:29-36, Acts 13:34, Romans 1:3, 2 Tim. 2:8, Revelation 3:7, Revelation 5:5, Revelation 22:16)

Four Major Promises of the Davidic Covenant for the Seed of David

1. I will make your name great
2. I will be his father, and he will be My son
3. I will build you a house
4. Your house, kingdom, and throne shall be forever

The promise to "*make your name great*" echoes back to God's promise to Abram in Genesis 12. In contrast to the people's effort at the Tower of Babel to make a name for themselves, God chose Abram and promised to make his name great. Here, He did the same for David. He recounted His relational history with David (see 2 Samuel 7:8-9), and then He offered him this covenant that recalled the Abrahamic covenant: "*Now I will make your name great like the names of the greatest men on Earth*" (2 Samuel 7:9). Like the Abrahamic covenant, this is a grant covenant. God seems to always want to make grant covenants. He gave them to Noah and Abraham, and He tried to give one to Israel (the free offer to be His Kingdom of priests), which turned into a kinship covenant (because of their rejection) and eventually lead to a vassal type covenant (because of their rebellion for 40 yrs). In the midst of this vassal covenant system, David arose as a man who genuinely wanted to honor the Lord (by building the Lord a house), and in response, the Lord honored him back (by promising him a house, a kingdom). So the first part of God's promise to David was that He would make his name great.

I will be his father, and he will be My son (2 Samuel 7:13-14)

These verses speak of Solomon as a shadow type, with the reality and substance being Christ.

I will build you a house (2 Samuel 7:11-12)

Your house, kingdom, and throne will be forever (2 Samuel 7:13-16)

The Davidic and Abrahamic covenants are the "covenants of promise" mentioned in Ephesians 2:12

A similarity between the Davidic and Abrahamic covenants is the appearance of a man named Melchizedek (his title, not his name). Noah's son Shem (the oldest living relative of Abraham at that time would have been the priest of the family that Abraham honored – Shem is Melchizedek, king of a literal city called Salem, and by meaning of his name "King of Righteousness", the true title for Jesus).

Only three places in Scripture mention Melchizedek. The first in Genesis 12, where Abram met him, and Melchizedek blessed him (Noah and his sons had been blessed by God, and Shem found Abraham to transfer the blessing to him which ultimately traveled to mankind through Jesus and those in Him). The second mention of his name is found is in Psalm 110, written by David. Third, the author of Hebrews mentions him several times, primarily in chapter 7 where he contrasts the Levitical priesthood to the priesthood after the order of Melchizedek. Therefore, Melchizedek is mentioned in the context of the Abrahamic and Davidic covenants, and as a contrast to the priesthood of the Mosaic covenant.

110 is the most quoted Psalm in the New Testament, quoted more than thirty times. Psalm 110 is a very important Psalm inside the New Covenant. It is written by David and mentions Melchizedek, which ties it back to Abraham. Therefore, the Abrahamic and Davidic covenants are the foundation of the New Covenant, as Matthew mentions in the opening line of his gospel.

The writer of Hebrews, who wrote to Jews who were struggling to make the transition from the old to the New Covenant, mentions Melchizedek as the priesthood, which is superior to the Levitical priesthood, because Jesus is a High Priest after the order of

Melchizedek, a Messianic promise. It's important to note that Melchizedek is mentioned only in context of the Abrahamic and Davidic covenants as they point to the New Covenant for fulfillment.

Chapter Eight
Bible chronology;
the history of Israel

The Chronology of the Old Testament and history of Israel goes like this:

- Garden of Eden

- Job (preflood)

- Noah and the flood

- Abraham, Isaac, Jacob (Israel)

- Joseph

- Israel goes to Egypt for 430 years – slavery

- Israel escapes Egypt - Passover, covenant initiated (a type of the Cross)

- Mt. Sinai, the Law (kinship covenant, 10 commandments, Tabernacle)

- Leviticus is for the Levitical priests (blessings and curses)

- Moses sends the 12 spies (10 give bad report, 2 give good report)

- 40 years in the wilderness (the book of Numbers)

- Deuteronomy (a change of leadership from Moses to Joshua, a change in covenant from kinship to vassal because on 40 years of rebellion in the wilderness). Deuteronomy becomes a covenant lawsuit based on the vassal covenant, and prophesies the eventual end of the Old Covenant (see the song of Moses, which was also sung in Revelation about the ending of the Old Covenant). Deuteronomy is written in a 5-part structure based on a vassal covenant treaty between a Great King and a Lesser King.

- Joshua takes over leadership. He accomplishes the conquest of the land that would become Israel's tribal inheritance.

- The times of the Judges. There were some victories and some defeats, based on obedience or disobedience to the vassal covenant. Several kings and kingdoms oppress Israel during this time.

- The story of Ruth reveals the family line of David.

- Saul is picked as king by the people, but later rejected by God for his disobedience. God then tells Samuel the prophet to anoint David as king. David waits his turn to take the throne, running from Saul and writing many of the Psalms during this timer.

- Saul is king for 40 years while David waits. This becomes a picture of something past and something future for Israel. Past, it's a picture of one generation dying in the wilderness after 40 years and one generation being prepared to enter into the land of inheritance. Future, it's a picture of unbelieving Israel who rejected the Cross "wandering in the wilderness" until the destruction of Jerusalem in 70 AD, while believing Israel is releasing the gospel to the world waiting for the Kingdom to be "present with power", which came after the fall of Jerusalem in 70 AD.

- David becomes king and reigns for 40 years. David and Israel's armies win the greater land promised to Abraham, from the Euphrates to the River in Egypt. David receives the plans for the Tabernacle but cannot build it for being a man of bloodshed. David plans for the next generation by storing up the materials for the future Tabernacle to be built by his son. David receives the promise of the Kingdom to come through his Seed (Jesus) to reign upon his throne.

- Solomon becomes king and reigns for 40 years. Peace with no wars. Solomon and Israel enjoy the greater land promised to Abraham. Solomon builds the Temple.

- After Solomon the kingdom divides between 2 men, Rehoboam (Solomon's son) and Jeroboam (son of Nebat)

Most people have a basic understanding of the Old Testament and chronology up to this point. It typically goes astray from here.

- Jeroboam took 10 tribes, which became known as the kingdom of Israel or the Northern kingdom.

- Rehoboam took 2 tribes, (Judah and Benjamin) which became known as the kingdom of Judah or the Southern kingdom. The Levites, who were priests and had no land inheritance, joined with the kingdom of Judah (see 2 Chronicles 11:13-17)

- The kingdom of Israel, the 10 tribes, the Northern kingdom: Many kings come and go. All the kings of Israel were bad or worse.

- Prophets during that time (bringing covenant lawsuit based on the vassal covenant and/or a future hope of the New Covenant to Israel) are Elijah, Elisha, Jonah, Amos, Hosea.

- The kingdom of Israel is taken captive by Assyria 722 BC. These became the lost tribes of Israel. A scattered remnant later returns to the land.

- Other names used among the prophets for the Northern kingdom are Ephraim and Samaria. Nineveh of Assyria, who took the kingdom of Israel captive, is later destroyed by Babylon.

- The kingdom of Judah, the 2 tribes with Levi, the Southern kingdom: Many kings come and go. Some are good, some - bad.

- Prophets during that time (bringing covenant lawsuit based on the vassal covenant and/or a future hope of the New Covenant to Israel) are Obadiah, Joel, Isaiah, Micah, Nahum, Zephaniah, Habakkuk, Jeremiah, Daniel, and Ezekiel.

- The kingdom of Judah is taken captive by Babylon in 586 BC. Isaiah, Jeremiah and Ezekiel prophesied the destruction of Jerusalem. Daniel and Ezekiel are taken captive into Babylon. Daniel becomes powerful there. Daniel prophesies about the Kingdom and the coming of Messiah. Ezekiel prophesies about a new, spiritual Temple and a new city of Jerusalem.

- While in Babylon, the Pharisees are formed, and become the ruling influence in Israel after the return from exile. Judah and Benjamin along with the Levites, and some other scattered tribes return to the land.

- The Persians take over Babylon and take the Jewish people captives. The story of Esther in Persia occurs.

- Cyrus the king of Persia releases the Jews back to their land.

- Ezra and Nehemiah return to the land to rebuild the Temple and the wall and to restore the religion of Israel, yet without an Ark of the Covenant.

- After the return to the land, 3 prophets arise: Haggai, Zechariah, and Malachi.

- Malachi deals with a corrupt Levitical priesthood, and prophesies about a curse and a drastic change coming to Israel.

- The drastic change becomes the message of the Kingdom and the New Covenant. Believing Jews carry this message after Jesus is crucified. A shift to what Israel was, from law to the Kingdom in Jesus, 12 apostles, a New Jerusalem, a new Temple, a new priesthood, a New Covenant.

- The curse becomes the destruction of Jerusalem (Genesis 12:3 and Galatians 3:16), the Temple and the priesthood in 70 AD by the Roman armies. This was the time of Jacob's trouble that Jeremiah prophesied about.

Chapter Nine
The prophets of the Old Covenant
(Covenant lawyers)

The prophets of the Old Covenant, under the vassal covenant, were like God's prosecuting attorneys. They brought a charge against the people of God, or against the priest, or king, for violating God's covenant.

If a vassal kingdom violated the terms of the covenant, the king would send messengers to the vassal, warning the offenders of coming judgment, in which the curse-sanctions of the covenant would be enforced. This turns out to be the function of the Biblical prophets in the Old Covenant; they were prosecuting attorneys, covenant lawyers, bringing God's message of Covenant Lawsuit to the offending nations of Israel and Judah.

The first prophecy that speaks of coming judgment upon His covenant people, Israel, is found in the book of Deuteronomy. Deuteronomy was written at the end of Moses' life. Much of it rehearses their rebellion in the wilderness for the past 40 years, and then adjusts the covenant for an addendum to it, the vassal covenant, where more rules, more blessings for obedience, and more curses for disobedience are added to what was previously given to them. Now the Law, if it wasn't before, became a heavy burden to them, which they could not bear, although God told them once,

If you obey the Lord your God and keep his commands and decrees that are written in this Book of the Law and turn to the Lord your God with all your heart and with all your soul. Now what I am commanding you today is not too difficult for you or beyond your reach. It is not up in Heaven, so that you have to ask,

"Who will ascend into Heaven to get it and proclaim it to us so we may obey it?" Nor is it beyond the sea, so that you have to ask, "Who will cross the sea to get it and proclaim it to us so we may obey it?" No, the word is very near you; it is in your mouth and in your heart so you may obey it. See, I set before you today life and prosperity, death and destruction. (Deuteronomy 30:10-15)

In the First century, with the offer of salvation in the New Covenant, if they had chosen life, it would have led them into the Kingdom of God with Jesus. Those who believed in Jesus, of Israel, were those who chose life.

The first prophecy that speaks of coming judgment upon His covenant people, Israel, is found in the book of Deuteronomy

Then the Lord appeared at the tent in a pillar of cloud, and the cloud stood over the entrance to the tent. And the Lord said to Moses: "You are going to rest with your ancestors, and these people will soon prostitute themselves to the foreign gods of the land they are entering. They will forsake me and break the covenant I made with them.

And in that day I will become angry with them and forsake them; I will hide my face from them, and they will be destroyed. Many disasters and calamities will come on them, and in that day they will ask, 'Have not these disasters come on us because our God is not with us?' And I will certainly hide my face in that day because of all their wickedness in turning to other gods.

"Now write down this song and teach it to the Israelites and have them sing it, so that it may be a witness for me against them. When I have brought them into the land flowing with milk and honey, the land I promised on oath to their ancestors, and when they eat their fill and thrive, they will turn to other gods and worship them, rejecting me and breaking my covenant.

And when many disasters and calamities come on them, this song will testify against them, because it will not be forgotten by their descendants. I know what they are disposed to do, even before I bring them into the land I promised them on oath." So Moses wrote down this song that day and taught it to the Israelites. (Deuteronomy 31:15-22)

Another prophecy about their coming destruction and loss of the land came to Solomon after he built the Temple:

"But if you or your descendants turn away from me and do not observe the commands and decrees I have given you and go off to serve other gods and worship them, then I will cut off Israel from the land I have given them and will reject this temple I have consecrated for my Name. Israel will then become a byword and an object of ridicule among all peoples.

This temple will become a heap of rubble. All who pass by will be appalled and will scoff and say, 'Why has the Lord done such a thing to this land and to this temple?' People will answer, 'Because they have forsaken the Lord their God, who brought their ancestors out of Egypt, and have embraced other gods, worshiping and serving them - that is why the Lord brought all this disaster on them.'" (1 Kings 9:6-9)

This prophecy is for Israel, and was fulfilled through the events of 70 AD and the war with the Roman armies. One of the promises contained in that section was *"This temple will become a heap of rubble"*. The judgment was that when they turn their backs on God, and serve other gods, then He will cut them off from the land and their house, Temple, will be destroyed. People will be astonished that pass by it, and ask *"Why has the Lord done this to this people?"* When first century Israel did not believe in Jesus, then those unbelievers became those who seek after other gods. Jesus was the way to righteousness and the way to the Father, and any other way would be both anti-Christ and the worship of an idol or false god.

The prophets of the Old Testament were typically prophesying 2 basic messages within their writings:

1. Coming judgment, either immediate, or in the future, for Jerusalem, Israel and Judah. The culmination of this came in 70 AD. Under the Old Covenant, God would judge surrounding nations to show He is God over all and to fight for His people because of the vassal covenant. He was both punisher and protector of His people under that type of covenant. This is a hard point for many to wrap their head around, but it's a key to understanding the whole Bible as God's covenant journey with humanity.

   Three examples of God judging a surrounding nation can be found in Isaiah 13:10,13 - God's judgment on Babylon, Isaiah 34:4 - God's judgment on Idumea, and Ezekiel 32:7,8 - God's judgment on Egypt. In Amos 8:9, we see God judging Israel. These were all judgments based on the vassal covenant, and in the New Covenant world we live in today, this is not how God operates. The New Covenant has revealed His love for humanity. It was always there, yet veiled, and confined to operate as a Judge under the Law covenant. Under the New Covenant, He is Father, and humanity is His children, many lost who need to come home, and some saved and filled with His love.

2. The coming New Covenant, Kingdom of God, with its blessings for humanity, and a restored Earth. Isaiah prophesied about this restored Earth under the New Covenant. They were never prophesying, in the Old Testament, some event to happen in our day or in our future. These were covenantal prophets, and their judgments pertained to Old Covenant Israel.

I believe the Earth and humanity are moving toward a restoration because of the New Covenant. It's because the Kingdom of God is spreading throughout the entire Earth, as leaven spreads in dough. Here are some prophecies from Isaiah concerning this restoration, and then a word from Peter in the book of Acts that confirms this:

He will judge between the nations and will settle disputes for many peoples. They will beat their swords into plowshares and their spears into pruning hooks. Nation will not take up sword against nation, nor will they train for war anymore. (Isaiah 2:4)

The wolf will live with the lamb, the leopard will lie down with the goat, the calf and the lion and the yearling together; and a little child will lead them. The cow will feed with the bear, their young will lie down together, and the lion will eat straw like the ox. The infant will play near the cobra's den, and the young child will put its hand into the viper's nest. They will neither harm nor destroy on all my holy mountain, for the Earth will be filled with the knowledge of the Lord as the waters cover the sea. (Isaiah 11:6-9)

"Never again will there be in it an infant who lives but a few days, or an old man who does not live out his years; the one who dies at a hundred will be thought a mere child; the one who fails to reach a hundred will be considered accursed. They will build houses and dwell in them; they will plant vineyards and eat their fruit. No longer will they build houses and others live in them, or plant and others eat. For as the days of a tree, so will be the days of my people; my chosen ones will long enjoy the work of their hands. They will not labor in vain, nor will they bear children doomed to misfortune; for they will be a people blessed by the Lord, they and their descendants with them. Before they call I will answer; while they are still speaking I will hear. The wolf and the lamb will feed together, and the lion will eat straw like the ox, and dust will be the serpent's food. They will neither harm nor destroy on all my holy mountain," says the Lord. (Isaiah 65:20-25)

...and that he may send the Messiah, who has been appointed for you - even Jesus. Heaven must receive him until the time comes for God to restore everything, as he promised long ago through his holy prophets. (Acts 3:20-21)

Isaiah also spoke on eschatological issues, which always deal with the ending of the Old Covenant as a system, with the removal of its Temple and land.

Isaiah is one of the prophets with many prophetic phrases, which pointed forward to the eschatological last days of Old Covenant Israel.

One thing we need to understand is that when Jesus came, He divided the nation of Israel. He divided them into unbelievers and believers. The unbelievers rejected Jesus and His Cross, and stubbornly held onto the Old Covenant, remaining in physical Jerusalem, their "holy city", while believing Israel left the Old Covenant, embraced Jesus and His Cross, and entered into something new, the spiritual, new Jerusalem, the spiritual Mt. Zion, which is the Kingdom of God.

It was believing Israel which took the gospel of the Kingdom to the Gentiles, and now to the whole world. We have been grafted into the remnant, believing Israel, so that all believers in Christ are the Israel of God in Christ.

Let's look at what Isaiah was talking about, concerning eschatology in Israel, in Isaiah 4:2-6

verse 2 - *In that day the Branch of the Lord shall be beautiful and glorious; and the fruit of the Earth shall be excellent and appealing for those of Israel who have escaped.*

The Branch is Jesus. "In that day" is speaking of the Eschatological last days of the Old Covenant, when Jerusalem was being destroyed and the Kingdom of God was ready to be revealed with power. This verse mentions "Those of Israel who have escaped". This is speaking of escaping the physical Jerusalem as it was being destroyed to enter the beauty of the New Jerusalem as a sign of His Presence and protection for us.

verse 3 - *And it shall come to pass that he who is left in Zion and remains in Jerusalem will be called holy - everyone who is recorded among the living in Jerusalem.*

The Zion and Jerusalem spoken of here is the Mt. Zion of the Kingdom and the New Jerusalem. This is made up of those who are made holy by the Holy Spirit, by the work of Jesus, and these are called "The Living".

verse 4 - *When the Lord has washed away the filth of the daughters of Zion, and purged the bloodshed of Jerusalem from her midst, by the spirit of judgment and by the spirit of burning.*

This verse speaks of the destruction of Jerusalem, where God poured out His wrath, used the Roman armies to judge, destroy, and burn the city and Temple to the ground.

This was the end of the Old Covenant system, and the end of the wrath of God. In God's eyes, He was washing away the filth of sin and purging the bloodshed, which had taken place in Jerusalem over the centuries, as the prophets were killed.

verse 5 - *then the Lord will create above every dwelling place of Mt. Zion and above her assemblies, a cloud and smoke by day and the shining of a flaming fire by night. For over all the glory there will be a covering (canopy).*

This verse speaks of the Glory of God dwelling among His people, the New Jerusalem, which came down out of Heaven to the Earth after the Old Covenant Harlot System was judged. The marriage has now happened between Jesus and His Bride. God uses the picture of the Tabernacle in the wilderness and how He was with them as a cloud and smoke by day and a fire by night.

verse 6 - *And there will be a tabernacle for shade in the daytime from the heat, for a place of refuge , and for a shelter from storm and rain.*

This verse is filled with prophetic symbolism, speaking of the protection of the Lord among His people.

Isaiah, Jeremiah, Ezekiel, as well as Daniel, Zechariah, and other prophets all spoke of the coming judgment on Israel and Jerusalem, which was ultimately fulfilled in 70 AD, and of the coming New Covenant Kingdom of God.

The Babylonian army destroyed Jerusalem in 586 BC. This was when they went into captivity for 70 years, which the angel told Daniel was actually a 490 year captivity. When Israel came out of Babylon and back to their own land, they never had freedom again. They were under the rule of the Persians, the Greeks and the Romans and then Jesus came shortly after Rome had become a kingdom with a dynastic line of Emperors, from Julius Caesarto Caesar Nero, the last in that family line. In the first century, Jerusalem had become Babylon, and Rome was the beast to destroy the harlot. We will cover all of this in later chapters.

The prophets of the Old Covenant, the vassal covenant, were God's prosecuting attorneys, sent to declare judgment based on covenant violation. Under the New Covenant, prophets are God's declarers of His love and forgiveness. A different covenant has a different law, a different priesthood, and the prophets have a different message. It's called the good news of the Kingdom of God.

Chapter Ten
Daniel's 70 weeks

Many charts have been made concerning the 70 weeks of Daniel's prophecy. It's important to understand that the prophecies of Daniel were fulfilled within Israel and ultimately Jesus, and is, therefore, not about our future. In order to understand the prophecy, for many have strayed off course with their charts, we must determine if it was for the covenant people of Old Covenant Israel, or for the whole world at some time in the future. This is the same question we must answer in order to understand the book of Revelation correctly.

My view is that the entire Bible is written with covenant Israel in mind, in the Old Covenant, and then the transition into the New Covenant throughout the New Testament, where what once was the physical bloodline of Abraham is now the children of Abraham according to faith in Jesus. So, the prophecies of Daniel are for Old Covenant Israel, and they speak of the Cross and destruction of Jerusalem in 70 AD. Daniel also speaks of the Resurrection of Jesus in the twelfth chapter.

The prophecy of Daniel's 70 weeks goes like this:

...in the first year of his reign, I, Daniel, understood from the Scriptures, according to the word of the Lord given to Jeremiah the prophet, that the desolation of Jerusalem would last seventy years. (Daniel 9:2)

This is the covenant lawsuit against Israel while under that vassal covenant:

All Israel has transgressed your law and turned away, refusing to obey you. "Therefore the curses and sworn judgments written in the Law of Moses, the servant of God, have been poured out on us, because we have sinned against you. You have fulfilled the words spoken against us and against our rulers by bringing on us great disaster.

Under the whole Heaven nothing has ever been done like what has been done to Jerusalem. Just as it is written in the Law of Moses, all this disaster has come on us, yet we have not sought the favor of the Lord our God by turning from our sins and giving attention to your truth. The Lord did not hesitate to bring the disaster on us, for the Lord our God is righteous in everything he does; yet we have not obeyed him. (Daniel 9:11-14)

Here is the prophecy, which was for Old Covenant Israel:

As soon as you began to pray, a word went out, which I have come to tell you, for you are highly esteemed. Therefore, consider the word and understand the vision: "Seventy 'sevens' are decreed for your people and your holy city to finish transgression, to put an end to sin, to atone for wickedness, to bring in everlasting righteousness, to seal up vision and prophecy and to anoint the Most Holy Place.

"Know and understand this: From the time the word goes out to restore and rebuild Jerusalem until the Anointed One, the ruler, comes, there will be seven 'sevens,' and sixty-two 'sevens.' It will be rebuilt with streets and a trench, but in times of trouble. After the sixty-two 'sevens,' the Anointed One will be put to death and will have nothing. The people of the ruler who will come will destroy the city and the sanctuary. The end will come like a flood: War will continue until the end, and desolations have been decreed. He will confirm a covenant with many for one 'seven.' In the middle of the 'seven' he will put an end to sacrifice and offering. And at the temple he will set up an abomination that causes desolation, until the end that is decreed is poured out on him." (Daniel 9:23-27)

First of all, we find Daniel worrying about the days he lived in, which God greatly cared about, but the angel came to tell Daniel of a time in the future, when a desolation would occur, but also the forgiveness of sins would come. This was the transition from old to New Covenant which happened in the first century, mainly from 30 AD to 70 AD, a 40-year generation.

The seventy weeks he mentions are to be understood as 70 times 7, or 490 years (There is agreement on this among scholars). For this 490-year span of time, the clock began ticking in 457 BC. The Jews were captive in Persia, and in that year, Artaxerxes, the king of Persia, decreed that the Jews were free to return to their homeland and rebuild Jerusalem and the Temple (Ezra 7:12-26).

The first seven weeks, or 49 years, of this prophecy were fulfilled in 408 BC, when Jerusalem was restored and rebuilt. This was after Israel began to return to their land.

The next set of weeks, the 62 weeks, or 434 years, takes us up to when Jesus began His ministry, around 27 AD. This was when *"the Most Holy was anointed"*. At the baptism of Jesus, when His ministry officially began, Jesus was baptized in the Holy Spirit.

In the middle of the last week, the 70th week, the crucifixion occurred. Jesus was crucified around 30 AD. This was when transgression was finished, He made an end to sins, reconciliation for iniquity, and through His Resurrection, He brought in everlasting righteousness. Jesus was the end of the Law for righteousness. He was the reality and substance that the Law with its rituals pointed to. Jesus was the Perfect Passover Lamb who delivers from death forever.

It speaks of the prince that shall come and destroy the city and sanctuary. This jumps forward to 70 AD, when General Titus came, while his father Vespasian reigned over the Roman Empire. The destruction of 70 AD was part of the first coming and finished work of Jesus. This was His completed first mission. General Titus burned Jerusalem to the ground, and plowed the ground up. It was later rebuilt, but Old Covenant Jerusalem was utterly destroyed, with only 3 of the original towers standing in the city today.

Jesus caused the sacrifice to cease, making the Old Covenant "obsolete" by His Cross, yet the Temple and Levitical priesthood continued to operate for 40 more years, until its destruction in 70 AD. The Law, though obsolete at the Cross, remained active, yet fading (see Hebrews 8:13). In the middle of the week, Jesus was crucified. But, the end of the week, when the 490 years were expired, what happened? That would have been around 34 AD.

That was when Stephen preached his sermon to the Jewish Temple rulers, and told them they were rejecting the Holy Spirit by rejecting the New Covenant. This was when the 490 years ended, and God's plan of judgment began, which culminated with Him using Roman armies to destroy the city in the infamous year of 70 AD. Stephen offered the system, which God was wrapping up, the opportunity to come into the Kingdom of God through the New Covenant. They rejected it. Let's look at what Stephen told them:

Now Stephen, a man full of God's grace and power, performed great wonders and signs among the people. Opposition arose, however, from members of the Synagogue of the Freedmen (as it was called)-Jews of Cyrene and Alexandria as well as the provinces of Cilicia and Asia-who began to argue with Stephen. But they could not stand up against the wisdom the Spirit gave him as he spoke.

Then they secretly persuaded some men to say, "We have heard Stephen speak blasphemous words against Moses and against God." So they stirred up the people and the elders and the teachers of the law. They seized Stephen and brought him before the Sanhedrin. They produced false witnesses, who testified, "This fellow never stops speaking against this holy place and against the law. For we have heard him say that this Jesus of Nazareth will destroy this place and change the customs Moses handed down to us." All who were sitting in the Sanhedrin looked intently at Stephen, and they saw that his face was like the face of an angel. (Acts 6:8-15)

Stephen was telling them that God was done with that covenant with its Temple, and this offended them. Stephen goes on to rehearse to them the history of Israel. It's a wonderful journey through the Bible in chapter 7 of Acts. But, I want us to focus on what Stephen told them at the end of the sermon:

Then the high priest asked Stephen, "Are these charges true?" To this he replied: "Brothers and fathers, listen to me! The God of glory appeared to our father Abraham while he was still in Mesopotamia, before he lived in Harran. (Acts 7:1-2)

When the high priest asked Stephen if these accusations against him were true, Stephen began to preach the history of Israel, to prove that what he had been saying was true. After his journey through their history, he rails on them for rejecting their hope of eternal life.

> *However, the Most High does not live in houses made by human hands. As the prophet says: "'Heaven is my throne, and the Earth is my footstool. What kind of house will you build for me? says the Lord. Or where will my resting place be? Has not my hand made all these things?' "You stiff-necked people! Your hearts and ears are still uncircumcised. You are just like your ancestors: You always resist the Holy Spirit! Was there ever a prophet your ancestors did not persecute? They even killed those who predicted the coming of the Righteous One. And now you have betrayed and murdered him - you who have received the law that was given through angels but have not obeyed it."*

> *When the members of the Sanhedrin heard this, they were furious and gnashed their teeth at him. But Stephen, full of the Holy Spirit, looked up to Heaven and saw the glory of God, and Jesus standing at the right hand of God. "Look," he said, "I see Heaven open and the Son of Man standing at the right hand of God." At this they covered their ears and, yelling at the top of their voices, they all rushed at him, dragged him out of the city and began to stone him. Meanwhile, the witnesses laid their coats at the feet of a young man named Saul. While they were stoning him, Stephen prayed, "Lord Jesus, receive my spirit." Then he fell on his knees and cried out, "Lord, do not hold this sin against them." When he had said this, he fell asleep.* (Acts 7:48-60)

Deuteronomy 30:6 told Israel of a coming time when their heart would be circumcised. Stephen uses that against them by reminding them that they are uncircumcised in heart and ears, and always resisting the Holy Spirit, even as their fathers, who killed the prophets, did. Their murder of him brought the judgment of God. He was the angel sent to them to bring them into the New Covenant, and they rejected it and killed the messenger.

The 490 years were now finished, and Babylon the harlot would be judged, which was first century Jerusalem. God had a new Bride for His Son to marry, a new Israel in Christ, and this marriage happened after the harlot city was destroyed.

Daniel also prophesied about the coming of the Messiah, His birth, the Rock of God, who would bring in a Kingdom, which would cover the Earth as a Mountain. Daniel 2 contains this prophecy:

In the second year of his reign, Nebuchadnezzar had dreams; his mind was troubled and he could not sleep. So the king summoned the magicians, enchanters, sorcerers and astrologers to tell him what he had dreamed. When they came in and stood before the king, he said to them, "I have had a dream that troubles me and I want to know what it means." Then the astrologers answered the king, "May the king live forever! Tell your servants the dream, and we will interpret it."

The king replied to the astrologers, "This is what I have firmly decided: If you do not tell me what my dream was and interpret it, I will have you cut into pieces and your houses turned into piles of rubble. But if you tell me the dream and explain it, you will receive from me gifts and rewards and great honor. So tell me the dream and interpret it for me." Once more they replied, "Let the king tell his servants the dream, and we will interpret it." Then the king answered, "I am certain that you are trying to gain time, because you realize that this is what I have firmly decided: If you do not tell me the dream, there is only one penalty for you. You have conspired to tell me misleading and wicked things, hoping the situation will change. So then, tell me the dream, and I will know that you can interpret it for me."

The astrologers answered the king, "There is no one on Earth who can do what the king asks! No king, however great and mighty, has ever asked such a thing of any magician or enchanter or astrologer. What the king asks is too difficult. No one can reveal it to the king except the gods, and they do not live among humans."

This made the king so angry and furious that he ordered the execution of all the wise men of Babylon. So the decree was issued to put the wise men to death, and men were sent to look for Daniel and his friends to put them to death.

When Arioch, the commander of the king's guard, had gone out to put to death the wise men of Babylon, Daniel spoke to him with wisdom and tact. He asked the king's officer, "Why did the king issue such a harsh decree?" Arioch then explained the matter to Daniel.

At this, Daniel went in to the king and asked for time, so that he might interpret the dream for him. Then Daniel returned to his house and explained the matter to his friends Hananiah, Mishael and Azariah. He urged them to plead for mercy from the God of Heaven concerning this mystery, so that he and his friends might not be executed with the rest of the wise men of Babylon.

The night the mystery was revealed to Daniel in a vision. Then Daniel praised the God of Heaven and said: "Praise be to the name of God for ever and ever; wisdom and power are his. He changes times and seasons; he deposes kings and raises up others. He gives wisdom to the wise and knowledge to the discerning. He reveals deep and hidden things; he knows what lies in darkness, and light dwells with him. I thank and praise you, God of my ancestors: You have given me wisdom and power, you have made known to me what we asked of you, you have made known to us the dream of the king."

Then Daniel went to Arioch, whom the king had appointed to execute the wise men of Babylon, and said to him, "Do not execute the wise men of Babylon. Take me to the king, and I will interpret his dream for him." Arioch took Daniel to the king at once and said, "I have found a man among the exiles from Judah who can tell the king what his dream means."

The king asked Daniel (also called Belteshazzar), "Are you able to tell me what I saw in my dream and interpret it?" Daniel replied, "No wise man, enchanter, magician or diviner can explain to the king the mystery he has asked about, but there is a God in Heaven who reveals mysteries. He has shown King Nebuchadnezzar what will happen in days to come.

Your dream and the visions that passed through your mind as you were lying in bed are these: "As Your Majesty was lying there, your mind turned to things to come, and the revealer of mysteries showed you what is going to happen. As for me, this mystery has been revealed to me, not because I have greater wisdom than anyone else alive, but so that Your Majesty may know the interpretation and that you may understand what went through your mind. "Your Majesty looked, and there before you stood a large statue-an enormous, dazzling statue, awesome in appearance.

The head of the statue was made of pure gold, its chest and arms of silver, its belly and thighs of bronze, its legs of iron, its feet partly of iron and partly of baked clay. While you were watching, a rock was cut out, but not by human hands. It struck the statue on its feet of iron and clay and smashed them. Then the iron, the clay, the bronze, the silver and the gold were all broken to pieces and became like chaff on a threshing floor in the summer. The wind swept them away without leaving a trace. But the rock that struck the statue became a huge mountain and filled the whole Earth.

"This was the dream, and now we will interpret it to the king. Your Majesty, you are the king of kings. The God of Heaven has given you dominion and power and might and glory; in your hands he has placed all mankind and the beasts of the field and the birds in the sky. Wherever they live, he has made you ruler over them all. You are that head of gold. "After you, another kingdom will arise, inferior to yours. Next, a third kingdom, one of bronze, will rule over the whole Earth.

Finally, there will be a fourth kingdom, strong as iron-for iron breaks and smashes everything-and as iron breaks things to pieces, so it will crush and break all the others. Just as you saw that the feet and toes were partly of baked clay and partly of iron, so this will be a divided kingdom; yet it will have some of the strength of iron in it, even as you saw iron mixed with clay. As the toes were partly iron and partly clay, so this kingdom will be partly strong and partly brittle. And just as you saw the iron mixed with baked clay, so the people will be a mixture and will not remain united, any more than iron mixes with clay.

"In the time of those kings, the God of Heaven will set up a kingdom that will never be destroyed, nor will it be left to another people. It will crush all those kingdoms and bring them to an end, but it will itself endure forever. This is the meaning of the vision of the rock cut out of a mountain, but not by human hands - a rock that broke the iron, the bronze, the clay, the silver and the gold to pieces. "The great God has shown the king what will take place in the future. The dream is true and its interpretation is trustworthy. "

Then King Nebuchadnezzar fell prostrate before Daniel and paid him honor and ordered that an offering and incense be presented to him. The king said to Daniel, "Surely your God is the God of gods and the Lord of kings and a revealer of mysteries, for you were able to reveal this mystery." Then the king placed Daniel in a high position and lavished many gifts on him. He made him ruler over the entire province of Babylon and placed him in charge of all its wise men. Moreover, at Daniel's request the king appointed Shadrach, Meshach and Abednego administrators over the province of Babylon, while Daniel himself remained at the royal court.

The statue from the dream represents a succession of kingdoms until you get to the Kingdom of God. It started at Babylon, to Persia, to the Greeks, to the Romans, and then the rock comes during the Roman kingdom, striking the feet, which were the 10 provinces of the Roman empire.

This is the prophecy of Jesus coming as the Rock of God, and His life and influence spreads as the Kingdom of God, as a Mountain, until it covers the whole Earth. We live inside the process of this happening now. We are the instruments God has chosen to use in order to bring His Kingdom and justice into the Earth. As I have previously spoken, a restoration of Earth and humanity is currently in process.

Chapter Eleven
Zechariah and
70 AD prophecy

Zechariah's prophecy is filled with fantastic spiritual imagery, of angelic horses riding across the skies keeping watch. These horses with riders seem to be keeping up with Israel's prophetic time clock. The horsemen of Revelation carry out the closing judgment on national Israel and the Old Covenant system.

I want to focus on the prophecies concerning Jesus and 70 AD. Zechariah prophesied after the Babylonian destruction of Jerusalem, and there was a rebuilding going on during that time. Therefore, Zechariah's prophecies about a coming destruction of Jerusalem were for the first century generation to experience.

The 2 olive trees:

Zechariah sees 2 olives trees feeding oil to the golden candlestick. We know in Revelation 11:3-4 that these 2 olive trees and 2 candlesticks are the 2 witnesses.

It was the Law and the prophets, which testified as 2 witnesses against Old Covenant Israel that Jesus is their Savior and Messiah. It was the Law and the prophets that declared He was the fulfillment of the Abrahamic and Davidic covenants. It was the Law and the prophets, which were as 2 olive trees standing before the throne revealing the Son prior to His incarnation. There is still gold to be mined concerning Jesus in the Law and the prophets for us today.

Revelation speaks of them prophesying and then being killed, raised up and taken up to Heaven. Jesus fulfilled the Law and the prophets, so symbolically, they were representing Him in that portion of Revelation, dying and rising up into Heaven. They spoke of Him, and it was He and His Cross, which Old Covenant Israel rejected.

113

We find the source of these 2 witnesses as the 2 olive trees in the prophecy of Zechariah

Then the angel who talked with me returned and woke me up, like someone awakened from sleep. He asked me, "What do you see?" I answered, "I see a solid gold lampstand with a bowl at the top and seven lamps on it, with seven channels to the lamps. Also there are two olive trees by it, one on the right of the bowl and the other on its left."

I asked the angel who talked with me, "What are these, my Lord?" He answered, "Do you not know what these are?" "No, my Lord," I replied. So he said to me, "This is the word of the Lord to Zerubbabel: 'Not by might nor by power, but by my Spirit,' says the Lord Almighty. "What are you, mighty mountain? Before Zerubbabel you will become level ground. Then he will bring out the capstone to shouts of 'God bless it! God bless it!'" (Zechariah 4:2-7)

The word in Zechariah describing this begins with the candlestick. The purpose of the candlestick or lampstand was to lead the High Priest into the presence of the Lord at the Ark of the Covenant. It was a light. Zechariah speaks of these 2 olives trees, the Law and the prophets, and the Messianic promises contained in them, are supplying oil for light. They were a light for a season, an age, to Israel. When the light of the world had come, the fulfillment of those promises and prophecies was finished.

The word of the Lord to Zerubbabel, who was part of laying the foundation for the rebuilt Temple (Christ being the chief cornerstone of the foundation of the real Temple, built upon the promises and teachings of the prophets and apostles based on Ephesians 2:20), was

"...not by might, nor by power but by My Spirit".

The Temple and Kingdom in Christ is not of flesh but of Spirit, by grace. The great mountain that Zerubbabel was before would represent the Old Covenant world. There was a shout coming forth to that old system, *"Grace, grace to it!"*

The 2 witnesses of Revelation are the Law and the prophets, symbolically represented by Moses and Elijah, who appeared to Jesus at His transfiguration. They witnessed against the wicked unbelievers of Israel, of Old Covenant Israel who rejected Jesus as Messiah and rejected His Cross.

I believe the 2 olive trees represent the Messianic promises for Israel, which witnessed against the unbelieving Jews of the first century. This is what fueled the early Church, and should fuel the Church today, the promises of God in the Old Covenant, meant for us in the New Covenant. In fact, the Church is built upon the apostles and prophets, meaning, the teaching of the Lord's apostles, and the Old Testament prophecies relating to the New Covenant. This is what we, as Gentiles, are grafted into. The olive tree, the Messianic promises for Israel, and the world, for those who believe in Jesus.

If some of the branches have been broken off, and you, though a wild olive shoot, have been grafted in among the others and now share in the nourishing sap from the olive root, do not consider yourself to be superior to those other branches. If you do, consider this: You do not support the root, but the root supports you.

You will say then, "Branches were broken off so that I could be grafted in." Granted. But they were broken off because of unbelief, and you stand by faith. Do not be arrogant, but tremble. For if God did not spare the natural branches, he will not spare you either. Consider therefore the kindness and sternness of God: sternness to those who fell, but kindness to you, provided that you continue in his kindness. Otherwise, you also will be cut off.

And if they do not persist in unbelief, they will be grafted in, for God is able to graft them in again. After all, if you were cut out of an olive tree that is wild by nature, and contrary to nature were grafted into a cultivated olive tree, how much more readily will these, the natural branches, be grafted into their own olive tree! (Romans 11:17-24)

Zechariah speaks of a coming new Temple that is not by might and power but by the Spirit of the Lord, with shouts of "*grace, grace, to it*". The great mountain was the Old Covenant Temple, which had to go.

Then the angel who talked with me returned and woke me up, like someone awakened from sleep. He asked me, "What do you see?" I answered, "I see a solid gold lampstand with a bowl at the top and seven lamps on it, with seven channels to the lamps. Also there are two olive trees by it, one on the right of the bowl and the other on its left." I asked the angel who talked with me, "What are these, my Lord?" He answered, "Do you not know what these are?" "No, my Lord," I replied. So he said to me, "This is the word of the Lord to Zerubbabel: 'Not by might nor by power, but by my Spirit,' says the Lord Almighty. "What are you, mighty mountain? Before Zerubbabel you will become level ground. Then he will bring out the capstone to shouts of 'God bless it! God bless it!'" Then the word of the Lord came to me: "The hands of Zerubbabel have laid the foundation of this temple; his hands will also complete it. Then you will know that the Lord Almighty has sent me to you. (Zechariah 4:1-9)

Zechariah spoke of Jesus, the Branch, being a priest and a king, which is after the order of Melchizedek. He is the one who builds the new Temple of the New Covenant, made up of believers. Verse 13 says He shall be a priest upon his throne, and the counsel of peace shall be between them both. This is a Kingdom promise, but a reality for us today. Jesus is the priest on the throne, and the peace of the Kingdom is upon it all. The Kingdom of God is a Kingdom of peace. The counsel of peace is between these 2 offices of priest and king, in the Kingdom of God.

Tell him this is what the Lord Almighty says: 'Here is the man whose name is the Branch, and he will branch out from his place and build the temple of the Lord. It is he who will build the temple of the Lord, and he will be clothed with majesty and will sit and rule on his throne. And he will be a priest on his throne.

And there will be harmony between the two.' The crown will be given to Heldai, Tobijah, Jedaiah and Hen son of Zephaniah as a memorial in the temple of the Lord. Those who are far away will come and help to build the temple of the Lord, and you will know that the Lord Almighty has sent me to you. This will happen if you diligently obey the Lord your God. (Zechariah 6:12-15)

In chapters 12, 13 and 14, the prophecies center more on the coming destruction of Jerusalem, which occurred in 70 AD. I will bring out a few of the high lights and try to explain them.

A prophecy: The word of the Lord concerning Israel. The Lord, who stretches out the Heavens, who lays the foundation of the Earth, and who forms the human spirit within a person, declares:

"I am going to make Jerusalem a cup that sends all the surrounding peoples reeling. Judah will be besieged as well as Jerusalem. On that day, when all the nations of the Earth are gathered against her, I will make Jerusalem an immovable rock for all the nations. All who try to move it will injure themselves. (Zechariah 12:1-3)

Jerusalem, seen as a harlot and unfaithful wife to God, and as Babylon the harlot, was being warned of coming judgment through the prophecies of Zechariah. Zechariah then goes on to prophesy about those who came into the New Covenant, relating it to the house of David, which is the line of Jesus. It's symbolic language speaking of Jesus being the Messiah, through the covenantal line of David and Judah.

"And I will pour out on the house of David and the inhabitants of Jerusalem a spirit of grace and supplication. They will look on me, the one they have pierced, and they will mourn for him as one mourns for an only child, and grieve bitterly for him as one grieves for a firstborn son". (Zechariah 12:10)

This similar language is used by John in Revelation, speaking of the "coming of Jesus" in judgment against Jerusalem:

"Look, he is coming with the clouds," and "every eye will see him, even those who pierced him"; and all peoples on Earth "will mourn because of him." So shall it be! Amen.
(Revelation 1:7)

This covenantal language is used to connect the prophecies together as pointing to the same event, the destruction of 70 AD. The Jewish believers of the first century would have understood this type of language and would have made the connection. Many times, and centuries later, and differences of cultures, we read these verses in Revelation and think it means something completely different than the original intention of John when he wrote it.

It's important to note that *"tribes of the land"* is the correct translation of that verse, and not *"peoples of the Earth"*, as if it's speaking of a worldwide destruction. It's localized to Israel and specifically, Jerusalem.

The next verse speaks of the New Covenant of forgiveness and cleansing coming to the inhabitants of Jerusalem:

On that day a fountain will be opened to the house of David and the inhabitants of Jerusalem, to cleanse them from sin and impurity. "On that day, I will banish the names of the idols from the land, and they will be remembered no more," declares the Lord Almighty. "I will remove both the prophets and the spirit of impurity from the land".
(Zechariah 13:1-2)

The house of David is in reference to Jesus being the Seed promised to David, making Jesus the Messiah and Son of God.

The next verse eludes to the Cross, and how Jesus was crucified by His own people"

If someone asks, 'What are these wounds on your body?' they will answer, 'The wounds I was given at the house of my friends.' (Zechariah 13:6)

Chapter 14 is also tied to the destruction of Jerusalem in 70 AD. There is some confusing, symbolic language used, but this is typical of prophets, and something for us to seek to understand.

A day of the Lord is coming, Jerusalem, when your possessions will be plundered and divided up within your very walls. I will gather all the nations to Jerusalem to fight against it; the city will be captured, the houses ransacked, and the women raped. Half of the city will go into exile, but the rest of the people will not be taken from the city. Then the Lord will go out and fight against those nations, as he fights on a day of battle. (Zechariah 14:1-3)

God used the Roman armies to destroy the wicked unbelievers in Jerusalem in 70 AD, but He also protected His New Covenant people from that same army.

The feast of tabernacles was a celebration of their exodus out of Egypt. Jerusalem in the first century had become like a new Egypt that the people of God need to escape from. The keeping of the feasts of tabernacles is symbolic language for the reality of living in the freedom of the New Jerusalem, the New Covenant, escaping the bondage of slavery.

Then the survivors from all the nations that have attacked Jerusalem will go up year after year to worship the King, the Lord Almighty, and to celebrate the Festival of Tabernacles. (Zechariah 14:16)

Again, the reference to the feast of tabernacles is symbolic in the sense of celebrating the escape from Egypt, or the escape from the bondage of the Old Covenant into the freedom of the New Covenant.

During that time, those who did not enter the New Covenant were judged and destroyed.

This will be the punishment of Egypt and the punishment of all the nations that do not go up to celebrate the Festival of Tabernacles. (Zechariah 14:19)

119

Many times, such as in Ezekiel's Temple vision, imagery of the Old Covenant with its rituals and vessels is mentioned. This is alluding to the types and shadows which those things represent, and pointing forward to the reality of these things in Christ in the New Covenant. The vessels of the Lord go from being "things" in the Temple of the Old Covenant, to being people who are as the furnishings of the new Temple in Christ.

A key to understanding Old Testament prophecy is found within something Jesus said:

For this is the time of punishment in fulfillment of all that has been written. (Luke 21:22)

The *"all things, which are written"* that were being fulfilled were the Old Testament prophecies concerning the destruction of Jerusalem and the New Covenant arriving. This was the shift in covenants, from physical to spiritual, from old to new, the 40-year period of covenant transition. Based on what Jesus said, every Old Testament prophecy was fulfilled or had arrived at the time of the days of vengeance, which was the great tribulation for Israel in 70 AD.

Chapter Twelve
Malachi and
the coming silence

In the books of Moses, you have Exodus, Leviticus, Numbers and Deuteronomy. Each book has a specific purpose in mind.

Exodus – The deliverance of Israel from Egypt and the establishing of the Mosaic, kinship covenant.

Leviticus – This book is the priestly code and duties, with requirements for the people of Israel, since it was the job of the priest to teach the people these things. It's full of many types and shadows, which usually point to the Cross for significance. There were blessings and curses in this book based on obedience and disobedience, for both the people and the priesthood.

Numbers – This book documents the 40 years in the wilderness, with instances of God's wrath at work, based on that kinship covenant.

Deuteronomy – This book was written at the end of Moses' life, when a change in leadership was about to occur, from Moses to Joshua. Because Moses was the mediator of the kinship covenant, his death brought reason for a change in the covenant, where God attached an addendum to the previous covenant. He added more rules, blessings and curses, and the covenant was downgraded to a vassal covenant. A vassal covenant is a treaty between a Great King and His servants. Israel now became the servants of the Lord, where He first offered them to be His Kingdom of priests. Paul seemed proud of this language, identifying himself as the bond slave of the Lord. It seems today we find more teaching on sonship than servantship, and I am not saying if that is good or bad. Just an observation. Much of Deuteronomy rehearses their 40 years of rebellion in the wilderness, and there fear of taking the Promised Land.

Joshua then covers their conquest of the land until they obtained the tribal promises of God for Israel:

So the Lord gave Israel all the land he had sworn to give their ancestors, and they took possession of it and settled there. The Lord gave them rest on every side, just as he had sworn to their ancestors. Not one of their enemies withstood them; the Lord gave all their enemies into their hands. Not one of all the Lord's good promises to Israel failed; everyone was fulfilled. (Joshua 21:43-45)

By the time we get to Malachi, a lot has happened. The kingdom of Israel formed, reigned, and then divided after Solomon's reign. Each kingdom went into captivity, both Israel and Judah, oppressed by the Assyrians and the Babylonians. It was only Judah, along with Benjamin and some Levites, who came back to the land after their captivity. When they came back to rebuild, a few of the other tribes may have wandered back, but mostly Israel consisted of the tribes of Judah and Benjamin, with some Levites.

The book of Malachi is mostly about the Levites and Temple duties. It shows how the priesthood was not living by example, and was misleading the people of God. It was in this book that God said He would send the curse, which became realized in 70 AD.

Malachi prophesied about the coming Sun, or King of Righteousness, and how He was coming to cleanse His Temple. This speaks of the destruction of 70 AD.

Let's look at a few Scriptures in Malachi:

"Oh, that one of you would shut the temple doors, so that you would not light useless fires on my altar! I am not pleased with you," says the Lord Almighty, "and I will accept no offering from your hands. My name will be great among the nations, from where the sun rises to where it sets. In every place incense and pure offerings will be brought to me, because my name will be great among the nations," says the Lord Almighty. "But you profane it by saying, 'The Lord's table is defiled,' and, 'Its food is contemptible.'

And you say, 'What a burden!' and you sniff at it contemptuously," says the Lord Almighty. "When you bring injured, lame or diseased animals and offer them as sacrifices, should I accept them from your hands?" says the Lord.

"Cursed is the cheat who has an acceptable male in his flock and vows to give it, but then sacrifices a blemished animal to the Lord. For I am a great king," says the Lord Almighty, "and my name is to be feared among the nations. (Malachi 1:10-14)

The prophet Malachi was bringing covenantal accusation against the Levite priests. God is finding fault with the priesthood of the Levites, and their sacrifices and offerings were shameful. God speaks of how He is wearied with them, and reminds them that He is also Lord of the Gentiles. This speaks into the coming New Covenant when language such as that is used.

Chapter 2 of Malachi is a complete indictment against the Levitical priesthood in Israel:

"And now, you priests, this warning is for you. If you do not listen, and if you do not resolve to honor my name," says the Lord Almighty, "I will send a curse on you, and I will curse your blessings. Yes, I have already cursed them, because you have not resolved to honor me.

"Because of you I will rebuke your descendants; I will smear on your faces the dung from your festival sacrifices, and you will be carried off with it. And you will know that I have sent you this warning so that my covenant with Levi may continue," says the Lord Almighty.

"My covenant was with him, a covenant of life and peace, and I gave them to him; this called for reverence and he revered me and stood in awe of my name. True instruction was in his mouth and nothing false was found on his lips. He walked with me in peace and uprightness, and turned many from sin.

"For the lips of a priest ought to preserve knowledge, because he is the messenger of the Lord Almighty and people seek instruction from his mouth. But you have turned from the way and by your teaching have caused many to stumble; you have violated the covenant with Levi," says the Lord Almighty.

"So I have caused you to be despised and humiliated before all the people, because you have not followed my ways but have shown partiality in matters of the law." Do we not all have one Father? Did not one God create us? Why do we profane the covenant of our ancestors by being unfaithful to one another? Judah has been unfaithful.

A detestable thing has been committed in Israel and in Jerusalem: Judah has desecrated the sanctuary the Lord loves by marrying women who worship a foreign god. As for the man who does this, whoever he may be, may the Lord remove him from the tents of Jacob -- even though he brings an offering to the Lord Almighty. Another thing you do: You flood the Lord's altar with tears. You weep and wail because he no longer looks with favor on your offerings or accepts them with pleasure from your hands.

You ask, "Why?" It is because the Lord is the witness between you and the wife of your youth. You have been unfaithful to her, though she is your partner, the wife of your marriage covenant. Has not the one God made you? You belong to him in body and spirit. And what does the one God seek? Godly offspring. So be on your guard, and do not be unfaithful to the wife of your youth.

"The man who hates and divorces his wife," says the Lord, the God of Israel, "does violence to the one he should protect," says the Lord Almighty. So be on your guard, and do not be unfaithful. You have wearied the Lord with your words. "How have we wearied him?" you ask. By saying, "All who do evil are good in the eyes of the Lord, and he is pleased with them" or "Where is the God of justice?" (Malachi 2:1-17)

We are not Levitical priests, and we are not operating under that covenant. It's good to know where you stand when you read and study the Word of God. We have a high standard in the New Covenant, but its empowered by grace in the Holy Spirit.

Malachi 3 is the famous chapter on tithing that many preachers have used to get offerings from the people. The ones who have done this I am sure do it in all sincerity of heart. But, the truth is, we are not under that covenant, and we are not giving to upkeep a Temple, and we are not giving food offerings for the priests, and so on. This chapter is completely Old Covenant, and there is no curse associated with anything in the New Covenant.

There is no condemnation in Christ. We give our resources and money to advance the Kingdom of God, and we are blessed people because we have faith in Jesus Christ. God is not sending curses or the devourer to us when we do not give. He is not eating up the produce of our crops, neither in the natural nor in the Spirit. We remain blessed people when we give or do not give. We are not under obligation, but we operate and live by faith and love. We should give to see the Kingdom advance.

"Will a mere mortal rob God? Yet you rob me. "But you ask, 'How are we robbing you?' "In tithes and offerings. You are under a curse-your whole nation-because you are robbing me. Bring the whole tithe into the storehouse, that there may be food in my house. Test me in this," says the Lord Almighty, "and see if I will not throw open the floodgates of Heaven and pour out so much blessing that there will not be room enough to store it. I will prevent pests from devouring your crops, and the vines in your fields will not drop their fruit before it is ripe," says the Lord Almighty. "Then all the nations will call you blessed, for yours will be a delightful land," says the Lord Almighty. (Malachi 3:8-12)

This was a rebuke to Old Covenant Israel, not something we need to preach today. Its history and covenantal, and if anything, we should learn what they did so that we can appreciate what we have so much more!

Chapter 4 is full of language pointing to the destruction of the Old Covenant system and the coming of the New Covenant Kingdom of God:

> *"Surely the day is coming; it will burn like a furnace. All the arrogant and every evildoer will be stubble, and the day that is coming will set them on fire," says the Lord Almighty. "Not a root or a branch will be left to them. But for you who revere my name, the sun of righteousness will rise with healing in its rays. And you will go out and frolic like well-fed calves. Then you will trample on the wicked; they will be ashes under the soles of your feet on the day when I act," says the Lord Almighty. "Remember the law of my servant Moses, the decrees and laws I gave him at Horeb for all Israel. "See, I will send the prophet Elijah to you before that great and dreadful day of the Lord comes. He will turn the hearts of the parents to their children, and the hearts of the children to their parents; or else I will come and strike the land with total destruction."* (Malachi 4:1-6)

The curse came in 70 AD, which was the finish of the Old Covenant with all of its trappings. It's impossible to ever recreate that system again. At best, it would be a counterfeit with no purpose and no power. God has moved on, and He lives inside His own covenant, the New Covenant, and He operates through love and forgiveness toward humanity, desiring all people to be saved and filled with the Holy Spirit.

At the end of Malachi's prophecy, not another prophetic word came to Israel for the next 400 years, as many found themselves awaiting the Messiah. As the gospel opens up, we see Simeon, and Zachariah and Elizabeth, Mary, Joseph, Anna, and others waiting with expectation for the Messiah to come. The Word itself became flesh, the Word that Israel had become hungry for. He had arrived. The Law covenant existed "until the Seed should come", and now that the Seed had come, the ending of the Law can now begin for Israel.

As Jesus comes on the scene, will they be willing to forsake their law and turn to Christ?

Chapter Thirteen
Jesus and the New Covenant

There were 12 tribes and Jesus called 12 apostles. Twelve is the number of government, and 12 is part of the Kingdom government as well. The New Covenant replaces the Old Covenant, and takes what was once about 12 tribes and makes it about the teachings of the 12 apostles. A reorganization of Israel is what happened from Old to New Covenant. If you are in Christ, you are a part of the true Israel of God, a Heavenly Israel, with a Heavenly Jerusalem, and a Heavenly Mt. Zion. Yet, these things have come to Earth now, and a greater connection between Heaven and Earth is progressively taking place.

Jesus is the fulfillment of the Seed promised to both Abraham and David. In Abraham's covenant, the Seed will bless the nations, and in David's covenant, the Seed will reign on the throne forever, and Shepherd His people. In order to understand the relationship between the Abrahamic, Mosaic and Davidic covenants, and how they relate to the New Covenant, then the story of 3 trains is appropriate:

3 trains leave the station, but only 2 arrive at their destination:

Imagine the Abrahamic covenant, the Mosaic covenant and the Davidic covenants were all trains that left a destination and were traveling to another destination. The Abrahamic and Davidic covenant trains contain no passengers, only promises.

The Mosaic covenant train is full of people, those of the physical bloodline of Abraham. When the Abrahamic and Davidic trains reach the Cross, the New Covenant, all the promises get off those trains, and get onto the New Covenant train, which has many people from all over the world piling on to it. When the Mosaic covenant reaches the New Covenant train station, unbelieving Jews remain on the train, but the believing Jews who embraced Jesus get off and onto the New Covenant train.

The Mosaic covenant train leaves that station with the unbelieving Jews still on it, and it derails later on down the track, crashes and explodes, 40 years after the Cross. The unbelieving Jews of Jesus' day became the wicked and adulterous generation that Jesus spoke out against, and it was they who stubbornly remained on that train (of the Old Covenant).

On the New Covenant train, the believing Jews along with Gentiles who joined them, believing in Jesus, found all those Abrahamic and Davidic promises. Now they are happy and blessed as they continue to travel down the track in the advancing Kingdom of God.

So, what exactly is the New Covenant? Let's look at the section of Scripture that best describes the New Covenant:

But in fact the ministry Jesus has received is as superior to theirs as the covenant of which he is mediator is superior to the old one, since the New Covenant is established on better promises. For if there had been nothing wrong with that first covenant, no place would have been sought for another. But God found fault with the people and said: "The days are coming, declares the Lord, when I will make a New Covenant with the people of Israel and with the people of Judah. It will not be like the covenant I made with their ancestors when I took them by the hand to lead them out of Egypt, because they did not remain faithful to my covenant, and I turned away from them, declares the Lord.

This is the covenant I will establish with the people of Israel after that time, declares the Lord. I will put my laws in their minds and write them on their hearts. I will be their God, and they will be my people. No longer will they teach their neighbor, or say to one another, 'Know the Lord,' because they will all know me, from the least of them to the greatest. For I will forgive their wickedness and will remember their sins no more." By calling this covenant "new," he has made the first one obsolete; and what is obsolete and outdated will soon disappear. (Hebrews 8:6-13)

In another place, David describes the New Covenant:

David says the same thing when he speaks of the blessedness of the one to whom God credits righteousness apart from works: "Blessed are those whose transgressions are forgiven, whose sins are covered. Blessed is the one whose sin the Lord will never count against them." (Romans 4:6-8)

In the New Covenant, our sins are forever forgiven, not imputed to our account in any way. The blood of Jesus has purged sin once and for all. The New Covenant is a covenant of forgiveness, grace, power, love, joy, righteousness, in the Holy Spirit, where Heaven flows into the Earth to bring about restoration of creation. The fullness of this will be our future bodily resurrection, when Heaven and Earth become one.

Taking the example of the previous covenants God has made, the New Covenant is cut between 2 parties: The Father King and the Son King. It's both a kinship and vassal type covenant, but the beauty of it is Jesus is the Perfect Son of Israel, and He fulfills every part of the Old Covenant types and shadows, and suffers and dies in His own body to establish the new. It's perfect. It cannot be diminished or improved upon, only received by grace through faith. We enter into this covenant through marriage to Jesus, becoming inheritors of the promises. This marriage is the faith relationship we have with Him and the Father in the Spirit. We become part of this Bride, and sons and daughters in Christ. We are also entrusted as ambassadors of Heaven's Kingdom spreading it throughout the Earth.

Prior to the Cross, Jesus enacted the New Covenant symbolically with bread and wine:

While they were eating, Jesus took bread, and when he had given thanks, he broke it and gave it to his disciples, saying, "Take and eat; this is my body." Then he took a cup, and when he had given thanks, he gave it to them, saying, "Drink from it, all of you. This is my blood of the covenant, which is poured out for many for the forgiveness of sins. I tell you, I will not drink from this fruit of the vine from now on until that day when I drink it new with you in my Father's kingdom." (Matthew 26:26-29)

129

This is the New Covenant, made in the broken body and shed blood of our Lord Jesus. His broken body obtained our healing, and His shed blood obtained our forgiveness. Our role is to receive this grace by faith, and then grow daily in that faith relationship with Him, experiencing our identity in Christ in the Kingdom. Jesus said He would not drink "*of the fourth*" cup "*until that day when I drink it new with you in My Father's Kingdom*". This is our fellowship and communion we have with Him. The fourth cup is the cup of restoration, completion and acceptance. We are perfectly married, as a corporate Body of believers, to Jesus Christ, our Husband in this New Covenant. Marriage is how we become partakers and inheritors of the covenantal blessings of eternal life. We can drink and eat with Him anytime, but especially during times of His manifest presence with us, during worship gatherings, etc. Dr. Stan Newton has written a good book on Kingdom Communion, where he explores this fourth cup of communion.

The New Covenant brings to us an inheritance in Christ. This inheritance was first spoken of to Abraham, about land, but Abraham knew there was more to it as he looked for the city of God, the New Jerusalem that has come in Christ. The inheritance promises that we have now in Christ were revealed to the seven Churches of Revelation. There are 14 promises. It's interesting that David's Hebraic and numeric name equals 14. This is why Matthew broke up Israel's history in 3 groups of 14 generations each. David is 14, and he is at the heart of who Jesus is and the Kingdom of God. His throne in Heaven is the throne of grace, which brings salvation.

A list of things we have inherited in Christ:

1. Eating from the tree of life, eternal life (a never ending source of life)
2. The crown of life (reign in life) - we have authority in Christ
3. Hidden Manna (fellowship meal of marriage) – we are One with Jesus
4. White Stone (innocence) with our new name written in it (a name of our new identity in Christ that only we can experience)

5. Power over the nations (we are the authority in the Earth)
6. The Morning Star - we are the light of the world
7. White clothing - we are the righteousness of God
8. Name written in Heaven never to be blotted out (our citizenship)
9. Our name confessed before the Father
10. Made a pillar in the Temple God - we live in the New Jerusalem as a living stone
11. Name of God written on us - we are His
12. Name of new city of Jerusalem given to us
13. New name written on us (identity experience)
14. We sit on the throne with Jesus as joint heirs with Him

Everything of the Old Testament can be seen through the lens of types and shadows to gain understanding in the New Covenant. In this New Covenant, God has done it all. It becomes our life journey to gain understanding and revelation of the things we have in Christ. As the father told his elder son,

> *"'My son,' the father said, 'you are always with me, and everything I have is yours.* (Luke 15:31)

We need not beg our Father for anything. It's received by faith with full assurance. There is plenty for us to figure out in this walk of faith. Paul says we walk by faith and not by sight. He is talking about walking and living in the Spirit. It's this living in the Spirit that creates problems for us on Earth, because we are in the flesh. So we must become spiritually discerning and perceiving. We must become people of faith.

The difference between the Law covenant and the New Covenant is not law vs. grace, but rather, law vs. faith. Faith came through Christ. Grace and truth came through Christ. The Law, which contains wrath, came through Moses. The biggest problem with the Law is the wrath for covenant violation and no hope of eternal life. If there was wrath at work now, people would be in trouble, but we are not under the Law. The wrath of God was finished, according to Revelation 15:1, through the judgments on Jerusalem in 70 AD.

The New Covenant is a Kingdom without wrath. It's where the love of God has been fully revealed. It was the Old Covenant, according to Paul, that veiled Jesus.

Therefore, since we have such a hope, we are very bold. We are not like Moses, who would put a veil over his face to prevent the Israelites from seeing the end of what was passing away. But their minds were made dull, for to this day the same veil remains when the Old Covenant is read. It has not been removed, because only in Christ is it taken away. Even to this day when Moses is read, a veil covers their hearts. But whenever anyone turns to the Lord, the veil is taken away. Now the Lord is the Spirit, and where the Spirit of the Lord is, there is freedom. And we all, who with unveiled faces contemplate the Lord's glory, are being transformed into his image with ever-increasing glory, which comes from the Lord, who is the Spirit. (2 Corinthians 3:12-18)

This word "veil" is key to understanding the transition from old to New Covenant. The "Revelation" of Jesus Christ is about the "unveiling" of Jesus, as Almighty God and King to Israel and the world. Jesus came to unveil the Father to those who would believe. The Old Covenant veiled God's love and veiled their minds from seeing Jesus as their Messiah. The New Covenant in Jesus shows us God's love by His Spirit.

"No one has ever seen God. But the unique One, who is himself God, is near to the Father's heart. He has revealed God to us" (John 1:18 NLT). Under the Old Covenant, *"No one has ever seen God"*, because His presence was behind the veil, and only the high priest could enter with blood once per year to sprinkle blood upon the mercy seat. Jesus put His own blood upon God's ark, the throne, and the mercy seat in Heaven, obtaining forgiveness for humanity. All have been forgiven in the New Covenant, but not all have received it by grace through faith. When the veil tore in two pieces from top to bottom at the crucifixion of Jesus, the religious Jews of the Temple sewed it back together and hung it up. The Spirit was signifying the way into the Holiest of all places was now accessible to those who believe.

For Christ did not enter a sanctuary made with human hands that was only a copy of the true one; he entered Heaven itself, now to appear for us in God's presence. (Hebrews 9:24)

Then God's temple in Heaven was opened, and within his temple was seen the ark of his covenant. And there came flashes of lightning, rumblings, peals of thunder, an Earthquake and a severe hailstorm. (Revelation 11:19)

This is the very throne of God, the Ark of His Covenant in Heaven, where Jesus put His own blood, the blood of the Lamb, the perfect Passover and perfect propitiation for sins.

The New Covenant is a grant covenant for us, though it seems to be a kinship and vassal type covenant between the Father and Son, 2 Great Kings. Noah, Abraham and David all had grant covenants. The Mosaic was a kinship and then a vassal covenant, far different than a grant covenant. A grant covenant is where the Greater takes on all obligations, and the lesser party is a receiver of the benefits through relationship. A grant covenant is the best type of all the covenants.

The Kingdom and purpose of God has always been to have a Bride for His Son. This is accomplished in the New Covenant, and growing as a reality throughout the Earth.

Jesus was dying for the forgiveness of sins on the Cross, but He was something else while on that Cross.

Jesus came to Israel as their God, their Husband. The Husband who had made a covenant with Israel at Mt. Sinai had now come from Heaven to Earth to make a New Covenant, a new marriage with Israel. Under the Law, the legal way to end a marriage was for the husband to die, releasing the wife to marry another. We see this language mentioned in Romans 7:1-4.

Do you not know, brothers and sisters - for I am speaking to those who know the law - that the law has authority over someone only as long as that person lives? or example, by law a married woman is bound to her husband as long as he is alive, but if her husband dies, she is released from the law that binds her to him. So then, if she has sexual relations with another man while her husband is still alive, she is called an adulteress. But if her husband dies, she is released from that law and is not an adulteress if she marries another man. So, my brothers and sisters, you also died to the law through the body of Christ that you might belong to another, to him who was raised from the dead, in order that we might bear fruit for God.

Therefore, in this case, Jesus came as the covenant God of Israel to die, as their Husband, in order to release her from the previous covenant, freeing her to marry anew. The goal was for Israel to embrace the Cross and Resurrection of Jesus, and enter into the New Covenant with their Husband, the resurrected Lord. Only a remnant, the believers of Israel, did this, and thus, this remnant carried the message of the Kingdom to the rest of the world. This is the Israel of God.

This is the glory of the New Covenant, a beautiful marriage. John, using prophetic symbolic language, speaks of this Bride as the New Jerusalem, a jeweled city with streets of pure gold, and gates of pearl. The names of the tribes of Israel on the gates signify that it's the remnant of Israel who opened the New Covenant to the rest of the world. The names of the apostles of the Lord on the foundations under these gates, signifying the city of this New Covenant marriage is built upon the teaching of the Lord's apostles, as well as, upon the New Covenant prophecies found in our Old Testament (see Ephesians 2:19-20).

Consequently, you are no longer foreigners and strangers, but fellow citizens with God's people and also members of his household, built on the foundation of the apostles and prophets, with Christ Jesus himself as the chief cornerstone.

This marriage is the culmination of God's covenant journey with humanity, which began in the Garden of Eden, Adam and Eve being a type and shadow of this marriage relationship.

For unbelieving Israel, they become the harlot of Babylon, refuses to accept the death of their husband and saying, as prophesied in Isaiah, and repeated in the Revelation of Jesus Christ:

Now then, listen, you lover of pleasure, lounging in your security and saying to yourself, 'I am, and there is none besides me. I will never be a widow or suffer the loss of children.' (Isaiah 47:8)

Give her as much torment and grief as the glory and luxury she gave herself. In her heart she boasts, 'I sit enthroned as queen. I am not a widow; I will never mourn.' (Revelation 18:7)

This is the shame associated with those covenant people who rejected the beautiful New Covenant, which was being offered to them.

For us, today, in Christ, we are the Bride, the New Jerusalem, and the Kingdom of God covering the whole Earth. We get to celebrate the beauty of the Cross and partake of communion, the bread and wine, in our gatherings. Yet, this covenant meal is more than just celebrating the death of our Lord. It's the marriage supper as well, where we celebrate the marriage, which came because of that Cross. When the harlot city fell in 70 AD, immediately after that was the marriage supper of the Lamb.

Then the angel said to me, "Write this: Blessed are those who are invited to the wedding supper of the Lamb!" And he added, "These are the true words of God." (Revelation 19:9)

We can find this same language in one of the Kingdom parables of Jesus in the Gospel of Matthew, chapter 22:1-9

The kingdom of Heaven is like a king who prepared a wedding banquet for his son. He sent his servants to those who had been invited to the banquet to tell them to come, but they refused to come. "Then he sent some more servants and said, 'Tell those who have been invited that I have prepared my dinner: My oxen and fattened cattle have been butchered, and everything is ready. Come to the wedding banquet.' "But they paid no attention and went off--one to his field, another to his business. The rest seized his servants, mistreated them and killed them. The king was enraged. He sent his army and destroyed those murderers and burned their city.

"Then he said to his servants, 'The wedding banquet is ready, but those I invited did not deserve to come. So go to the street corners and invite to the banquet anyone you find.' So the servants went out into the streets and gathered all the people they could find, the bad as well as the good, and the wedding hall was filled with guests.

The Bible contains the beautiful story of this marriage of Jesus and His Bride. The New Covenant is the reality and evidence of this event. As His Bride, we are co-heirs with our Husband the King. As the Bride, we are the authority in the Earth being one Spirit with our Husband, even as Adam and Eve were one flesh. We live in the days of the ever advancing, ever increasing Kingdom of God, covering the whole Earth, as the waters cover the sea.

Chapter Fourteen
The Gospels and 70 AD

Most Christians are surprised to learn of the amount of 70 AD information we find in the gospels, in the words of Jesus and in the parables He taught. The Mosaic covenant was coming to an end, and the New Covenant was on the horizon. Jesus taught and spoke often about these things. Jesus had the key of David, to open and to shut, and He did this in many of the things He taught. Many of His parables contained the language that a judgment was coming, and a subsequent new day.

Let's look at the first instance of the 70 AD reference in the gospels.

So all the generations from Abraham to David are fourteen generations; and from David until the carrying away into Babylon are fourteen generations; and from the carrying away into Babylon unto Christ are fourteen generations. (Matthew 1:17)

You might wonder how this verse can tie into the judgment and new day that was coming, but the number 14 is significant here. Fourteen is the numeric value of David's Hebraic name. Matthew was showing the Davidic covenant concerning the Kingdom when he broke up Israel's history in 3 sections of 14 generations each. David, the Beloved, whom Jesus is the Seed of, the King, the Shepherd, the worshipful Psalmist, the prophet, the leader. David loomed large in the hearts and minds of the Jewish people, and Jesus being the long awaited Son who would open the New Covenant and end the Old Covenant, was now here. The Son of David had arrived!

This next section of Scripture is very significant to understanding the covenant transition that was taking place to Israel. John baptizes Jesus, and there is so much quality information, concerning covenant and Kingdom, within this passage of Scripture:

In those days John the Baptist came, preaching in the wilderness of Judea and saying, "Repent, for the kingdom of Heaven has come near." This is he who was spoken of through the prophet Isaiah: "A voice of one calling in the wilderness, 'Prepare the way for the Lord, make straight paths for him.'" John's clothes were made of camel's hair, and he had a leather belt around his waist. His food was locusts and wild honey. People went out to him from Jerusalem and all Judea and the whole region of the Jordan. Confessing their sins, they were baptized by him in the Jordan River.

But when he saw many of the Pharisees and Sadducees coming to where he was baptizing, he said to them: "You brood of vipers! Who warned you to flee from the coming wrath? Produce fruit in keeping with repentance. And do not think you can say to yourselves, 'We have Abraham as our father.' I tell you that out of these stones God can raise up children for Abraham. The ax is already at the root of the trees, and every tree that does not produce good fruit will be cut down and thrown into the fire.

"I baptize you with water for repentance. But after me comes one who is more powerful than I, whose sandals I am not worthy to carry. He will baptize you with the Holy Spirit and fire. His winnowing fork is in his hand, and he will clear his threshing floor, gathering his wheat into the barn and burning up the chaff with unquenchable fire. (Matthew 3:1-12)

The very idea of preaching the Kingdom outside of the Temple was offensive to the religious leaders. John the Baptist was born a Levite, and his family probably thought he would be a Levite priest like his father, but God had another plan for John. John was called to be the prophet who would herald the coming of the Lamb of God, baptizing Him. John first declared the Kingdom being near, being at hand. John the Baptist even fulfilled a prophecy of Isaiah, "...*the voice of one crying in the wilderness*". John came in the Spirit and Power of Elijah, or a carrier of the same grace as a prophet.

Elijah came against a pagan system declaring the judgment of God, and John was also coming against a system that was ready to die, which had become corrupt and called a harlot by God and His prophets. This *"winnowing fork"* of Jesus was part of the key of David, to judge and shut down the Old Covenant system.

John asks the Pharisees and Sadducees, *"O generation of vipers, who warned you to flee from the wrath to come?"* The book of Deuteronomy called the generation that would experience the judgment of God, perverse and crooked, in whom is no faith. The ones who did not have faith in Jesus had no faith at all as the New Covenant system was becoming available to them. They were the ungodly, wicked sinners that God would judge in the great tribulation.

They are corrupt and not his children; to their shame they are a warped and crooked generation. (Deuteronomy 32:5)

"I will hide my face from them," he said, *"and see what their end will be; for they are a perverse generation, children who are unfaithful".* (Deuteronomy 32:20)

God did not hide His face from Jesus at the Cross, but He did hide His face from Old Covenant Israel when they rejected Jesus.

Jesus rebukes that ungodly and wicked generation in many places, using that Old Covenant language, which they knew well:

He answered, "A wicked and adulterous generation asks for a sign! But none will be given it except the sign of the prophet Jonah". (Matthew 12:39)

"If anyone is ashamed of me and my words in this adulterous and sinful generation, the Son of Man will be ashamed of them when he comes in his Father's glory with the holy angels." (Matthew 8:38)

Jesus went on to say, "To what, then, can I compare the people of this generation? What are they like?" (Luke 7:31)

"You unbelieving and perverse generation," Jesus replied, *"how long shall I stay with you and put up with you? Bring your son here."* (Luke 9:41)

That's just a sample, but Jesus was connecting to the Song of Moses section of Scripture in Deuteronomy 32, which prophesied the judgment of 70 AD. Israel was the people of God, and Jesus came to them to offer them a New Covenant and rescue them from Roman oppression by giving them the power of the Kingdom, but only a remnant of Israel, the 144,000 seen in Revelation, followed the Lamb, and became born again. Paul calls this "*the remnant according to grace*".

Romans 4:15 tells us "*the law brings wrath*". Wrath is not a part of God's heart, but it was a part of the Law Covenant. As a Righteous Judge, He executed wrath, it says, "*through the means of angels*". The culmination of this wrath was when the Old Covenant law system was destroyed in 70 AD.

The state of the people of Israel when Jesus came to them was that they were lost, without faith, needing help, sick, demon-possessed, corrupt, walking in darkness, and He came to them, to deliver them. We can see His heart in the language of the Beatitudes:

Blessed are the poor in spirit, for theirs is the kingdom of Heaven. Blessed are those who mourn, for they will be comforted. Blessed are the meek, for they will inherit the Earth. Blessed are those who hunger and thirst for righteousness, for they will be filled. Blessed are the merciful, for they will be shown mercy. Blessed are the pure in heart, for they will see God. Blessed are the peacemakers, for they will be called children of God. Blessed are those who are persecuted because of righteousness, for theirs is the kingdom of Heaven. (Matthew 5:3-10)

Jesus was calling them into comfort, into healing, into power, righteousness, the mercy of God, a pureness in heart by His blood, and into a Kingdom of peace where they would be the children of God. There is application for us as well, but I am focusing on how they heard what He said, in the Beatitudes, and what they were feeling when He spoke to them. They were poor in spirit, mourning because of the Law, and desiring the Kingdom to come. It creates a greater appreciation for covenant Israel and the heart of

God when we view Scripture in this way. Jesus longed to draw all of Israel to Himself.

This next section of Scripture is very interesting and easy to miss if you are not following the line of thought with Jesus. Let me explain. Jesus begins to dismantle the old Temple system and establish and build a new Temple system through His words. He draws their attention to the furnishings of the Temple, and replaces those "things" with people. The new Temple is a Temple of people in the Lord:

> *You are the salt of the Earth. But if the salt loses its saltiness, how can it be made salty again? It is no longer good for anything, except to be thrown out and trampled underfoot. You are the light of the world. A town built on a hill cannot be hidden. Neither do people light a lamp and put it under a bowl. Instead they put it on its stand, and it gives light to everyone in the house. In the same way, let your light shine before others, that they may see your good deeds and glorify your Father in Heaven.* (Matthew 5:13-16)

He first takes them to the place of sacrifice, the brazen altar. This is where the Levite priest put salt on the sacrifice as it burned to the Lord, a sweet smelling savor. Jesus calls them "*the salt of the Earth*". You are not the salt of the sacrifice, but you are the salt of the Earth, as living sacrifices. Go and transform the Earth!

Then Jesus takes them into the first chamber, in their minds, the Holy Place, where there was the table of showbread, the lampstand and the altar of incense. He draws their attention to the lampstand and tells them "*you are the light of the world*", so go shine! You are now the light that leads people to the presence of God. Jesus goes on to call the Church the lampstand in the book of Revelation. We, corporately, are the Church, the Body of Christ on Earth, and we, together, shine the light of the glorious gospel, through our words and life.

As Jesus is talking about the Temple, dismantling the old and building something new, He tells them something significant about the Temple and the Law:

Do not think that I have come to abolish the Law or the Prophets; I have not come to abolish them but to fulfill them. For truly I tell you, until Heaven and Earth disappear, not the smallest letter, not the least stroke of a pen, will by any means disappear from the Law until everything is accomplished. Therefore anyone who sets aside one of the least of these commands and teaches others accordingly will be called least in the kingdom of Heaven, but whoever practices and teaches these commands will be called great in the kingdom of Heaven. For I tell you that unless your righteousness surpasses that of the Pharisees and the teachers of the law, you will certainly not enter the kingdom of Heaven. (Matthew 5:17-20)

Jesus speaks of a fulfillment coming to the Law. The ultimate fulfillment, though He had already been fulfilling many types and shadows of Israel and the Law, would be His death as the Perfect Passover Lamb fulfilling the Law. His death made the Law obsolete, through fulfillment. So He tells them, *"Do not think that I came to destroy the law"*. He did not come to only remove it, but to fulfill it, as a legal means to end it. Christ is the end of the Law for righteousness for those who believe. This is part of the key of David to close up the Law.

The Jews called the Temple "Heaven and Earth". We covered this in a previous chapter. Jesus uses that type of language here, telling them that until the Temple is gone, the Law will still be in force. Therefore, keep the Law, but rather, keep the spirit of the Law, which He then begins to teach them about. He is calling them into a greater righteousness, one that comes through Him.

The next stop as they walk through the Temple in their minds is the Most Holy Place, where the Ark of the Covenant sat, though at this time in history, the Ark was not there. The Babylonians had taken it in battle many years earlier. Some believe the prophet Jeremiah may have hid it, but no one knew where it was. They have been looking for it for many years. But, within the Ark of the Covenant, were the 10 commandments, which is the standard of the Law. Now that He has drawn their attention to the commandments of the Law, look at what He tells them:

You have heard that it was said to the people long ago, 'You shall not murder, and anyone who murders will be subject to judgment.' But I tell you that anyone who is angry with a brother or sister will be subject to judgment. Again, anyone who says to a brother or sister, 'Raca,' is answerable to the court. And anyone who says, 'You fool!' will be in danger of the fire of hell. (Matthew 5:21-22)

He takes the commandment to not kill and turns into a matter of the heart and of how we treat other people. He warns them that in breaking the Law you can be called before the Sanhedrin, but then warns them of something most people have missed, concerning 70 AD. The term "hell" here is actually the Hebrew word Gehenna. Gehenna was a place in Jerusalem that was called the Valley of the Sons of Hinnom. It had an ancient history to Israel. It was once used as a place to sacrifice children to Molech while under the influence of Babylonian religions. When Jesus came, it was a trash heap and graveyard that smoldered and burned constantly. The fires kept burning. It was a picture of the coming destruction of Jerusalem, which would happen in 70 AD. He does not warn them that they will die and go to hell, but He warns them they if they do not change, be converted in heart, they will die in the fires of the coming wrath and destruction.

He then draws their attention to the commandment against adultery, and raises the standard on that one, to that of the heart:

You have heard that it was said, 'You shall not commit adultery.' But I tell you that anyone who looks at a woman lustfully has already committed adultery with her in his heart. (Matthew 5:27-28)

We have the grace of God to overcome sin, and the intimacy and leading of the Holy Spirit. If we listen to His promptings, we will be in good shape. If we step over His direction, then we may suffer the consequences of grieving the Spirit and whatever trouble has come along with our bad decision. This is how the Lord teaches us and disciplines us, when we get into sin. He does not send wrath and judgment. We have a completely different relationship than Israel had, but Jesus is calling them into this new relationship. With that said, we have grace to not commit adultery.

But, if we do, God does not cast us to hell, as many have taught. He lifts us out of our mess, and helps us become successful again.

Jesus begins to transition them into a Kingdom mindset, yet with remaining stipulations of the Law around them:

This, then, is how you should pray: 'Our Father in Heaven, hallowed be your name, your kingdom come, your will be done, on Earth as it is in Heaven. Give us today our daily bread. And forgive us our debts, as we also have forgiven our debtors. And lead us not into temptation, but deliver us from the evil one.' For if you forgive other people when they sin against you, your Heavenly Father will also forgive you. But if you do not forgive others their sins, your Father will not forgive your sins. (Matthew 6:9-15)

Jesus begins more so to call them out of the physical, or temporal, and into the Spirit, or the eternal.

Do not store up for yourselves treasures on Earth, where moths and vermin destroy, and where thieves break in and steal. But store up for yourselves treasures in Heaven, where moths and vermin do not destroy, and where thieves do not break in and steal. For where your treasure is, there your heart will be also. (Matthew 6:19-21)

Jesus is not instructing them to not have any wealth, but rather, He is drawing their attention away from the physical Temple that had so dominated their minds, to the Kingdom of God in the Spirit. The Kingdom of God is in the Spirit, not in a building. And our heart is the connection to it as the Holy Spirit is in us. Jesus calls them to place their heart into the Spirit, and let that become our treasure. Not temples of gold in the natural, but in the Spirit.

In the next set of verses, the workers of iniquity to Jesus were the religious Jews who rejected Him. They were the wicked, adulterous, perverted and crooked generation spoken of in Deuteronomy and the gospels. Jesus is addressing them in this section of Scripture, and telling them they if they do not come to Him, they will miss the Kingdom.

Not everyone who says to me, 'Lord, Lord,' will enter the kingdom of Heaven, but only the one who does the will of my Father who is in Heaven. Many will say to me on that day, 'Lord, Lord, did we not prophesy in your name and in your name drive out demons and in your name perform many miracles?' Then I will tell them plainly, 'I never knew you. Away from me, you evildoers!' (Matthew 7:21-23)

The Pharisees would cast out a demon using the name of God, and they always had to get the name of the demon before they could adjure it to leave. They did many works for God under the Old Covenant, but if they do not come to Jesus, they will miss the Kingdom.

Jesus then ends His teaching, that dealt with the old Temple, the new Temple and Kingdom of God with words about a house (they called the Temple the house of God).

Therefore everyone who hears these words of mine and puts them into practice is like a wise man who built his house on the rock. The rain came down, the streams rose, and the winds blew and beat against that house; yet it did not fall, because it had its foundation on the rock. But everyone who hears these words of mine and does not put them into practice is like a foolish man who built his house on sand. The rain came down, the streams rose, and the winds blew and beat against that house, and it fell with a great crash. (Matthew 7:24-27)

If you do not come to Jesus, then the destruction of Jerusalem, which is coming, will destroy the house you are trusting in, but if you listen to Me, and come to Me, then you will be safe. That is the basic message of Matthew 7. He wraps up everything He has been saying with the conclusion to all His words. Come to Me, escape the destruction, and carry on in the Kingdom.

There are many other things I can say about 70 AD from the book of Matthew, but I will let you discover those things as you read through it. I will give you a hint on one thing: In the parable of the wheat and tares, the unbelieving Jews who rejected Jesus were the tares who would be burned in the fires of the destruction, but the wheat were those who embraced Jesus and the New

Covenant, the sons of the Kingdom, the true Israel of God. The end of the age was dealing with the Mosaic age of the Old Covenant. The harvest was the ending of this age, where the transition was taking place. That section of Scripture is not about the end of the world nor is it about a coming great harvest of believers. It's about the transition, which was like a woman travailing in birth, from Old Covenant to New Covenant, in order for the Kingdom to come.

I want to look at a parable of a wedding in Matthew 22. It's one of the clearest examples of Jesus speaking about the coming destruction of the city of Jerusalem and the coming Kingdom. We must realize, the Kingdom became present with power after the fall of Jerusalem, because that is when the wedding occurred.

Jesus spoke to them again in parables, saying: "The kingdom of Heaven is like a king who prepared a wedding banquet for his son. He sent his servants to those who had been invited to the banquet to tell them to come, but they refused to come.

"Then he sent some more servants and said, 'Tell those who have been invited that I have prepared my dinner: My oxen and fattened cattle have been butchered, and everything is ready. Come to the wedding banquet.' "But they paid no attention and went off-one to his field, another to his business. The rest seized his servants, mistreated them and killed them. The king was enraged. He sent his army and destroyed those murderers and burned their city.

"Then he said to his servants, 'The wedding banquet is ready, but those I invited did not deserve to come. So go to the street corners and invite to the banquet anyone you find.' So the servants went out into the streets and gathered all the people they could find, the bad as well as the good, and the wedding hall was filled with guests.

"But when the king came in to see the guests, he noticed a man there who was not wearing wedding clothes. He asked, 'How did you get in here without wedding clothes, friend?' The man was speechless. "Then the king told the attendants,

146

'Tie him hand and foot, and throw him outside, into the darkness, where there will be weeping and gnashing of teeth.' "For many are invited, but few are chosen." (Matthew 22:1-14)

The certain King here is God the Father who has prepared a marriage for His Son. He called Old Covenant Israel to the New Covenant, but many of them did not come. He uses the picture of them making excuses. Then after the Cross, He sent His apostles and other disciples to preach the gospel to Israel, but they fought against them. Then, God calls them to go to the rest of the world, the Gentiles, and bring them into the New Covenant. The wedding occurred after the city fell.

The armies God used were the Roman armies. This was under the Old Covenant, with its final display of wrath. God used Babylonian armies to destroy the Temple in 586 BC. He used Roman armies to utterly destroy it in 70 AD. Jesus then gives the picture of someone not worthy trying to get into the wedding, and not properly dressed. This would be an Old Covenant Jewish person that thought they could be a part of the Kingdom without being clothed in Christ. The outer darkness, weeping and gnashing of teeth would have been the destruction of the Jerusalem and the Temple in 70 AD, the worst time in Israel's history. This was the great tribulation.

We see that the idea of the coming destruction is a theme woven through most of what Jesus talked about. It was a theme among the prophets of old, and Jesus had come with the key of David to establish the New Covenant, and bring an end to the Old Covenant. "His coming" spoken of many times in Scripture, was in relation to His coming in judgment through the events of 70 AD. Here is an example of that:

The chief priests and the whole Sanhedrin were looking for false evidence against Jesus so that they could put him to death. But they did not find any, though many false witnesses came forward. Finally, two came forward and declared, "This fellow said, 'I am able to destroy the temple of God and rebuild it in three days.'"

Then the high priest stood up and said to Jesus, "Are you not going to answer? What is this testimony that these men are bringing against you?" But Jesus remained silent. The high priest said to him, "I charge you under oath by the living God: Tell us if you are the Messiah, the Son of God." "You have said so," Jesus replied. "But I say to all of you: From now on you will see the Son of Man sitting at the right hand of the Mighty One and coming on the clouds of Heaven."

Then the high priest tore his clothes and said, "He has spoken blasphemy! Why do we need any more witnesses? Look, now you have heard the blasphemy. What do you think?" "He is worthy of death," they answered. Then they spit in his face and struck him with their fists. Others slapped him and said, "Prophesy to us, Messiah. Who hit you?" (Matthew 26:59-68)

When Jesus told the high priest that he himself would see Jesus sitting on the right hand of power and coming in the clouds of Heaven, He was using Old Testament, prophetic language. God coming on the clouds was a common way of saying that God is bringing judgment upon a city. This is the same language Jesus uses to the high priest. They would see Him as King and God through the events of 70 AD. He won and they lost!

Daniel spoke of this Messiah as coming on the clouds of Heaven, so Jesus declares to them that He is that Man! To them, what He said was blasphemy!

We see in verse 68 that they are mocking His claim to be the Messiah, by saying, *"Prophesy to us, if you are the Christ. Who hit you?"*

These were those Jews who did not believe, who became the wicked and perverse, adulterous generation.

A quote from the historian, Josephus, concerning the state of Jerusalem during the time prior to the destruction:

"I am of the opinion that had the Romans deferred the punishment of these wretches, either the Earth would have opened, and swallowed up the city, or it would have been swept away by a deluge, or have shared in the thunderbolts of the land of Sodom. For it produced a race far more ungodly than those who were thus visited in Sodom."

Chapter Fifteen
Paul, James, Peter, Jude, John and 70 AD

Let's look at the apostolic eschatology of Paul, James, Peter, Jude and John, but first: What is eschatology?

Eschatology is a word meaning "the study of last things". For too long, Bible scholars and theologians have misunderstood the meaning of the word to mean the study of the last things of planet Earth.

Ideas and thoughts usually accompany that form of thinking creating cataclysmic events in our future, a great tribulation, a rebuilt Temple in Jerusalem, and a coming rapture. All of those are misguided and false ideas.

The heart of "eschatology" (study of last things) is the shift that took place from 30 AD to 70 AD when the Old Covenant became obsolete and fading (at the Cross), and the New Covenant began to arise brighter and brighter. After 70 AD the Kingdom of God came present with power.

Eschatology is not about cataclysmic events in our future. Eschatology reveals the dying of one covenant and the coming to life of a New Covenant, which continues to spread and grow throughout the Earth today. This is the Kingdom of God's activity today.

The entire New Testament was written during this eschatological time frame from the Cross to the destruction of Jerusalem, which is 30 AD to 70 AD. This is the framework of the New Testament teaching of the apostles. The warnings of wrath had to do with the coming destruction of the Temple and city of Jerusalem in their generation, not ours. There is no wrath in this New Covenant Kingdom.

So, be at peace. The Kingdom is here. No longer is it "at hand", but here! Who are we? We are the ambassadors of Heaven's Kingdom, advancing the Kingdom as it spreads like leaven working its way through the dough. Darkness is a reality, but the Light of the Kingdom is a much bigger and much better reality.

It's time to cast off the fear, doom and gloom teachings, which have permeated the Churches' pulpits and embrace an optimistic view of the days we live in and the times ahead of us. This is an apostolic eschatology, which is always victorious in its approach.

What we learn about the writings in the New Testament is that there was an underlying theme: the coming judgment, which happened in 70 AD. We cannot ignore it or overlook it, but rather, learn it and grow from the knowledge. There is a Greek word that is used throughout the writings of the New Testament that sheds light on what they were expecting:

Apokalupsis (ap-ok-al'-oop-sis); From G601; disclosure: appearing, coming, lighten, manifestation, be revealed, revelation. This word also means, "unveiling" - to remove the cover, and remove what's preventing the eye to see.

It was the Old Covenant, with it's rituals, laws, Temple and priesthood, that was veiling Jesus, and thus veiling the Father (2 Corinthians 3:13-16). The veil in the Holy of Holies, that separated God from man, became a veil in the heart and mind of Jewish people in the first century so that many of them could not see Jesus, "blinded" by the Law covenant. To be blinded because of a harlot is what Samson lived through in his life, being a prophetic picture of first century, unbelieving Israel.

Let's look at where this word "apokalupsis" appears:

But because of your stubbornness and your unrepentant heart, you are storing up wrath against yourself for the day of God's wrath, when his righteous judgment will be revealed. (Romans 2:5)

This *"day of God's wrath"* was coming within their generation, and it was the great tribulation, which happened from 66 to 70 AD. Nero actually began his fierce persecution of Christians in 64 AD.

The purpose of this wrath was to remove every physical symbol of the Old Covenant, mainly the Temple and priesthood. This coming wrath was also "the revelation of Jesus Christ", or Christ being "revealed", unveiled. The Old Covenant was veiling Jesus, who was the representation of the Father's heart. To enter into the New Covenant is to believe on Jesus and know the Father's heart.

Therefore you do not lack any spiritual gift as you eagerly wait for our Lord Jesus Christ to be revealed. (1 Corinthians 1:7)

...and give relief to you who are troubled, and to us as well. This will happen when the Lord Jesus is revealed from Heaven in blazing fire with his powerful angels. (2 Thessalonians 1:7)

Therefore, with minds that are alert and fully sober, set your hope on the grace to be brought to you when Jesus Christ is revealed at his coming. (1 Peter 1:13)

This particular "coming" of Jesus was prophetic and covenantal language, which speaks of the hand of God in the judgment on a city. I personally believe in a final coming of Jesus, but much of the references to "His coming" in the New Testament were related to the judgment of 70 AD.

But rejoice inasmuch as you participate in the sufferings of Christ, so that you may be overjoyed when his glory is revealed. (1 Peter 4:13)

The revelation from Jesus Christ, which God gave him to show his servants what must soon take place. He made it known by sending his angel to his servant John (Revelation 1:1)

There was the expectation that Jesus would be unveiled, or revealed, with the removal of the Old Covenant and the Kingdom coming present with power. Let me explain what I mean when I speak of the Kingdom coming present with power.

153

And he said to them, "Truly I tell you, some who are standing here will not taste death before they see that the kingdom of God has come with power." (Mark 9:1)

Jesus was saying that some of them would witness the events of 70 AD. It was after the events of 70 AD that the Kingdom came present with power. The birth pangs spoken of in the New Testament was in the birthing of the Kingdom of God in its fullness, so that it may spread and cover the whole Earth. What the Church has done with this power has not always been fruitful through the past centuries. I will discuss that in a later chapter.

Let's look at how John saw the coming new age and the passing away of the old age:

Yet I am writing you a new command; its truth is seen in him and in you, because the darkness is passing and the true light is already shining. (1 John 2:8)

John saw the old age as fading into darkness, and the new coming age of Jesus and the New Covenant Kingdom as a light shining brighter and brighter. We are not waiting, today, for this light to come. The Kingdom of God is here and spreading, and we must learn to embrace it in our thinking and theology.

Let's look at how James saw these things:

Be patient, then, brothers and sisters, until the Lord's coming. See how the farmer waits for the land to yield its valuable crop, patiently waiting for the autumn and spring rains. (James 5:7)

How strange would it be for James to give the exhortation to *"be patient until the Lord's coming"*, to people who live 2000 years after this was written? James was speaking to his audience, writing about specific things, that we can gain knowledge and application from, but the warnings of the Lord's coming and wrath were for them, not us.

His coming would be through the events of the destruction. It was this destruction that brought a great liberation among the true Israel of God, believers in Christ, at that time in history. As you can see, it's extremely significant to the Scriptures. A good understanding of eschatology, not dispensational futurism, but a system of theology based more in history and covenant. I find Partial Preterism to be the most biblically accurate means of understanding the Bible. When you learn what the historical and covenantal terms mean, then it becomes easier to understand the context.

Terms such as "latter days", "last days", "end of the age", "latter times", "time of the end" all relate to the same time in history: **the last days of the Old Covenant Temple system**.

Terms such as "day of the Lord", "the day of God", "the coming day", all relate to the day of destruction in 70 AD, not some time in our future. We live in the New Covenant. God is not going to destroy anything. We can all relax. God is love. God is light. God is a Good Father. He is saving His humanity, to make them children in His family.

The end of all things is near. Therefore be alert and of sober mind so that you may pray. (1 Peter 4:7)

Peter was talking to his audience about the soon coming end of the Old Covenant. The Temple system loomed large throughout the Roman Empire. Many Gentiles wanted the God of Israel, and felt He was the true God. Much of the early Church was Jewish, but there was a mixture of Gentiles among them often times. Gentiles were also a part of Temple worship since they had their own court, the "court of the Gentiles."

The term last days in context of the last days of the Jewish Old Covenant:

Your gold and silver are corroded. Their corrosion will testify against you and eat your flesh like fire. You have hoarded wealth in the last days. (James 5:3)

Once again, these are warnings to a first century generation of people, Jewish people. The Temple was also used as a bank, and wealthy people stored gold and valuables there. When the Temple falls, all their stored up wealth would be gone.

Above all, you must understand that in the last days scoffers will come, scoffing and following their own evil desires. (2 Peter 3:3)

This also was a first century warning concerning the "last days" of the Jewish Temple and city. We cannot take a Scripture like this and apply it to us today. We are not living in any sort of "last days". We are part of the Kingdom of God covering the Earth. We serve and advance this Kingdom for our life span. Another term used in regard to the coming wrath they were anticipating was "the day of the Lord." The day of the Lord was the expectation of this coming destruction:

But the day of the Lord will come like a thief. The Heavens will disappear with a roar; the elements will be destroyed by fire, and the Earth and everything done in it will be laid bare. (2 Peter 3:10)

The Heavens and Earth being destroyed in the above Scripture was speaking of the Jewish Temple. They called it Heaven and Earth, because it was the place where Heaven met Earth, where God met with man. We do live in the new Heaven and new Earth today, where God lives in believers.

...as you look forward to the day of God and speed it's coming. That day will bring about the destruction of the Heavens by fire, and the elements will melt in the heat. (2 Peter 3:12)

As we discussed before, the Heavens and Earth burning, and the elements melting with fervent heat all related to the Temple system, and the fire it was about to undergo. The Greek word used for "elements" is 'stoicheion'.

Both Paul and Peter use this word, and every time Paul used it, he was referring to the religion and ritual of the Old Covenant. Peter used it in the same way, but when we do not understand what "Heavens and Earth" meant to them, then we also fail to realize how the word "elements" is being used. Heavens and Earth was the Temple system, and elements were the religion and rituals of the Old Covenant.

Jude rails on those Jewish unbelievers who persecute the Church and attempt to infiltrate the Church and cause the Church to fail. Jude even quotes from Enoch, who prophesied about those very days that Jude was living in:

Yet these people slander whatever they do not understand, and the very things they do understand by instinct-as irrational animals do-will destroy them. Woe to them! They have taken the way of Cain; they have rushed for profit into Balaam's error; they have been destroyed in Korah's rebellion. These people are blemishes at your love feasts, eating with you without the slightest qualm-shepherds who feed only themselves. They are clouds without rain, blown along by the wind; autumn trees, without fruit and uprooted-twice dead. They are wild waves of the sea, foaming up their shame; wandering stars, for whom blackest darkness has been reserved forever. Enoch, the seventh from Adam, prophesied about them:

See, the Lord is coming with thousands upon thousands of his holy ones to judge everyone, and to convict all of them of all the ungodly acts they have committed in their ungodliness, and of all the defiant words ungodly sinners have spoken against him." These people are grumblers and faultfinders; they follow their own evil desires; they boast about themselves and flatter others for their own advantage. But, dear friends, remember what the apostles of our Lord Jesus Christ foretold. They said to you, "In the last times there will be scoffers who will follow their own ungodly desires." These are the people who divide you, who follow mere natural instincts and do not have the Spirit. (Jude 1:10-19)

The early Church dealt with a lot of imposters, false teachers, Gnostics, Judaizers, and those who would seek to seduce and gain power in this new Church system. The apostles fought against the lies by teaching sound doctrine. The early Church was a Jewish Church, and Jude reminds them of their history by mentioning Cain, Korah, and then Enoch's prophecies. All those things pointed to the days they were living in, the last days of the Old Covenant, and judgment was coming upon that region.

More on the "elements"

The following is a section of Scripture that many have misunderstood, built wrong end times theology out of, and created fear in the hearts of believers. First read these Scriptures and then I will explain the historical context of what Peter was saying in these verses. I pray it brings you revelation, understanding and great peace to learn the truth I am about to share:

> But the day of the Lord will come as a thief in the night; in the which the Heavens shall pass away with a great noise, and the elements shall melt with fervent heat, the Earth also and the works that are therein shall be burned up. Seeing then that all these things shall be dissolved, what manner of persons ought ye to be in all holy conversation and godliness, Looking for and hasting unto the coming of the day of God, wherein the Heavens being on fire shall be dissolved, and the elements shall melt with fervent heat? (2 Peter 3:10-12)

Wow, a lot going on there. It would seem Jesus is going to come back and destroy and burn everything, and then recreate this new Heaven and Earth system that we can all live in. But, is that really what these verses are saying? Is this really what Peter was saying to his first century audience?

Remember, as Peter wrote this, somewhere around the early 60's ad, the idea of a coming destruction of Jerusalem and the Temple was a buzz of conversation in the air. Jesus had prophesied such a thing in Matthew 24, Mark 13, and Luke 21, and now Peter knew the time was certainly closer than ever before. Let's look at a few terms that will help bring understanding.

The term "Heaven and Earth", to a first century Jewish person meant the Temple system (see Matthew 5:18). The holy of holies was called Heaven, the place God dwelled on the Ark of the Covenant, the place only the high priest could visit once per year (see Hebrews 9:24). The holy place was called land, where the common priesthood could enter and do their duties. And the bronze laver was called the sea, where the priests would wash off (see 2 Chronicles 4:6).

Thus, the Temple system under the Old Covenant was actually called "Heaven and Earth" to the religious Jews. The model has always been "on Earth as it is in Heaven" and this applied for the Temple, which was itself a copy of Heavenly things (see Hebrews 8:5).

With that foundation laid, we can understand that Peter was talking about a coming destruction on the Temple system, the Heaven and Earth of that day, so that a new Heaven and new Earth could then emerge out of those ashes, or more accurately, as John saw, *"descending out of Heaven as a bride adorned for her Husband"*, which is what we know as the glory of the New Covenant today. But what about this word "elements"?

It's not speaking of the elements we learned about in science class. These elements actually come from a word in the Greek meaning "traditions of men, religious rules, bondage to a religious system, and principles of a teaching" (see Galatians 4:3,9; Colossians 2:8, 20; Hebrews 5:12).

In other words, the "elements" that Peter said would melt with fervent heat were the "trappings" of the religious, Old Covenant system. Ah, we can all relax now, because God is not going to send Jesus back to destroy and burn up the Heavens and Earth that is under our feet and over our head. He was speaking of the destruction of a religious system that dominated the culture of that day. That system had become "the harlot of Babylon" in God eyes, and the harlot or whore that the Old Covenant prophets had spoken of.

One might ask, "Why does this even matter?" Why, because entire end times' teachings that are false have come out of misunderstanding these Scriptures, and knowing the real truth about something will always set you free. So go be free with this new knowledge you have just learned. Blessings to you, in Jesus name!

I believe the New Testament is the canon story of the New Covenant, which begins at the Birth of Jesus and ends at the destruction of Jerusalem and the marriage of the King and His Bride, the New Jerusalem. It has a context, and it's not written in the context of future history or for our time. It's written in the context of Jewish Israel but then takes that and turns it into a worldwide enterprise as the Kingdom of God advances across the Earth. John Robinson wrote a good book on Redating the New Testament, and gives many proofs as to the validity of it being written prior to the destruction of 70 AD. David Chilton, Kenneth Gentry, Jonathan Welton, Harold Eberle, and Stan Newton have also written good books that fit in with the historical and covenantal context of the Bible.

Chapter Sixteen
The covenantal and theological letter to the Romans and understanding Israel both then and now

Romans was written by Paul to Jewish believers who were "among the Gentiles" (Romans 1:5). Romans is probably the most written about, talked about, and taught about in the theological world. Pages and pages of commentary have been written concerning the theology and doctrine contained in the book of Romans.

The book of Romans has a contextual flow that is important to follow. Paul was building an argument that Jesus is the Christ and He came to the Jews first but now is preached to the Gentiles, and that God is calling people from all over creation to come into the Kingdom of God. That's the overall theme of the book. Paul begins by addressing his mostly Jewish audience by stating whose Seed Jesus is of:

> ...regarding his Son, who as to his Earthly life was a descendant of David, and who through the Spirit of holiness was appointed the Son of God in power by his resurrection from the dead: Jesus Christ our Lord. Through him we received grace and apostleship to call all the Gentiles to the obedience that comes from faith for his name's sake. (Romans 1:3-5)

It was the Davidic covenant that first gives us the idea of "the Son of God", and Paul makes that point as well. He mentions the Holy Spirit and the Resurrection of Jesus from the dead. Paul mentions those covenantal fulfillments from David's covenant in the opening words of his letter to the Romans. This is one proof that his audience was mostly Jewish believers.

The contextual flow to the book of Romans goes like this:

1. The Davidic covenant is fulfilled in Christ.

2. The New Covenant is open to all people.

3. Being a natural Jew will not save you.

4. God will bring divine wrath, in the first century, upon the system, which rejected the Cross of His Son.

5. Sin has been a problem since Adam.

6. God has dealt with sin through judgments in the past.

7. Jew and Gentile stand before God equally guilty because of sin.

8. The Abrahamic covenant is fulfilled in Christ.

9. His Cross is the solution for the sin problem.

10. In Adam, you die, but in Christ you live and reign.

11. Grace is not an excuse to sin, but is the power to overcome sin.

12. All are freed from the Law because of the Cross.

13. We are free from condemnation and are now sons of God in Christ.

14. A remnant of Jewish believers will be saved in the first century.

15. There is an election according to grace of believing Jews in the first century.

16. Paul expresses his desire for his own countrymen to be saved in the first century.

17. The Old Covenant has become a blinding influence until the Gentiles come to destroy the city and Temple in the first century.

18. Be transformed by the Holy Spirit in your mind.

Before we get into the contextual flow of Romans, I want to bring up 13 important points to understand about the book of Romans, the audience Paul was writing to, and the shift in their minds that was taking place because of transitioning from the Old Covenant world into the New Covenant world, from the letter of the Law to the power of the Spirit.

1. There was once a division between Jews and Gentiles. The gospel removes the division.

2. The gospel has leveled the playing field between Jew and Gentile. There is no favoritism with God, in the New Covenant.

3. God does not favor Jews over Gentiles. There is not a blessing attached with blessing Israel, based on Genesis 12:3. The one who was blessed and cursed was Jesus, and the curse they endured was the destruction of 70 AD, and the blessing they received was eternal life.

4. Jews who did not come to Christ in the first century were being "bad Jews".

5. There is a backdrop of a few things throughout the writings of the New Testament.

6. The Kingdom is near, the shift in covenants beings at hand.

7. The coming Kingdom of God when the Old Covenant is removed.

8. A war between the Judaizers and Paul's teachings on freedom (those of the circumcision vs. uncircumcision).

9. The book of Romans was written to Jewish people, who knew the Law, who also lived among Gentiles.

10. The gospel was to the Jew first and then to the Gentile. The goal was to get Israel saved, and add Gentiles as you go along. Today, the gospel is equally for everyone. God is not crying out to Israel as a nation to come to Christ no more than He is any other nation. It's the cry of His heart for the nations to be saved, but no single nation has an

elevated place in His heart. We are all equal because of the Cross.

11. The Jews of the first century who received the promises made to Abraham and David through faith in Jesus showed they were the true descendants of Abraham.

12. The advantage of being a Jew back then was the long history Israel had with God. The nation of Israel today is not the covenant people of God. They are simply a nation of mostly Jewish people, who have lost connection with which tribe they belong to and they do not practice true Judaism. They have a moral teaching of Rabbinical Judaism, but no redemption through blood. Redemption through good works is not an option. The religious Jews today still await the coming of their Messiah.

13. A Jew was someone who had been circumcised and was a physical descendant to Abraham. Abraham was at first a Gentile. He was uncircumcised when God met Him. Circumcision made Abraham a Jew. He was counted righteous before he was circumcised, while still a Gentile. This shows a picture of the gospel being for both Gentile and Jew. Circumcision also points forward to the New Covenant circumcision of the heart by the Holy Spirit.

Now that I got those 13 things into your thinking, **the first main point** of Romans is **"The Davidic covenant is fulfilled in Jesus Christ, through His birth and His Resurrection."**

...regarding his Son, who as to his Earthly life was a descendant of David, and who through the Spirit of holiness was appointed the Son of God in power by his resurrection from the dead: Jesus Christ our Lord. (Romans 1:3-4)

In order to understand what Paul is talking about, we have to know what covenant promises were made to David:

"When your days are over and you go to be with your ancestors, I will raise up your offspring to succeed you, one of your own sons, and I will establish his kingdom. He is the one who will build a house for me, and I will establish his throne forever. I will be his father, and he will be my son. I

will never take my love away from him, as I took it away from your predecessor. I will set him over my house and my kingdom forever; his throne will be established forever". (1 Chronicles 17:11-14)

When Jesus was born, He fulfilled part of this. He fulfilled the part about the Seed. His Resurrection fulfilled the Kingdom aspects of this covenant promise. The angel Gabriel repeats the covenantal promise made to David, to Mary, as she finds out she is pregnant with Jesus:

"You will conceive and give birth to a son, and you are to call him Jesus. He will be great and will be called the Son of the Most High. The Lord God will give him the throne of his father David, and he will reign over Jacob's descendants forever; his kingdom will never end." (Luke 1:31-33)

I have already covered the Davidic covenant in chapter seven, so go back and read it if you need to get more familiar with the Davidic covenant. Jesus being the fulfillment of those covenant promises was big to the Jewish believers. The expected Messiah was called the Son of David, and you can see several times when people called Jesus that, when they wanted Him to heal them. Also, being the Son of David according to that covenant promise meant He was also the Son of God, which we know Jesus is, but they seemed to miss it. One day Peter had the revelation from the Father that Jesus is the Son of God. It's good to understand the promise it connects to when it's part of our belief system.

The second point is **"The New Covenant is open to all people".** We may not have as much trouble grasping that, but a first century Jew would have struggled with understanding it. Peter did and Paul rebuked him. Even after Peter was saved, he had racial problems, separating Jews from Gentiles:

When Cephas came to Antioch, I opposed him to his face, because he stood condemned. For before certain men came from James, he used to eat with the Gentiles. But when they arrived, he began to draw back and separate himself from the Gentiles because he was afraid of those who belonged to the circumcision group. The other Jews joined him in his

165

hypocrisy, so that by their hypocrisy even Barnabas was led astray. When I saw that they were not acting in line with the truth of the gospel, I said to Cephas in front of them all, "You are a Jew, yet you live like a Gentile and not like a Jew. How is it, then, that you force Gentiles to follow Jewish customs? (Galatians 2:11-14)

Paul was basically asking Peter, "Why do you live in the freedom of the New Covenant, but you still treat Gentiles like you live in the Old Covenant?"

Paul goes on to speak of the gospel message being for everyone, with the only response being that of faith which is accepted. Bloodline no longer matters, but rather, righteousness, which comes by faith, and it's that faith we are to walk in.

For I am not ashamed of the gospel, because it is the power of God that brings salvation to everyone who believes: first to the Jew, then to the Gentile. For in the gospel the righteousness of God is revealed - a righteousness that is by faith from first to last, just as it is written: "The righteous will live by faith." (Romans 1:16-17)

The third point to make about Romans is **"Being a natural Jew will not save you."** Jesus had a conversation about this with some Pharisees, in the gospel of John.

I know that you are Abraham's descendants. Yet you are looking for a way to kill me, because you have no room for my word. I am telling you what I have seen in the Father's presence, and you are doing what you have heard from your father." "Abraham is our father," they answered. "If you were Abraham's children," said Jesus, "then you would do what Abraham did. As it is, you are looking for a way to kill me, a man who has told you the truth that I heard from God. Abraham did not do such things. You are doing the works of your own father." "We are not illegitimate children," they protested. "The only Father we have is God himself." Jesus said to them, "If God were your Father, you would love me, for I have come here from God.

I have not come on my own; God sent me. Why is my language not clear to you? Because you are unable to hear what I say. You belong to your father, the devil, and you want to carry out your father's desires. He was a murderer from the beginning, not holding to the truth, for there is no truth in him. When he lies, he speaks his native language, for he is a liar and the father of lies. Yet because I tell the truth, you do not believe me! Can any of you prove me guilty of sin? If I am telling the truth, why don't you believe me? Whoever belongs to God hears what God says. The reason you do not hear is that you do not belong to God." The Jews answered him, "Aren't we right in saying that you are a Samaritan and demon-possessed?" "I am not possessed by a demon," said Jesus, "but I honor my Father and you dishonor me. (John 8:37-49)

They claimed to be the children of Abraham, but Jesus tells them if they were the children of Abraham they would have believed on Him. To be a good Jew during that time period was to accept Jesus as Messiah. He came to them and for them, so they could be the blessing to the world. Then they claimed God was their Father. Jesus tells them again, if they were God's children they would have loved Him. He told them who their father was: the devil. These were the Jewish, Old Covenant people of God who Jesus said their father was the devil. In order for them to continue being the Israel of God, they had to accept Jesus.

Paul makes this point clear too, as we go through the book of Romans. So much bad teaching over the past several decades, mainly since 1948 when Israel became a nation again, concerning national Israel being the true people of God, and the Church is under another covenant. It's all non-sense! The truth of the Word tells a different story. Dispensationalism has crippled the Church for too long, and I hope books like this one will help bring the needed change to such teachings.

Under the Old Covenant, circumcision of the flesh brought someone into the Mosaic covenant, and circumcision of the heart brings someone into the New Covenant. Both systems operated/operate by the blood of a Lamb, but only the blood of Jesus is eternal.

The fourth point to make about the contextual flow to the book of Romans is **"God will bring divine wrath in the first century upon the Old Covenant system which rejected the Cross of His Son."** The issue about wrath is that it's completely tied to the Old Covenant system, which is no more. Therefore, wrath is no more.

...because the law brings wrath. And where there is no law there is no transgression. (Romans 4:15)

Wrath came in the Old Covenant because of covenant violation. As I will explain later in this book, the book of Revelation was about the ending of the Old Covenant, which finally happened in 70 AD. When you understand that, then you can understand what it means when it says this:

I saw in Heaven another great and marvelous sign: seven angels with the seven last plagues - last, because with them God's wrath is completed. (Revelation 15:1)

According to Revelation 15:1, the wrath of God was finished when the judgments of God were poured out on the harlot, Babylonian system that Jerusalem had become. When we read about wrath in the New Testament, its always talking about the coming wrath, which came in the great tribulation of 66 to 70 AD. The Christian persecution by Nero throughout the Roman Empire started in 64 AD. That's when Peter and Paul were killed, and John was banished to Patmos. That's when he wrote the Revelation. Nero killed himself in 68 AD, and John was released and went into Ephesus and distributed the 7 letters to the 7 Churches. Israel's great tribulation began in 66 AD when Roman armies sieged the city of Jerusalem and began to starve them out, not allowing anyone to come or go. The destruction to Jerusalem and the Temple happened in 70 AD, forty years after Jesus gave the prophecy in Matthew 24. Within one generation, God had made a complete change from Old Covenant, Temple system, to the Kingdom coming in power with the new Heaven and new Earth.

The wrath of God is being revealed from Heaven against all the godlessness and wickedness of people, who suppress the truth by their wickedness. (Romans 1:18)

Paul relates those who hold the truth (of Jesus) in unrighteousness were those unbelieving Jews still trapped in the Old Covenant. Israel's purpose was to receive their Messiah and bring His Kingdom to the whole world. God judged, with wrath, that Mosaic system that rejected the Cross of Jesus.

The fifth point about Romans is that **"Sin has been a problem since Adam".**

This next portion of Scripture speaks into the unbelieving Jews who rejected Jesus, but it also goes back in the history of Israel, with mentions of the Egyptians, Sodom and Gomorrah, and the Babylonians, all who worshipped pagan deities:

...since what may be known about God is plain to them, because God has made it plain to them. For since the creation of the world God's invisible qualities - his eternal power and divine nature - have been clearly seen, being understood from what has been made, so that people are without excuse. For although they knew God, they neither glorified him as God nor gave thanks to him, but their thinking became futile and their foolish hearts were darkened. Although they claimed to be wise, they became fools and exchanged the glory of the immortal God for images made to look like a mortal human being and birds and animals and reptiles. Therefore God gave them over in the sinful desires of their hearts to sexual impurity for the degrading of their bodies with one another. They exchanged the truth about God for a lie, and worshiped and served created things rather than the Creator-who is forever praised. Amen.

Because of this, God gave them over to shameful lusts. Even their women exchanged natural sexual relations for unnatural ones. In the same way the men also abandoned natural relations with women and were inflamed with lust for one another. Men committed shameful acts with other men, and received in themselves the due penalty for their error. Furthermore, just as they did not think it worthwhile to retain the knowledge of God, so God gave them over to a depraved mind, so that they do what ought not to be done.

They have become filled with every kind of wickedness, evil, greed and depravity. They are full of envy, murder, strife, deceit and malice. They are gossips, slanderers, God-haters, insolent, arrogant and boastful; they invent ways of doing evil; they disobey their parents; they have no understanding, no fidelity, no love, no mercy. Although they know God's righteous decree that those who do such things deserve death, they not only continue to do these very things but also approve of those who practice them. (Romans 1:19-32)

The above Scripture shows how God dealt with humanity because of sin and before the Cross. Paul writes a history of sin's effects on humanity.

The wrath and judgment that Paul was talking about was going to be fulfilled in the 70 AD destruction of Jerusalem. Paul mentioned sin historically, mentioning various instances of specific sin, but the judgment that was coming upon that generation was about removing the visible signs of the Old Covenant.

The sixth point about Romans is that **"God has dealt with sin through judgments in the past"**. Again, as you read through verses 19 through 32 of Romans chapter one, you can see Paul going through the history of sin and the response of God. The issue he will eventually get to is that God is no longer judging sin, because Christ has become the propitiation and Passover for our sins. Jesus is the final offering for sin, and this is important to understand for the sake of the gospel, and this is why Paul is methodically going through these things in Romans.

The seventh point about Romans is that **"Jew and Gentile both stand before God equally guilty because of sin."**

You, therefore, have no excuse, you who pass judgment on someone else, for at whatever point you judge another, you are condemning yourself, because you who pass judgment do the same things. Now we know that God's judgment against those who do such things is based on truth. So when you, a mere human being, pass judgment on them and yet do the same things, do you think you will escape God's judgment? Or do you show contempt for the riches of his kindness, forbearance and patience, not realizing that God's kindness is intended to lead you to repentance? But because of your stubbornness and your unrepentant heart, you are storing up wrath against yourself for the day of God's wrath, when his righteous judgment will be revealed. God "will repay each person according to what they have done." To those who by persistence in doing good seek glory, honor and immortality, he will give eternal life. But for those who are self-seeking and who reject the truth and follow evil, there will be wrath and anger. There will be trouble and distress for every human being who does evil: first for the Jew, then for the Gentile; but glory, honor and peace for everyone who does good: first for the Jew, then for the Gentile. For God does not show favoritism. All who sin apart from the law will also perish apart from the law, and all who sin under the law will be judged by the law. (Romans 2:1-12)

Gentiles were also involved in Temple worship in Jerusalem, having their own court. Paul makes it clear that sin is now the issue for humanity, whether one is a Jew or a Gentile. For the Jewish people, this may have been shocking to learn, and for the Gentile, a responsibility to come to Christ and be enlightened by the Holy Spirit had become available. Again, the language of judgment and coming wrath in these verses, both dealt with the entire Roman Empire, and then specifically Jerusalem. Gentiles were involved in both areas.

The eighth point begins the solution to the sin problem, which began in the garden and was the cause of the flood, that **"The Abrahamic covenant is fulfilled in Christ."** It was through the promises given to Abraham and then fulfilled in Christ Jesus that the hope for redemption and glory comes back to humanity. Even when Abraham took his only son Isaac up the mountain to sacrifice him, it was a type and shadow of the crucifixion, the ram caught in the thicket ultimately being the picture of Christ, the Lamb of God. In the New Covenant, we are children of Abraham by faith in Christ, making this a new Israel.

Paul first approaches the point of being a Jew who has been circumcised, yet does not obey the Law. How is that person any better than a Gentile who does not have the Law, yet lives a good life? Paul goes on to talk about a circumcision of the heart, which makes someone a true Jew, and a true child of Abraham:

You who boast in the law, do you dishonor God by breaking the law? As it is written: "God's name is blasphemed among the Gentiles because of you." Circumcision has value if you observe the law, but if you break the law, you have become as though you had not been circumcised. So then, if those who are not circumcised keep the law's requirements, will they not be regarded as though they were circumcised? The one who is not circumcised physically and yet obeys the law will condemn you who, even though you have the written code and circumcision, are a lawbreaker. A person is not a Jew who is one only outwardly, nor is circumcision merely outward and physical. No, a person is a Jew who is one inwardly; and circumcision is circumcision of the heart, by the Spirit, not by the written code. Such a person's praise is not from other people, but from God. (Romans 2:23-29)

In Chapter 3 of Romans, Paul talks about being a Jew and being under the Law, but he then levels the playing field again, making all equally guilty before God:

...for all have sinned and fall short of the glory of God, and all are justified freely by his grace through the redemption that came by Christ Jesus. (Romans 3:23-24)

Paul goes on to chapter 4 where he speaks of Abraham and his relationship with God, and how Abraham's covenant is the foundation of the grace covenant we have in Christ:

What then shall we say that Abraham, our forefather according to the flesh, discovered in this matter? If, in fact, Abraham was justified by works, he had something to boast about - but not before God. What does Scripture say? "Abraham believed God, and it was credited to him as righteousness." (Romans 4:1-3)

The ninth point is that **"His Cross is the solution for the sin problem."**

David says the same thing when he speaks of the blessedness of the one to whom God credits righteousness apart from works: "Blessed are those whose transgressions are forgiven, whose sins are covered. Blessed is the one whose sin the Lord will never count against them." Is this blessedness only for the circumcised, or also for the uncircumcised?

We have been saying that Abraham's faith was credited to him as righteousness. Under what circumstances was it credited? Was it after he was circumcised, or before? It was not after, but before! And he received circumcision as a sign, a seal of the righteousness that he had by faith while he was still uncircumcised.

So then, he is the father of all who believe but have not been circumcised, in order that righteousness might be credited to them. And he is then also the father of the circumcised who not only are circumcised but who also follow in the footsteps of the faith that our father Abraham had before he was circumcised. It was not through the law that Abraham and his offspring received the promise that he would be heir of the world, but through the righteousness that comes by faith.

For if those who depend on the law are heirs, faith means nothing and the promise is worthless, because the law brings wrath. And where there is no law there is no transgression. Therefore, the promise comes by faith, so that it may be by grace and may be guaranteed to all Abraham's offspring - not only to those who are of the law but also to those who have the faith of Abraham. He is the father of us all. As it is written: "I have made you a father of many nations." He is our father in the sight of God, in whom he believed - the God who gives life to the dead and calls into being things that were not. (Romans 4:6-17)

I like how Paul goes to the Davidic covenant, in the Psalms, to bring out a New Covenant reality, the forgiveness of sins. Under the Law there was only a temporary, year by year, system of sacrifice and forgiveness. The High Priesthood of Jesus has forgiven all sin once and for all. That is the glory of the gospel. In fact, everyone who has ever lived and ever will live has already been forgiven, because the blood was shed through the Spirit of the ages, bringing eternal life for those who believe in Jesus. The first century Jews were told to have the faith of Abraham, which would lead them to believe in Jesus. We then have the faith of Jesus, which is the New Covenant.

Paul begins to contrast the Law covenant with the grace and faith covenant. He shows that the promises of inheritance made to Abraham came by way of promises he believed and not according to the Law covenant. It's the Law covenant, which also worked wrath-bringing death, but the New Covenant is a covenant of righteousness, peace and joy in the Holy Spirit, the Spirit of Life.

The New Covenant is also called the Law of the Spirit of Life, the Law of Christ, the Kingdom of God, The New Heaven and New Earth, the New Jerusalem, Spiritual Mt. Zion, The Israel of God, Our Inheritance in Christ, Our Marriage in Christ. These are all words, phrases and thoughts that lead to the same thing, Jesus the King and the believer's union to Him.

Paul also begins to speak of circumcision, which came from Abraham, but was carried on under the Law, since they were the seed of Abraham. In the New Covenant, Paul will progress and show how the circumcision that matters is the circumcision of the heart, which means to be crucified with Christ and live as a new creation in Him.

The word **propitiation** has been misunderstood for so long. When defined according to the historical Greek mindset, it means, "to appease the wrath of an angry god." The Greeks had many angry gods, and they offered sacrifice for propitiation purposes, but Jesus is the "atoning sacrifice". God was not angry, but was "*in Christ, reconciling the world to Himself, not holding their sins against them.*" The Cross was an act of love and forgiveness, not an act of God's wrath put upon Jesus in order to spare us.

Actually, the gospel says we also died with Christ, so He did not die in our place, but we did die with Him. He died for us, but not in our place since we died with Him. It was the great exchange, the righteous for the unrighteous.

God did not forsake Jesus, even though Psalm 22 says that. Jesus quoted the first verse of that Psalm to draw the Hebrew people to the entirety of that Psalm. Jesus, I am sure, felt forsaken, but God did not forsake Him. As you read the entire Psalm, you learn that God was with Him through it all, and Paul picks this thought up in 2 Corinthians 5:17-21.

Therefore, if anyone is in Christ, the new creation has come: The old has gone, the new is here! All this is from God, who reconciled us to himself through Christ and gave us the ministry of reconciliation: that God was reconciling the world to himself in Christ, not counting people's sins against them. And he has committed to us the message of reconciliation. We are therefore Christ's ambassadors, as though God were making his appeal through us. We implore you on Christ's behalf: Be reconciled to God. God made him who had no sin to be sin for us, so that in him we might become the righteousness of God. (2 Corinthians 5:17-21)

The tenth point is that **"In Adam you died, but in Christ you live and reign."**

Therefore, since we have been justified through faith, we have peace with God through our Lord Jesus Christ (Romans 5:1)

Therefore, just as sin entered the world through one man, and death through sin, and in this way death came to all people, because all sinned - To be sure, sin was in the world before the law was given, but sin is not charged against anyone's account where there is no law. Nevertheless, death reigned from the time of Adam to the time of Moses, even over those who did not sin by breaking a command, as did Adam, who is a pattern of the one to come. But the gift is not like the trespass. For if the many died by the trespass of the one man, how much more did God's grace and the gift that came by the grace of the one man, Jesus Christ, overflow to the many! Nor can the gift of God be compared with the result of one man's sin: The judgment followed one sin and brought condemnation, but the gift followed many trespasses and brought justification.

For if, by the trespass of the one man, death reigned through that one man, how much more will those who receive God's abundant provision of grace and of the gift of righteousness reign in life through the one man, Jesus Christ! Consequently, just as one trespass resulted in condemnation for all people, so also one righteous act resulted in justification and life for all people.

For just as through the disobedience of the one man the many were made sinners, so also through the obedience of the one man the many will be made righteous. The law was brought in so that the trespass might increase. But where sin increased, grace increased all the more, so that, just as sin reigned in death, so also grace might reign through righteousness to bring eternal life through Jesus Christ our Lord. (Romans 5:12-21)

In Christ, we have become so many things, which make up our identity. Even the armor of God spoken of in Ephesians is our identity in Him. One aspect of our identity is that we are ambassadors of Heaven's Kingdom on Earth. We represent Christ, being His Body, and walking in His Spirit, His love and His authority.

Paul explains that sin entered the world. We are not born with sin living in us. Sin seems to be something we all grow in to. The fact is, we are all born in to Adam, and we must be born again in to Christ in order to have eternal life. Sin entered, and condemnation with sin, but in Christ, the sin is forgiven, atoned for, and righteousness is given to us. There is no condemnation, only forgiveness, for those who are in Christ by faith.

Paul tells us that because of the gift of righteousness and the abundance of grace, we now reign in life. We are seated with Him on the throne, and He is above all powers, whether on Earth or in

Heaven. We are One Spirit with Jesus, and as He is, so are we in this world. Greater is He who is in us than he who is in the world. We are ambassadorial kings, priests, and sons of our Father. Our Father is the Greatest, and Jesus is the perfect representation of the Father. Though we are being conformed to the image of the Son, our ultimate goal is the heart of the Father. The heart of the Father is love and grace.

The eleventh point is that **"Grace is not an excuse to sin, but is the power to overcome sin."** Paul begins chapter six speaking of grace and sin. Paul also relates another symbol to our born again experience: **Baptism**. I believe the water baptism is meant to be a picture of not only the death, burial and Resurrection of Jesus, but also of our baptism in the Spirit, the water representing the Holy Spirit that we become immersed in to.

What shall we say, then? Shall we go on sinning so that grace may increase? By no means! We are those who have died to sin; how can we live in it any longer? Or don't you know that all of us who were baptized into Christ Jesus were baptized into his death? We were therefore buried with him through baptism into death in order that, just as Christ was raised from the dead through the glory of the Father, we too may live a new life.

For if we have been united with him in a death like his, we will certainly also be united with him in a resurrection like his. For we know that our old self was crucified with him so that the body ruled by sin might be done away with, that we should no longer be slaves to sin - because anyone who has died has been set free from sin. (Romans 6:1-7)

Paul simply rehearses what has happened spiritually in their lives. They have been saved, given grace, born again, in Christ, changed, transformed. Now live up to your calling! This is the message of the gospel for the believer: With all that has been done in you, now live up to your calling in Christ Jesus.

Grace is the gift of God that changes us, empowers us, and lifts us up into our identity. Grace is the fuel of the Spirit who lives in us. Paul said it wasn't he that worked more than them all, but the grace of God with him. Paul understood that grace was the energy to fulfill the calling. Grace and faith work together to do the good works ordained for us to do in Christ.

The twelfth point is that **"All are freed from the Law because of the sin".** Romans was written to a largely Jewish audience. It was only the Jews who were under the Law covenant, not Gentiles. There was never a law for Gentiles to abide by, other than the conscience, which is given by God. Gentiles may have tried then and now to follow the Old Covenant law, but it will never work, and there is nothing achieved in doing so. We have one goal: to live in Christ. Where the Spirit of the Lord is there is freedom. We are very free in Christ, and Paul was talking to these people who were also told that they were free from the Law:

Do you not know, brothers and sisters - for I am speaking to those who know the law - that the law has authority over someone only as long as that person lives? For example, by law a married woman is bound to her husband as long as he is alive, but if her husband dies, she is released from the law that binds her to him. So then, if she has sexual relations with another man while her husband is still alive, she is called an adulteress. But if her husband dies, she is released from that law and is not an adulteress if she marries another man.

So, my brothers and sisters, you also died to the law through the body of Christ that you might belong to another, to him who was raised from the dead, in order that we might bear fruit for God. For when we were in the realm of the flesh, the sinful passions aroused by the law were at work in us, so that we bore fruit for death. But now, by dying to what once bound us, we have been released from the law so that we serve in the new way of the Spirit, and not in the old way of the written code. (Romans 7:1-6)

In Romans 7:7-25, Paul goes on to speak about his own life when he was without Christ and under the Law. He was powerless to do the right thing and also had guilt and condemnation hanging over his head. He was not free. But, in Christ, he has found freedom and declares that there is no condemnation for those who are saved in Christ. Romans 7 is not about the struggle of the Christian life. It was clearly about life under the Law without the power of the Spirit which Paul himself experienced.

The thirteenth point is that **"We are free from condemnation and now are sons of God in Christ."**

Romans 8 is such a wonderful, New Covenant chapter, yet it also makes contrasts with the Law, calling it flesh, and the New Covenant, calling it Spirit. He speaks of Christ fulfilling the righteous requirement of the Law in us. The righteous requirement of the Law is the forgiveness of sin and redemption. Jesus did this by dying on the Cross. We have forgiveness of sin once and for all in Christ, evidenced by the indwelling Holy Spirit. Because we have this Spirit, we are no longer in the flesh, but in the Spirit. We are neither lost any longer, nor are we Jews under the Law, whatever the context would have been. This brings us into the reality of being sons of God in Christ, with freedom, not fear and bondage.

Therefore, there is now no condemnation for those who are in Christ Jesus, because through Christ Jesus the law of the Spirit who gives life has set you free from the law of sin and death. For what the law was powerless to do because it was weakened by the flesh, God did by sending his own Son in the likeness of sinful flesh to be a sin offering. And so he condemned sin in the flesh, in order that the righteous requirement of the law might be fully met in us, who do not live according to the flesh but according to the Spirit. (Romans 8:1-4)

For those who are led by the Spirit of God are the children of God. The Spirit you received does not make you slaves, so that you live in fear again; rather, the Spirit you received brought about your adoption to sonship. And by him we cry, "Abba, Father." The Spirit himself testifies with our spirit that we are God's children. Now if we are children, then we are heirs - heirs of God and co-heirs with Christ, if indeed we share in his sufferings in order that we may also share in his glory. (Romans 8:14-17)

179

Paul goes on to speak of the creation itself groaning for the sons of God to be manifested in the Earth. This is what we work toward always, growing into our identity in Christ. Today, 1/3 of humanity claims to be Christian, that's over 2 billion people, but the need for Kingdom understanding, knowing one's identity in Christ, discipleship, growing in the Spirit, gifts of the Spirit, and so on, all of these things are priorities to work on. Also today, many "Justice Ministries" are arising with great faith to go into areas and seek to stop wars, bring peace, bring education, bring dignity back to the lives of people, rescuing young girls from prostitution and slavery, and helping restore the sanctity of families again. These are things required for the Kingdom of God to advance in the Earth.

The idea that Jesus is coming soon is completely wrong. There is so much work to be done to make this Earth look like God's Kingdom, but we are moving toward that goal.

The freedom that we have in Christ also deals with being a free citizen, as opposed to a slave. We are free, as citizens and sons of the Kingdom of God.

The fourteenth point is "A remnant of Jewish believers will be saved in the first century."

This next portion of Scripture is time sensitive to the covenant transition period that Paul was living and writing within. He longed for his Jewish brethren to step into the New Covenant and be saved from the coming wrath. Let me share an article I wrote on this topic:

When you read through Romans chapters 9, 10 and 11, it becomes very clear, that, number one, Paul wrote this during the covenant transition period, prior to 70 AD, and his simple desire was that his Old Covenant brothers in the flesh would embrace this New Covenant. He goes on to say that there is no difference between a Jew and a Greek, because they both need salvation in Christ. He then mentions that God has not cast away His Old Covenant people, because he himself was a Jew, and he got saved. But, he makes it clear that it's those who are of faith in Christ that are of Israel, which is the Israel of God by faith. He also mentions that blindness is on Israel until the fullness of the Gentiles happens. The blindness is the veil of the Old Covenant. The fullness of the Gentiles, at that time which he wrote it, was a prophetic, future event for them, in which the Roman armies would sack the Temple and city of Jerusalem, and then the blindness of the Old Covenant veiling system would be removed. It's not about future revival of Jewish people. It was Paul's heart's desire that the Jewish people of Israel would be saved, but he also knew that it was only by the election of "grace", and that only a remnant of Old Covenant Jews would embrace the New Covenant. This was prophesied about in the Old Testament, and Paul understood this, although his heart longed for things to be different.

During the days of covenant transition (from 30 AD to 70 AD), the gospel was meant to be preached, "to the Jew first." This has biblical precedent, since God was initially dealing with them.

These twelve Jesus sent out with the following instructions: "Do not go among the Gentiles or enter any town of the Samaritans. Go rather to the lost sheep of Israel. (Matthew 10:5-6)

For I am not ashamed of the gospel, because it is the power of God that brings salvation to everyone who believes: first to the Jew, then to the Gentile. (Romans 1:16)

But, in time, a greater revelation began to emerge, that this gospel was bigger than first realized, and the New Covenant is for everyone.

Then Paul and Barnabas answered them boldly: "We had to speak the word of God to you first. Since you reject it and do not consider yourselves worthy of eternal life, we now turn to the Gentiles. (Acts 13:46)

Eventually, they began to realize that there is no difference, and that everyone needs to be saved. God has no favorites, and Jesus died for the sins of the whole world.

For there is no difference between Jew and Gentile - the same Lord is Lord of all and richly blesses all who call on him. (Romans 10:12)

The word "Israel" is used 2,576 times in our Bible, and in 2,301 verses. We should learn what it means. This is at the heart of the New Covenant message. Who is Israel? The word is taken from a root word meaning, "to prevail, have power." The word Israel literally means "He will rule as God." This is fulfilled in the New Covenant, as we reign in life through Christ.

There is a connection between Romans 9,10 and 11, and Deuteronomy 30 and 32. Paul ties elements of these things together. Deuteronomy ended with Moses on his way out, a future judgment being pronounced upon Israel if they did not embrace the future New Covenant, and then Paul writing in the midst of these very things going on around him and drawing attention to this reality. It was the remnant of the 12 tribes (represented by the symbolic number 144,000), which were saved and embraced the Lamb of the New Covenant (Passover Lamb which was Christ), and this was the election of grace for salvation. It's amazing how things become so clear when you understand God's covenant journey with mankind.

If you believe that Israel, as a nation, is still the people of God, then you also believe that they have salvation while they reject Jesus Christ. It's been almost 2000 years since Jesus died for the sins of everyone, and for those who receive Him by faith and are born again, the same have redemption through His blood. Over those 2000 years, very, very few national Jewish people have accepted Him as Messiah, yet there are those who still think they are the people of God. This goes against any understanding of covenant, of forgiveness, of God's holiness, and God's justice. "Israel" refers to a people of faith. In the Old Covenant, it was the 12 tribes of Israel. In the New Covenant, it's those who have faith in Jesus Christ (the message of the 12 apostles) for the forgiveness and redemption of their sins. It's not about race anymore, or nationality any longer. It's about a new creation!

Jesus divided Israel into 2 groups of people: believers in Him and unbelievers. The believers in Jesus became the new and true Israel of God. The unbelievers either died in the destruction of Jerusalem or were taken into slavery throughout the Roman Empire. It was this true Israel of believing Jews that carried the gospel message to the rest of the world. Israel today is a global enterprise of all nations who are in Christ, in the New Covenant. The nation of Israel today that was restarted in 1948 is not the covenant Israel of God.

I hope that there can be peace there between all people one day, but the covenant Israel of God is in the Spirit, the New Jerusalem, believers in Christ. This is His Wife, co-heirs with Jesus.

The fifteenth point is that **"There is an Election According to Grace of believing Jews in the first century"**. Many misunderstandings of predestination have been birthed out of not understanding the historical context of the Scriptures and the audience Paul was speaking to.

So too, at the present time there is a remnant chosen by grace. (Romans 11:5)

What then? What the people of Israel sought so earnestly they did not obtain. The elect among them did, but the others were hardened. (Romans 11:7)

As far as the gospel is concerned, they are enemies for your sake; but as far as election is concerned, they are loved on account of the patriarchs. (Romans 11:28)

Paul speaks of "at this present time" meaning the time frame in which he and others were living (around 56 AD). It was a unique time in history, which was a covenant transition period of 40 years for that Israel. The election Paul speaks of was the believing Jews. Are we elect? Absolutely, we belong to God, but in context, Paul was speaking of believing Jews. Paul says it was the unbelieving Jews, which were blinded, and what blinded them, according 2 Corinthians 3, was the Old Covenant system. The Temple with its priesthood and sacrifices blinded them from seeing God, because to see God was to see Jesus. Without Jesus, they had no God. When God said, *"I will be your God and you shall be My people"*,

He was speaking of this new relationship through Jesus in the New Covenant. That is an eternal relationship. The offer was to all of Israel. It was their job to bring the gospel the rest of the world. A remnant according to grace believed and did the job of spreading the gospel of the Kingdom throughout the Roman Empire and beyond.

The sixteenth point is that **"Paul expresses his desire for his own countrymen to be saved in the first century".**

I speak the truth in Christ - I am not lying, my conscience confirms it through the Holy Spirit - I have great sorrow and unceasing anguish in my heart. For I could wish that I myself were cursed and cut off from Christ for the sake of my people, those of my own race, the people of Israel. Theirs is the adoption to sonship; theirs the divine glory, the covenants, the receiving of the law, the temple worship and the promises. Theirs are the patriarchs, and from them is traced the human ancestry of the Messiah, who is God over all, forever praised! Amen.

It is not as though God's word had failed. For not all who are descended from Israel are Israel. Nor because they are his descendants are they all Abraham's children. On the contrary, "It is through Isaac that your offspring will be reckoned." In other words, it is not the children by physical descent who are God's children, but it is the children of the promise who are regarded as Abraham's offspring. (Romans 9:1-8)

It was the fervent desire of Paul that all of physical Israel at that time would have embraced Jesus and the New Covenant, but many of them did not. Only a remnant according to grace received Jesus. This is how Paul opens up chapter nine of Romans. He explains their history with God as the one people group on Earth who God made a covenant with, and gave them promises through Abraham's and David's covenant, with many types and shadows of their inheritance in the Mosaic covenant. The adoption as children was for them, if they would have accepted Christ. Paul tells them it was you who Jesus came to, God in the flesh, but those who rejected Jesus also rejected God. The Old Covenant was

184

in its last days. Paul explains to them that everyone in Israel is not a child of Abraham, but only those who receive Christ and become children of God through the promise.

The seventeenth point is that **"The Old Covenant has become a blinding influence until the Gentiles come to destroy the city and Temple in the first century."**

One of the errors of translation concerning future times, or "end times" is the use of the term coined "the fullness of the Gentiles." The concept of this is actually used in 3 places in our Bible:

They will fall by the sword and will be taken as prisoners to all the nations. Jerusalem will be trampled on by the Gentiles until the times of the Gentiles are fulfilled. (Luke 21:24)

I do not want you to be ignorant of this mystery, brothers and sisters, so that you may not be conceited: Israel has experienced a hardening in part until the full number of the Gentiles has come in. (Romans 11:25)

But exclude the outer court; do not measure it, because it has been given to the Gentiles. They will trample on the holy city for 42 months. (Revelation 11:2)

Each instance, this is referring to a time when the Gentiles (the Romans) would take over Jerusalem and the Temple and would destroy it. Jerusalem and the Temple were holy places for the Jews, and for the Gentiles to take over that holy thing meant tragedy for the Jewish nation. The fullness of the Gentiles has nothing to do with waiting for all us Gentiles to get saved in this "dispensation" of the age of grace, which is a popular interpretation of that phrase.

It was about the destruction of Jerusalem and the Temple by the Gentile Roman armies in the 70 AD era. It's already happened. We have moved far beyond those days and we live in the days of the ever advancing and increasing Kingdom of God.

Paul speaks of how the Old Covenant blinds the minds of unbelieving Israel:

But their minds were made dull, for to this day the same veil remains when the Old Covenant is read. It has not been removed, because only in Christ is it taken away. Even to this day when Moses is read, a veil covers their hearts. But whenever anyone turns to the Lord, the veil is taken away. Now the Lord is the Spirit, and where the Spirit of the Lord is, there is freedom. And we all, who with unveiled faces contemplate the Lord's glory, are being transformed into his image with ever-increasing glory, which comes from the Lord, who is the Spirit. (2 Corinthians 3:14-18)

The veil, which hung between the Holy Place and Holy of Holies, separated God from His people. They had to go through the priest to have relationship with God. God wanted them all to be priests, with no veil, but the Old Covenant called for the veil, when they rejected His offer at Mt. Sinai, to be His Kingdom of priests. In Christ, the veil is removed, and our minds and heart become free to enter into the Kingdom. In Christ, we are the Kingdom of priests that God wanted.

You can go back and read the story of Samson in a previous chapter of this book, and see the life picture of Samson being a type of Old Covenant Israel, that embraced the harlot, lost strength, became blinded and weak, and then enslaved. Israel's house eventually fell on them, symbolically, as the Temple and city were burned to the ground in 70 AD. Samson also died from a house he pushed down falling upon him. You might say unbelieving Israel caused their own demise, as they were warned prophetically for centuries.

I would like to mention a few teachers and authors that I have gained knowledge from in my journey with God: *Dr. Jonathan Welton, Dr. Stan Newton, Dr. Martin Trench, Dr. Kenneth Gentry, Gary DeMar, Harold Eberle, David Chilton, N.T. Wright, Scott Hahn, and Kelly Varner are a few of the authors I have gained understanding from.*

The final and **eighteenth point** that I have gleaned from the book of Romans is that Paul encourages all to be **"Be transformed by the Holy Spirit in your mind."**

It's the indwelling of the Holy Spirit that makes us One with Jesus. The Holy Spirit saves us, washes us, empowers us, leads us, talks to us, reveals truth to us, and connects us to Heaven with faith. The Holy Spirit is our Jesus on Earth with us.

Therefore, I urge you, brothers and sisters, in view of God's mercy, to offer your bodies as a living sacrifice, holy and pleasing to God - this is your true and proper worship. Do not conform to the pattern of this age, but be transformed by the renewing of your mind. Then you will be able to test and approve what God's will is - his good, pleasing and perfect will. (Romans 12:1-2)

Paul desires that the mind, the thinking of God's new people in Christ would be Kingdom oriented. Setting our minds on things above (the Kingdom), and not on things of the Earth. Earth is being transformed, but it happens as we set our minds on the Kingdom, on things above.

Paul puts great emphasis on the Spirit, for He is our life and peace, and reality in Christ. We are spiritual people in the New Covenant, ambassadors of a Kingdom that exists in a realm we cannot always see or feel, but God gives us glimpses of a greater glory that we are moving toward.

I hope this has helped put the book of Romans into the historical and covenantal context in which the Spirit would have us understand. Only by knowing the journey of God with His people Israel can we understand who we are as His Body on Earth today.

Many false doctrines have arisen over not understanding the historical and covenantal context of many parts of the Bible, Romans being one of those places where doctrinal divisions can occur.

This is the apostolic message of the Kingdom, from old to new, to a restored creation and humanity. This is the apostolic eschatology Jesus and His apostles declared.

We live in days where wars and persecutions should be diminishing. Where a greater light begins to shine because of the Kingdom. We live in days where rapes and divorce should be diminishing. Where poverty should be in its last days, and prosperity, peace and unity begin to take over the hearts and minds of people who are coming to Christ in His Kingdom.

Chapter Seventeen
The Last Days warning letter to the Hebrews

The author of the letter to the Hebrews is unknown. It has been speculated that Paul, or Barnabas, or Apollos could have written this letter to the Jewish people who were living in Jerusalem around 65 AD. The Jewish people were in the last days of the Old Covenantal system, and destruction was soon coming to remove every visible sign of that covenant, from its Temple to its Levitical priesthood, to the city they all lived in, Jerusalem. Jerusalem began to be called Babylon by those Jewish people who escaped into the New Covenant. Peter even addresses the Church in Jerusalem as such:

She who is in Babylon, chosen together with you, sends you her greetings, and so does my son Mark. (1 Peter 5:13)

Peter spent most of his time as an apostle in Jerusalem and that region, and only at the end of his life did he travel to Rome, where he died by the hand of Nero. Peter was mentioning the Church at Jerusalem and calling her *"She who is in Babylon"*.

Whoever wrote Hebrews was writing it in order to urge the remaining Jewish people who had not embraced Jesus to come into the glorious Kingdom of God and be saved, both from the soon coming destruction and from sin and death too. The writer wrote it in the context of the last days of the Old Covenant. The end of the age was at hand, and a new age of the Kingdom was practically here. Paul wrote about it as if it was already fully here, but they were awaiting its full arrival with the revelation of Jesus Christ, or His unveiling.

The book of Hebrews can be broken up into 3 sections, all of which exalt the Lordship and Supremacy of Jesus Christ:

1. Hebrews 1–7: **Jesus is better than the Old Covenant**

    a. Hebrews 1–2 Jesus the God-man is greater than angels.

    b. Hebrews 3–4:13 Jesus the apostle is greater than Moses.

    c. Hebrews 4:14–6:12 Jesus the High Priest is better than Aaron.

    d. Hebrews 6:13–7 Jesus is better than Melchizedek.

2. Hebrews 8–10: **The New Covenant is better than the Old Covenant**

    a. Hebrews 8 The New Covenant is based on better promises.

    b. Hebrews 9:1–10 The New Covenant has a better sanctuary.

    c. Hebrews 9:11–28 The New Covenant has a better sacrifice.

    d. Hebrews 10:1–18 The New Covenant has better results.

3. Hebrews 11–13: **Faith is our response to Jesus in the New Covenant**

    a. Hebrews 10:19–39 Faith is the natural response to the *"better things"* of the New Covenant, and we connect with that New Covenant through faith.

    b. Hebrews 11 Adam, Noah, Enoch, and many others give us examples of connecting by faith.

    c. Hebrews 12 Faith is the basis of a better relationship.

    d. Hebrews 13 Faith is a better manner of life.

Before we get into explaining the 3 sections of Hebrews, I want to begin with looking at timeframe, audience, and the exaltation of Jesus above the Old Covenant. The Temple with its rituals and priesthood had become an idol to Israel. Those willing to repent, change their thinking, were able to come into the Kingdom through Jesus, but those unwilling to repent, seeing no need for repentance, remained in the Old Covenant. There were those who were caught in the middle. Seeing the New Covenant, but being comfortable with the Old Covenant. I believe it's this last group, those caught in the middle that the writer of Hebrews is focusing on.

The history, or covenant journey of God with Israel:

In the past God spoke to our ancestors through the prophets at many times and in various ways... (Hebrews 1:1)

God used to deal with Israel by sending a prophet to them to tell them how they have been violating the covenant and what they need to do to fix the problem. In the New Covenant, the Cross fixes the problem of sin once and for all, and God no longer sends prophets to warn His people of covenant violation.

Rather, He sends prophets to encourage, exhort and comfort with New Covenant blessings. In their last days, the Old Covenant is coming to an end, and something new is on the horizon - the Kingdom of God, which is embodied in His Son, Jesus:

...but in these last days he has spoken to us by his Son, whom he appointed heir of all things, and through whom also he made the universe. (Hebrews 1:2)

The writer of Hebrews calls his time *"these last days"*, because he and other Jewish believers understood that the Old Covenant with its Temple and priesthood were in their last days.

Because of the New Covenant, Jesus is the King. This is the New Covenant Kingdom of God, and the writer shows the supremacy of Jesus over all creation:

The Son is the radiance of God's glory and the exact representation of his being, sustaining all things by his powerful word. After he had provided purification for sins, he sat down at the right hand of the Majesty in Heaven. So he became as much superior to the angels as the name he has inherited is superior to theirs. (Hebrews 1:3-4)

Jesus is being revealed to this audience as the Son of God, Messiah, but also God Himself. He lays the groundwork for the New Covenant, which is through the purging of sins in His blood. Now, He has been seated at the right hand of God, of Majesty on High.

Through my studies, I have come to the conclusion of a few things concerning angels:

1. Angels were created before mankind.

2. Angels were first called sons of God, or sons of Heaven, before man was created.

3. Angels are male and they can transform their bodies into that of a human, thus being able to have sexual relations with a woman.

4. It's through these sexual relations spoken of by Jude and in Genesis 6, was the race of giants produced that Enoch wrote about.

5. In the Old Covenant, angels dispensed the judgments of God, as the Law covenant was ordained of angels.

6. In the New Covenant, we are in Christ, above the angels, and they are to serve us.

7. Mankind, in Christ, are sons of God.

Moses was great in the minds of every Jewish person, but Jesus is being presented as He who is greater than Moses.

For every house is built by someone, but God is the builder of everything. "Moses was faithful as a servant in all God's house," bearing witness to what would be spoken by God in the future. But Christ is faithful as the Son over God's house. And we are his house, if indeed we hold firmly to our confidence and the hope in which we glory. (Hebrews 3:4-6)

Under Moses was Aaron, his brother. Aaron is Israel's first high priest under the initial Old Covenant. Jesus is the High Priest of the New Covenant, and He is greater than Aaron. Aaron died but Jesus lives forever.

Therefore, since we have a great high priest who has ascended into Heaven, Jesus the Son of God, let us hold firmly to the faith we profess. (Hebrews 4:14)

The exhortation to them is to hold on to their faith, especially in the coming tribulation, which was near.

And no one takes this honor on himself, but he receives it when called by God, just as Aaron was. (Hebrews 5:4)

Even as Aaron was called of God to initiate the Old Covenant, so Jesus is now called of God to initiate this New Covenant. Jesus was both High Priest and Lamb of God for the establishing of the New Covenant.

Then we come to the man Melchizedek, in Hebrews chapter 7. The writer is contrasting the priesthoods of Levi, Melchizedek and now Jesus. The writer elevates the priesthood of Melchizedek over Levi, but then shows that Jesus is greater than Melchizedek. I have discussed Melchizedek in a previous chapter but I will go over it again.

The comparisons of Christ to Melchizedek in Hebrews 7, and the answers to those hard questions are below. Many say, "It says he has no mother and no father", it says, "He lives forever", it says, "He did not have beginning of days nor end of life". All of these comparisons relate to the Old Covenant requirements of being a Levite priest and the New Covenant substance of the true priesthood in the Kingdom.

1. Levite priests were required to carry papers proving their heritage at all times (who was their father and mother), as well as their birth certificate because they were only able to be a priest from 30-50 years old. This answers the question of having no father or mother and having no beginning of days or end of life. It was related to the priesthood of Levi vs. Melchizedek.

2. Whereas Jesus in the order of Melchizedek, didn't need to prove His genealogy, and His priesthood didn't end at 50, it is eternal.

3. Abraham would have given tithe only to his oldest male ancestor as the priest.

What we also come to realize through study of the Scriptures is that the terminal generation of 30 AD to 70 AD was compared to Israel going through the wilderness for 40 years under Moses. It was unbelieving Israel who was compared to that previous generation. Therefore, there is also a warning of a coming destruction, which is compared to the flood and uses imagery of the plagues and Egypt and other Old Testament examples, which show up in the book of Revelation. Here is the first warning to Israel:

So, as the Holy Spirit says: "Today, if you hear his voice, do not harden your hearts as you did in the rebellion, during the time of testing in the wilderness, where your ancestors tested and tried me, though for forty years they saw what I did. That is why I was angry with that generation; I said, 'Their hearts are always going astray, and they have not known my ways.' So I declared on oath in my anger, 'They shall never enter my rest.' " See to it, brothers and sisters, that none of you has a sinful, unbelieving heart that turns away from the living God. But encourage one another daily, as long as it is called "Today," so that none of you may be hardened by sin's deceitfulness. (Hebrews 3:7-13)

That was a warning for those Jews who felt caught in the middle of the old and New Covenant. The writer of Hebrews quotes from David in the Psalms. David's covenant is foundational to the New Covenant Kingdom, and David wrote of many New Covenant realities while living in the midst of the vassal covenant between God and Israel.

The New Covenant is based on better promises than the Old Covenant.

But now hath he obtained a more excellent ministry, by how much also he is the mediator of a better covenant, which was established upon better promises. (Hebrews 8:6)

The promise of the New Covenant is forgiveness and eternal life, which is our redemption. But, there are other things we get to enjoy by being in this New Covenant with Jesus. Jesus revealed our inheritance when He spoke to the 7 Churches in Revelation:

A list of things we have inherited in Christ:

1. Eating from the tree of life, eternal life (a never ending source of life)

2. The crown of life (reign in life) - we have authority in Christ

3. Hidden Manna (fellowship meal of marriage) – we are One with Jesus

4. White Stone (innocence) with our new name written in it (a name of our new identity in Christ that only we can experience)

5. Power over the nations (we are the authority in the Earth)

6. The Morning Star - we are the light of the world

7. White clothing - we are the righteousness of God

8. Name written in Heaven never to be blotted out (our citizenship)

9. Our name confessed before the Father

10. Made a pillar in the Temple God - we live in the New Jerusalem as a living stone

11. Name of God written on us - we are His

12. Name of new city of Jerusalem given to us

13. New name written on us (identity experience)

14. We sit on the throne with Jesus as joint heirs with Him

The Old Covenant hid God's love, but the New Covenant reveals God's love, which began to break forth into humanity at the Cross. God has always been love, but the Law covenant had built into it the aspect of wrath.

Paul tells us that the Old Covenant was ordained of angels, so I believe it was the angels who administered the judgments due under the Old Covenant. The Law put a demand on the worshipper to be righteous, but the New Covenant provides grace and righteousness as free gifts to us.

Grace is power to live in the Spirit and walk in love, to do the ministry God has gifted and called us to do. We have an abundance of grace in the New Covenant, whereas the Old Covenant was not a covenant of grace. The New Covenant is a grant type of covenant, which means the Greater party is obligated to provide what is necessary to the lesser party.

The New Covenant is between the Perfect Father King and His Perfect Son King, and we partake of the inheritance through marriage (faith relationship). The Old Testament and Old Covenant is full of types and shadows but the New Covenant is the reality and substance realized in Christ, which those old things pointed to.

The New Covenant has a better sanctuary, a better sacrifice and better results. The Temple is God Himself, and it's the Kingdom in the Spirit, the New Jerusalem, and the Bride. The New Jerusalem is in the shape of a perfect cube, just like the Holy of Holies was. The New Jerusalem, the Bride, the Wife of Jesus, made up of believers, is the Temple of God, the dwelling place of God Himself. This New Jerusalem is the new Holy of holies.

The better sacrifice, of course, is Jesus, the Lamb of God. Jesus was 6 things while on the Cross:

1. He was the High Priest for humanity offering the sacrifice for forgiveness.

2. He was the Lamb of God for humanity's sins.

3. He was the Passover Lamb delivering from death and fulfilling the type and shadow of the Old Covenant for Israel.

4. He was God in the flesh dying as the Husband to Israel to release them from their previous marriage covenant so they could marry anew the resurrected Lord.

5. He was the Son of God dying as Adam to take the old creation to death and offer a new creation by His Resurrection.

6. He was the covenant partner with His Father establishing a New Covenant of forgiveness without wrath.

The New Covenant has better results as well. We are not servants, but children of God, with family rights. It's our identity in Christ that defines us, and not our failures or present struggles. We are the righteousness of God in Christ, and no weapon formed against us shall prosper. We have many promises in the Bible that find their meaning and release in Christ, and they are yes and amen in Him.

Faith is our reality, while on Earth in the flesh, in the New Covenant. One day we will have resurrected bodies and the relationship will no longer be faith based, yet still love based. Faith works through love, so love is the foundation and fruit of our relationship with the Lord.

There are many types and shadows found in the Old Testament stories and in the Old Covenant rituals that point to Christ. Every lamb and all the blood shed through sacrifice pointed to the final sacrifice in the blood of Jesus, which brings eternal redemption. The flood was a picture of death, burial, baptism and new life. The book of Hebrews mentions how the Old Covenant was like shadows and figures, but the New Covenant is the reality and substance:

Now the main point of what we are saying is this: We do have such a high priest, who sat down at the right hand of the throne of the Majesty in Heaven, and who serves in the sanctuary, the true tabernacle set up by the Lord, not by a mere human being. Every high priest is appointed to offer both gifts and sacrifices, and so it was necessary for this one also to have something to offer. If he were on Earth, he would not be a priest, for there are already priests who offer the gifts prescribed by the law. They serve at a sanctuary that is a copy and shadow of what is in Heaven. This is why Moses was warned when he was about to build the tabernacle: "See to it that you make everything according to the pattern shown you on the mountain." But in fact the ministry Jesus has received is as superior to theirs as the covenant of which he is mediator is superior to the old one, since the New Covenant is established on better promises. (Hebrews 8:1-6)

Under the Old Covenant, their faith was in a coming Messiah, which was represented by many types and shadows within that Old Covenant system, but in the New Covenant, we have the substance. The definition we use concerning the word faith, taken from Hebrews 11:1 contains the language of faith now being the substance (and no longer the shadow):

Now faith is confidence (substance) in what we hope for and assurance about what we do not see. (Hebrews 11:1)

Paul tells us that in Christ has true faith come, and before Him the Law covenant was not of faith.

Before the coming of this faith, we were held in custody under the law, locked up until the faith that was to come would be revealed. So the law was our guardian until Christ came that we might be justified by faith. Now that this faith has come, we are no longer under a guardian. (Galatians 3:23-25)

This describes the Old Covenant law as a prison guard, keeping Israel until Jesus and faith would come. Once Jesus comes, it will no longer be a law type relationship but rather, a faith-based relationship, the marriage of the New Covenant.

The writer of Hebrews is attempting to get them to see that the old has served its purpose, and pointed us all to Christ. Now, it's time to let go of the Law, and fully enter the New Covenant. Let me give a few more examples concerning the warnings of judgment for first century Israel if they do not heed the words of Christ, their Messiah:

It is impossible for those who have once been enlightened, who have tasted the Heavenly gift, who have shared in the Holy Spirit, who have tasted the goodness of the word of God and the powers of the coming age and who have fallen away, to be brought back to repentance. To their loss they are crucifying the Son of God all over again and subjecting him to public disgrace. Land that drinks in the rain often falling on it and that produces a crop useful to those for whom it is farmed receives the blessing of God.

But land that produces thorns and thistles is worthless and is in danger of being cursed. In the end it will be burned. (Hebrews 6:4-8)

That section of Scripture is very specific to the coming judgment of those who reject Christ, of those Hebrew people. The judgment came in 70 AD, and Hebrews was written around 65 AD. Five years after the warnings of this letter the entire Jewish world was turned upside down. Hebrews 6:4-6 speaks of those who are wavering in their faith and going back and forth between the Body of Christ and the Temple. The mindset of needing to sacrifice is like crucifying Jesus over and over.

The idea is to accept the once and for all final sacrifice of the Son of God for all sin. Hebrews 6:7-8 is speaking of the land, mainly the land of Israel and Jerusalem. Those who receive Christ will be blessed, but those who reject Him will be cursed and burned in the fires of 70 AD. They saw the land as their special inheritance, but in Christ, we have a land in the Spirit, a New Jerusalem, which has come down to Earth out of Heaven. We are pillars in this new Temple structure.

"This is the covenant I will make with them after that time", says the Lord. "I will put my laws in their hearts, and I will write them on their minds." Then he adds: "Their sins and lawless acts I will remember no more." And where these have been forgiven, sacrifice for sin is no longer necessary. Therefore, brothers and sisters, since we have confidence to enter the Most Holy Place by the blood of Jesus, by a new and living way opened for us through the curtain, that is, his body, and since we have a great priest over the house of God, let us draw near to God with a sincere heart and with the full assurance that faith brings, having our hearts sprinkled to cleanse us from a guilty conscience and having our bodies washed with pure water.

Let us hold unswervingly to the hope we profess, for he who promised is faithful. And let us consider how we may spur one another on toward love and good deeds, not giving up meeting together, as some are in the habit of doing, but encouraging one another - and all the more as you see the

Day approaching. If we deliberately keep on sinning after we have received the knowledge of the truth, no sacrifice for sins is left, but only a fearful expectation of judgment and of raging fire that will consume the enemies of God. Anyone who rejected the Law of Moses died without mercy on the testimony of two or three witnesses. How much more severely do you think someone deserves to be punished who has trampled the Son of God underfoot, who has treated as an unholy thing the blood of the covenant that sanctified them, and who has insulted the Spirit of grace? For we know him who said, "It is mine to avenge; I will repay," and again, "The Lord will judge his people." It is a dreadful thing to fall into the hands of the living God. (Hebrews 10:16-31)

Hebrews 10:16-31 begins by defining the New Covenant for Israel as being one of forgiveness and mercy. It speaks of the blood of Jesus, which has done the final work, and how Jesus is the High Priest over this new Temple. It speaks of maintaining faith in Jesus and not forsaking their assembling together. That was a very important admonition for them because of the evil days they lived in.

The Holy Spirit would speak words of comfort, direction and warning through ministers and prophets in their meetings, and it was imperative to hear the Spirit's relevant words for them. He then goes on to speak of the coming judgment upon the Mosaic system, which brings wrath (Romans 4:15). Those who are rejecting Jesus and His Cross are insulting the Spirit of Grace, which purchased them. Verse 30 quotes from the Song of Moses, found in Deuteronomy 32.

The Song of Moses was the prophetic song, which declared the coming destruction of the Old Covenant system and national Israel as a people of God. In the New Covenant, the people of God would be found in Christ, not by bloodline, but by the circumcision of the heart. For those who would reject Christ, would receive the wrath of God stored up and poured out upon that harlot system. This judgment of 70 AD is as important as the Virgin Birth, the Cross and the Resurrection in understanding the story of the New Covenant gospel of Jesus Christ. We, as Gentiles, were grafted into *"believing Israel"*, those Jewish people who were born again in Christ and then carried the apostolic message of the Kingdom into the rest of the world. The True Israel today, in the Spirit, is not about Jew and Gentile, but about a new creation, which comes by the Holy Spirit and faith in Jesus Christ. Only in the New Covenant do we have a Heavenly Father who loves us as He loves Jesus.

We do not live in the same type of days as those people did back then, especially in America and parts of Europe and Asia. Life is pretty good. Most of us do not have the dark cloud of persecution or looming judgment. Because of the advancing Kingdom of God, persecutions should diminish more and more as years go by, wars shall become less and less, cancers, aids, and other diseases and viruses will be healed and medicines and cures will be discovered. It's the restoration of all things of God's creation that we are after. We do not sit and think that things are getting worse; that the world is going to hell, and our only hope is the rapture. There is no rescue rapture. We await and participate in the work of bringing justice and love into the world and the Kingdom of God being established in the hearts and minds of humanity.

The book of Hebrews makes the comparison between the Old Covenant and the New Covenant. I guess my favorite portion of the book of Hebrews would be this:

You have not come to a mountain that can be touched and that is burning with fire; to darkness, gloom and storm; to a trumpet blast or to such a voice speaking words that those who heard it begged that no further word be spoken to them, because they could not bear what was commanded: "If even an animal touches the mountain, it must be stoned to death." The sight was so terrifying that Moses said, "I am trembling with fear."

But you have come to Mount Zion, to the city of the living God, the Heavenly Jerusalem. You have come to thousands upon thousands of angels in joyful assembly, to the Church of the firstborn, whose names are written in Heaven. You have come to God, the Judge of all, to the spirits of the righteous made perfect, to Jesus the mediator of a New Covenant, and to the sprinkled blood that speaks a better word than the blood of Abel. The New Covenant is not one where we "fear" God, but rather, we "love" God. We are not punished for sin, but rather, we have been forgiven. We are not accepted by our behavior, but rather, we have been perfectly accepted in the Beloved, Jesus Christ. It's very clear we have come to Mt. Zion, the Spirit Kingdom of God, and that kingdom is being demonstrating, manifested, and is growing and expanding throughout the Earth. (Hebrews 12:18-24)

Chapter Eighteen
The unveiling of Jesus Christ

I chose to use the word "unveiling" in the title to this chapter because it describes what "The Revelation of Jesus Christ" is actually about. His unveiling, being revealed, as Messiah, King, and Almighty God. Jesus is both the fulfillment of the Seed promise to Abraham and David, and He is God in the flesh, come to die and marry Israel anew.

One of the biggest issues among scholars and preachers today is the dating of the book of Revelation. When was it written? This matters tremendously. If it was written before 70 AD, then its about the destruction of Jerusalem and the Temple through the Roman war of 66-73 AD. If it was written after 70 AD, then it must be about a tribulation and destruction in our future. Here is a short list of things that prove, to me, that it was written before 70 AD.

1. It's the closing canon of the New Testament. The canon or story of the New Testament is that Jesus is born, fulfilling prophecy and His death and Resurrection bring the Kingdom of God to Israel, for those who believe. Revelation is the closing of the Old Covenant system, where the Song of Moses is sang by the saints, and the New Jerusalem is descending from Heaven to Earth to expand the Kingdom of God throughout the whole Earth. Revelation is the culmination of the tremendous shift, which took place in 70 AD.

2. After 70 AD, the Church flourished without Jewish persecution, because all the Jews were either Christian, dead from the destruction, or taken into slavery throughout the Roman Empire. Prior to 70 AD, only seven major Churches in that region would be reasonable.

Also, there is mention of the synagogue of Satan, which were the Judaizers persecuting the newly formed Christian Church made up of mostly Jewish people, among a few Gentiles. There would have been no synagogue of Satan (unbelieving Jews) after 70 AD to persecute the Church.

3. The Temple was still standing, because John is told to go measure it. If it were written after 70 AD, John would not have mentioned a Temple without also speaking of the most horrific thing to ever happen to the Jewish nation, which was the destruction of their holy city and holy Temple in 70 AD.

4. The mention of 666.

This calls for wisdom. Let the person who has insight calculate the number of the beast, for it is the number of a man. That number is 666. (Revelation 13:18)

In Hebrew, the numeric value of Caesar Nero is 600 plus 60 plus 6, or 666. Nero reigned over the Roman Empire from 54 AD to 68 AD. He killed himself in 68 AD. He began the Christian persecution throughout his empire in 64 AD, at which time both Peter and Paul were killed, and John was exiled to Patmos. He began the great tribulation for the Jewish nation in 66 AD, by sending his armies to siege their city.

5. The mention of the kings in Revelation 17:10 allows us to take history and tie it to what John wrote concerning the Roman Empire.

They are also seven kings. Five have fallen, one is, the other has not yet come; but when he does come, he must remain for only a little while. (Revelation 17:10)

Five are fallen, meaning five kings have come and died. The Roman Empire began with Julius Caesar. He was the first in the family line of emperors for Rome during this period of time. The Roman Senate declared him an eternal emperor. When you go back to Julius Caesar, the first emperor of Rome, five have fallen at the time John was writing this, around 65 AD:

- **Julius Caesar** (49 BC-44 BC) – The Roman Empire begins.

- Civil war broke out from 44 to 27 BC

- **Augustus** (27 BC-14 AD) Jesus was born under the reign of Augustus after the first census when Rome had annexed Israel.

- **Tiberius** (14 AD-37 AD)

- **Caligula** (37 AD-41 AD)

- **Claudius** (41 AD-54 AD)

Those five had died, so five had fallen.

Then the verse says, *"one is"*. That means there is one reigning now at the time John was writing, which would have been **Nero**. Let me mention something about Nero:

Nero so affected the imagination that the pagan writer Apollinius of Tyana, a contemporary of Nero, specifically mentions that Nero was called a *"beast"*: *"In my travels, which have been wider than ever man yet accomplished, I have seen many, many wild beasts of Arabia and India; but this beast, that is commonly called a Tyrant, I know not how many heads it has, nor if it be crooked of claw, and armed with horrible fangs... And of wild beasts you cannot say that they were ever known to eat their own mother, but Nero has gorged himself on this diet."*

Nero was referred to by many in the empire as *"the beast"*. He killed his mother and a wife. He had a 9 year old boy castrated and married him, parading him around the city in the queen's robes. He had sex with his mother, and kicked his pregnant wife. He had parties at night and used the live bodies of Christians to light the grounds. The Christians were tarred and lit on fire as they were impaled upon a stake.

The Seven Churches of Revelation:

When we get to the seven letters to the Seven Churches, we must realize that these were historical Churches with real people. In 64 AD, Nero unleashed a severe persecution against Christians, which lasted until the events of 70 AD played out. We also need to be reminded that the Bible is written through the lens of Hebraic, covenantal context. We are reading a story about a people group that Jesus came from and came to. The Bible and the book of Revelation are written within the context of Israel, but we, through faith in Jesus, have been grafted into what has become a global Kingdom enterprise. The Seven Letters actually follow a type of history of Israel, which to them, began in the garden.

Most of what is in this next section came from truth I gleaned from authors David Chilton and Jonathan Welton.

Demystifying the book of Revelation:

Revelation was written to 7 Churches about things, which were ready to happen in their generation. Daniel, who wrote about the coming of Jesus, His atonement and the destruction of the Temple, was told to seal his writing for it was a long way off, about 400 years. John was told to not seal his writing because it was at hand. The events of Revelation unfolded within a few years after John wrote.

The book of Revelation is about 3 basic things:

1.   The ending, wrapping up, of the Old Covenant Temple system, which had become a harlot committing adultery in the marriage. The Old Covenant veiled Jesus (2 Corinthians 3-4).

2.   The unveiling of Jesus as Almighty God and King of the Kingdom of God.

3. The revealing of the New Covenant Bride, the Body of Christ, made up of all nations, through a new marriage in a New Covenant.

The book of Revelation is speaking of a harlot (Old Covenant Jerusalem) that will soon be judged: *"And the ten horns which you saw, and the beast (the Roman Empire), these will hate the harlot (Old Covenant Jerusalem with her temple) and will maker her desolate and naked, and will eat her flesh and will burn her up with fire"* (Revelation 17:16).

The great city to perish *"shortly"* after John writes is Jerusalem. Josephus records for us that in A.D. 70 Titus *"gave orders that they should now demolish the entire city and temple"* and that *"it was so thoroughly laid even with the ground by those that dug it up to the foundation, that there was left nothing to make those that came thither believe it had ever been inhabited"*. This was anticipated in the New Testament (Matthew 22:7, 23:36, 24:2, Luke 19:44).

Our inheritance in Christ as revealed through the letters to the 7 Churches

Ephesus:

Inheritance Promise: To eat from the tree of life (eternal life).

Cultural relevance: The city of Ephesus had a temple to Diana/Artemis. It had 127 stone columns, called eternal trees and a sacred grove. If a criminal ran into the temple and clung to one of the trees, he was safe from arrest. Jesus promised to eat from the real source of eternal life, the tree of life, which is found in Himself.

(*Note*: Each of these 7 cities had a statue of the Emperor Nero at the entrance to the agora (market place). One had to burn incense to the statue as an act of worship in order to earn the right to enter the agora to buy and sell. The citizens of those cities referred to Nero as the beast, for being such an awful tyrant. Smearing ash from the incense on the forehead or right hand was called taking the mark of the beast.)

Smyrna:

Inheritance Promise: The crown of life (to reign in life through Christ).

Cultural relevance: Jesus told the Church at Smyrna that He knew their poverty. In this city, if one did not worship the pagan deity of the city, or the pagan deity over their particular trade that they worked at, then they could lose their job. There was tremendous persecution in this city by the synagogue of Satan, the Judaizers which hated the Christians. The Christians faced death, but Jesus

207

also promised them that they would not be hurt by the second death (which is the lake of fire).

Remember, Jesus told the Pharisees that they were of their father the devil. In the book of Revelation, these Jews who rejected Christ were called anti-Christ and a synagogue of Satan. From a covenant perspective, Jew and Israel are covenant terms related to a people in covenant with God, the New Covenant.

Pergamon:

Inheritance Promise: Hidden Manna. This relates to the Ark of the Covenant, and the covenant meal of communion, which reveals the marriage between Jesus and His Bride. Also, there's the promise of the white stone and our new name written on it. In the courts, if one was found innocent, then a white stone was given to them, but a black stone represented guilt. The new name written on it signifies the new experience of personal relationship with Jesus Christ, our new identity of being in Him. Only we can experience our own new name and new identity in Him, and we each have this in Christ.

Cultural Relevance: It's referred to as the place where Satan's throne dwells. Pergamon had 3 thrones. It was the capital of the Roman province of Asia, a governmental throne. It had the throne of Zeus with his temple. It had the throne of Asclepios the serpent healer, which had a cult of drug use and other practices built around it. Paganism was in the face of the Christians, and it was the place where Satan's throne and authority seemed to be rampant.

The term "Jezebel" was a Hebrew idiom being used to draw their attention back to a time in Israel's history when Jezebel led them to compromise and worship idols. This was the threat in their city as well, to join in with the pagan Romans and worship idols.

Other aspects of our inheritance:

Messianic promises were being given to the Christians of their connection to Jesus, their new identity in Him, their marriage to Him as co-heirs, their authority in Him, etc. The promise was that deliverance was soon coming. I am convinced that where there is great persecution today, if believers will learn by way of revelation their identity in Christ, who they really are, and what that means, then deliverance will come, and they will conquer.

Power over the nations (we are the authority in the Earth representing our King), the Morning Star (conquering light), White clothing (the pagan worshippers wore red or black dyed robes in their festivals, Thyatira was a city that had dyes as one of its industries), Name written in Heaven never to be blotted out (a Christian could lose citizenship in Sardis and have their name blotted out of the citizenry books), our name confessed before the Father as one of His own children, made a pillar in the Temple of God (many temples in Philadelphia with huge pillars), name of God written on us (the temples had the name of the Emperor on them), name of new city of Jerusalem given to us (our citizenship in the city of God), new name written on us (our experience in this new identity in Christ), sit with Jesus on the throne as joint heirs with Him.

Laodicea was nearby 2 other cities, Heiropolis and Colossae. Hot, healing springs were in Heiropolis and flowed down to Laodicea. Cold, refreshing springs were in Colossae and flowed down to Laodicea. By the time the waters converged and reached Laodicea, they were lukewarm, full of bacteria, and would make one sick to drink from it. Jesus was warning the Church to not be like this in the Spirit. Either be hot or cold. Hot springs had good healing properties, and cold springs were refreshing and good to drink. Lukewarm is good for no one.

Dispensationalists have wrongly assigned the 7 Churches to represent "ages" of Church history, but the language of the 7 Churches actually relates to Israel's history, from the garden to 70 AD. David Chilton discovered this, and Jonathan Welton documents it in his book "The Art of Revelation". Let me briefly explain:

1. The Church at Ephesus relates to the Garden of Eden. This was the time of leaving the first love as Adam and Eve did, of Christ walking among the lampstands as God walked in the garden, the judgment of removing the lampstand as compared

209

to the judgment of banishing Adam and Eve from the Garden, but then the promise of the tree of life to him who overcomes.

2. The Church at Smyrna relates to Israel's time during the 10 plagues of Egypt compared to the "tribulation of 10 days" mentioned to those in Smyrna.

3. The Church at Pergamum relates to Israel's time in the wilderness as compared to the enemies of the Church being as Balaam and Balak tempting them into idolatry, as Israel experienced in the wilderness.

4. The Church at Thyatira relates to Israel's monarchy, which had glory in David's day, the foundational covenant of Jesus announcing Himself as the Son of God to that Church, and the comparison to Jezebel as the enemies of the Church seducing them into sin. It ends with the promise of having authority over the nations, a true Kingdom/monarchy promise.

5. The Church at Sardis relates to the captivity period in Israel's history. The call was to strengthen the things that remain, which is an acknowledgement that there are a few people who have remained faithful, all are reminiscent of prophetic language about the remnant in a time of apostasy.

6. The Church at Philadelphia relates to their return to the land after captivity and the rebuilding of the Temple and city of Jerusalem. This was done during a time of testing, as the Church is also warned, with the encouragement language eluding to the Temple and city, as "pillars in the Temple" and the blessings of the New Jerusalem.

7. The Church at Laodicea relates to the last day's period of unbelieving Israel where they rejected Christ, (vomiting out of His mouth), and were lukewarm and in apostasy, yet boasting of great wealth. Israel and the Church alike are urged to repent and return to Christ, and in doing this will receive the dominion of His throne, being seated with Him.

Jesus was addressing seven Churches, which were on the route of the Roman armies as they came through their cities on their march to Jerusalem from the homeland. They were on their way, in 66 AD, to destroy the city of Jerusalem, and eventually its Temple, because of the many uprisings against Rome by the Jewish people.

As they went, in 66 AD, they would find and kill as many Jews as they could as they went through these seven cities. Rome wanted to bring a final end to the Jewish revolts within the Empire. Jesus sends warning, comfort, correction and advice to these seven Churches, made up of mostly Jewish people. The seven Churches find themselves in the midst of this great tribulation. John was banished to Patmos around 64 AD and more than likely wrote Revelation in 65 AD, around the same time Hebrews was being written, with its warnings. The goal was to save the lives of as many Christians as possible. In Jerusalem, because they heeded the words of Jesus from Matthew 24, every Christian made it out of the city alive, while 1.1 million Jews were killed and about 97,000 were taken into slavery.

Prophecy and judgment against Jerusalem in 70 AD:

...then let those who are in Judea flee to the mountains. Let no one on the housetop go down to take anything out of the house. Let no one in the field go back to get their cloak. How dreadful it will be in those days for pregnant women and nursing mothers! Pray that your flight will not take place in winter or on the Sabbath. For then there will be great distress, unequaled from the beginning of the world until now - and never to be equaled again. "If those days had not been cut short, no one would survive, but for the sake of the elect those days will be shortened. (Matthew 24:16-22)

The elect were Jewish believers in Christ during that first century time. We are elect as well, children of God, but in context, it's speaking to those specific people for the purpose of warning and advice. *"When you see the armies surrounding the city, flee to the mountains of Judea"*. They fled to Mt. Pella in that region and were safe. This happened in 66 AD in Jerusalem and throughout the land of Israel.

Jesus gives the Christians in these seven Churches promises of Himself, the inheritance they have in Christ. The Kingdom was in their midst, but in 70 AD, something happened in the Spirit that affected the hearts and minds of believers, and the Kingdom came present with power. The early Church, after 70 AD, eventually toppled the power of the Roman Empire as they embraced Christ and Christianity and departed from paganism. The Kingdom continues to capture the hearts and minds of billions of people on Earth today.

Here's a list of the things promised to them in the first century - things we have inherited in Christ:

1. Eating from the tree of life, eternal life (a never ending source of life)

2. The crown of life (reign in life) - we have authority in Christ

3. Hidden Manna (fellowship meal of marriage) – we are One with Jesus

4. White Stone (innocence) with our new name written in it (a name of our new identity in Christ that only we can experience)

5. Power over the nations (we are the authority in the Earth)

6. The Morning Star - we are the light of the world

7. White clothing - we are the righteousness of God

8. Name written in Heaven never to be blotted out (our citizenship)

9. Our name confessed before the Father

10. Made a pillar in the Temple God - we live in the New Jerusalem as a living stone

11. Name of God written on us - we are His

12. Name of new city of Jerusalem given to us

13. New name written on us (identity experience)

14. We sit on the throne with Jesus as joint heirs with Him

It's important to understand that the great tribulation, that many TV preachers and authors are warning us about, has already happened.

When Jesus prophesied about the coming great tribulation that would hit Israel about 37 years after He spoke it, and would last about 3 1/2 years, He made a statement about prophecy in the Old Testament...

For this is the time of punishment in fulfillment of all that has been written. (Luke 21:22)

The "*all that has been written*" was referring to the Old Testament Scriptures. Any lingering prophecies found in the Old Testament would find its fulfillment through the events of the great tribulation of 66-70 AD.

The purpose of prophecy is a fulfillment, not multiple fulfillments. Even concerning His prophecies about the great tribulation, He knew there would be those who would think it could happen again, so He clarified it with a statement:

For then there will be great distress, unequaled from the beginning of the world until now - and never to be equaled again. (Matthew 24:21)

His purpose in prophesying these events was a warning to those He was speaking to, to flee the city, and save themselves, when they saw the Roman armies approaching. This was never meant to be a scary warning for us today.

Therefore, every Old Testament Scripture has been fulfilled, based on Luke 21:22, yet there are many of those prophecies which pertain to the New Covenant, and we are living inside the fulfillment of those prophecies, as if "riding the wave" of their continuing and progressive fulfillment. We are advancing the Kingdom and we need the prophetic Scriptures to inspire and empower us to keep going.

Jesus said a few times that they would see Him coming in the clouds of Heaven, but what did He mean by that, and when would who see Him?

Jesus said over and over in the gospels that He would come. His disciples asked Him, in Matthew 24, what would be the sign of His coming. He began to tell them about the events that would surround the destruction of the Temple, the city of Jerusalem, and the coming great tribulation. The Revelation of Jesus Christ, which is about this destruction of 70 AD, tells us that He was soon to come on the clouds. Jesus, in Matthew 24, also mentions signs in the sun, moon, and stars in relation to His coming. So, what does it all mean?

First, let's look at some Old Testament examples of God "coming" in judgment upon a city...

Concerning the destruction of Babylon

The stars of Heaven and their constellations will not show their light. The rising sun will be darkened and the moon will not give its light. Therefore I will make the Heavens tremble; and the Earth will shake from its place at the wrath of the Lord Almighty, in the day of his burning anger. (Isaiah 13:10, 13)

Concerning the destruction of Idumea

All the stars in the sky will be dissolved and the Heavens rolled up like a scroll; all the starry host will fall like withered leaves from the vine, like shriveled figs from the fig tree. My sword has drunk its fill in the Heavens; see, it descends in judgment on Edom, the people I have totally destroyed. (Isaiah 34:4-5)

Concerning judgment upon Egypt

When I snuff you out, I will cover the Heavens and darken their stars; I will cover the sun with a cloud, and the moon will not give its light. All the shining lights in the Heavens I will darken over you; I will bring darkness over your land, declares the Sovereign Lord. (Ezekiel 32:7-8)

When David was delivered from Saul

The Earth trembled and quaked, and the foundations of the mountains shook; they trembled because he was angry.

Smoke rose from his nostrils; consuming fire came from his mouth, burning coals blazed out of it. He parted the Heavens and came down; dark clouds were under his feet. He mounted the cherubim and flew; he soared on the wings of the wind. He made darkness his covering, his canopy around him - the dark rain clouds of the sky. (Psalm 18:7-11)

Concerning God's judgment upon Jerusalem

Look! He advances like the clouds, his chariots come like a whirlwind, his horses are swifter than eagles. Woe to us! We are ruined! (Jeremiah 4:13)

What we see is fantastic, symbolic, prophetic language being used, with pictures of sun, moon, stars falling, being shaken, going dark, mountains trembling, the Earth moving, and clouds being a picture of the coming of God, His Presence, to punish or deliver.

Historically, we know that the Roman armies sieged Jerusalem in 66 AD, and eventually burned the city and Temple to the ground in 70 AD. This was the final end of the Old Covenant system with its trappings and elements. We can even see this in parable language, from Matthew 22:

The rest seized his servants, mistreated them and killed them. The king was enraged. He sent his army and destroyed those murderers and burned their city. (Matthew 22:6-7)

Let's look deeper at how the Hebrew people viewed the coming of God, from an episode in Elijah's life:

He replied, "I have been very zealous for the Lord God Almighty. The Israelites have rejected your covenant, torn down your altars, and put your prophets to death with the sword. I am the only one left, and now they are trying to kill me too." The Lord said, "Go out and stand on the mountain in the presence of the Lord, for the Lord is about to pass by." Then a great and powerful wind tore the mountains apart and shattered the rocks before the Lord, but the Lord was not in the wind. After the wind there was an Earthquake, but the Lord was not in the Earthquake. After the Earthquake came a fire, but the Lord was not in the fire. And after the fire came a gentle whisper. (1 Kings 19:10-12)

In the Hebrew mindset, it was understood that God could "come" in various ways. In a destructive wind, in an Earthquake, and in a fire, and of course, in the still small voice which Elijah encountered. When Jesus came in 70 AD, as He promised, He was a coming in judgment, to end and remove the Old Covenant system. He was done with it, and He was ready for the marriage with His bride to occur, which would release His Kingdom to be present with power.

Jesus came "*in the destruction of the city and temple*", through the armies of Rome! The destruction, the armies surrounding the city, and all the events happening during that time, were all "*the sign of His coming*". The fact that this destruction was taking place, according to His own prophetic words, proved He was King and as King, He was doing what He said He would do, as spelled out in many Scriptures, but especially in Matthew 22:1-8.

This was the coming of Jesus, on the clouds of judgment, symbolically, prophetically, fantastically, it all occurred. As a partial preterist, I believe there are other Scriptures which speak of His return to Earth, in our future, once the Kingdom has covered the Earth, at which time He will bring resurrection to us bodily. No more death! Until then, we advance the Kingdom, knowing that the great tribulation has happened, and is in our past, not future! Things are getting better because of the advancing Kingdom of God. Those who think things are getting worse have not taken an honest look at history. We live in a golden age of cultural and societal advances, with continuing breakthroughs in technology and medicine.

We see a drama played in the book of Revelation when John is caught up, in the Spirit, the throne of Heaven. He sees the throne, One sitting on it, 24 angelic elders, and 4 angelic beasts. When the Lamb emerges from the midst of the throne, the 24 elders cast their crowns at His feet and worship Him. What happened in this scene that caused them to do that? Why were they wearing crowns? In order to understand that, we need to look in the Old Testament at something David said.

I mentioned earlier in this book that angels were first called "sons of God" or "sons of Heaven", and were considered to be "of Elohim", and referred to as "gods" in the Old Testament. Man was made a little lower than the angels for the suffering of death. When Jesus resurrected, He became elevated above all principalities and powers, thrones and dominions, both in Heaven and on Earth. He is the King, and we are in Him, so we are now higher than the angels in rank, being the true sons of God by faith in Christ.

It is not to angels that he has subjected the world to come, about which we are speaking. But there is a place where someone has testified: "What is mankind that you are mindful of them, a son of man that you care for him? You made them a little lower than the angels; you crowned them with glory and honor and put everything under their feet." In putting everything under them, God left nothing that is not subject to them. Yet at present we do not see everything subject to them. But we do see Jesus, who was made lower than the angels for a little while, now crowned with glory and honor because he suffered death, so that by the grace of God he might taste death for everyone. (Hebrews 2:5-9)

God presides in the great assembly; he renders judgment among the "gods": (Psalm 82:1)

The term "gods" in Psalm 82:1 is referring to angelic authorities, such as the 24 angelic elders seen in the book of Revelation:

Surrounding the throne were twenty-four other thrones, and seated on them were twenty-four elders. They were dressed in white and had crowns of gold on their heads. (Revelation 4:4)

This was a Heavenly Sanhedrin that had authority while under the Old Covenant. Twice, we are told that angels are stewards of the Law covenant:

Why, then, was the law given at all? It was added because of transgressions until the Seed to whom the promise referred had come. The law was given through angels and entrusted to a mediator. (Galatians 3:19)

For since the message spoken through angels was binding, and every violation and disobedience received its just punishment. (Hebrews 2:2)

In this section of Revelation, we are witnessing the coronation of Jesus as King because of His death and Resurrection:

Each of the four living creatures had six wings and was covered with eyes all around, even under its wings. Day and night they never stop saying: "'Holy, holy, holy is the Lord God Almighty,' who was, and is, and is to come." Whenever the living creatures give glory, honor and thanks to him who sits on the throne and who lives for ever and ever, the twenty-four elders fall down before him who sits on the throne and worship him who lives for ever and ever. They lay their crowns before the throne and say: "You are worthy, our Lord and God, to receive glory and honor and power, for you created all things, and by your will they were created and have their being." (Revelation 4:8-11)

This is a praise to Jesus, because it is He who was, and is, and is to come. Also, the reference of Him *"who lives forever and ever"*, is in context of His Resurrection where He has defeated sin and death.

This next section is very interesting and very important to understand. There is mention of a scroll in the hand of the One on the throne. No one is worthy to take the scroll and open it, but One. The One who has died and rose again. This scroll is the divorce decree against Israel. I will explain a little more on that later, but this scroll contains the judgments due an unfaithful, harlot wife, under the Law covenant. This is the final judgment of the Law, upon the wife who rejected Her husband. Jesus died, as the Husband to Israel, to legally release them from the Law/marriage covenant, so they could be married to the Resurrected Christ anew in the New Covenant.

Then I saw in the right hand of him who sat on the throne a scroll with writing on both sides and sealed with seven seals. And I saw a mighty angel proclaiming in a loud voice, "Who is worthy to break the seals and open the scroll?" But no one in Heaven or on Earth or under the Earth could open the scroll or even look inside it. I wept and wept because no one was found who was worthy to open the scroll or look inside.

Then one of the elders said to me, "Do not weep! See, the Lion of the tribe of Judah, the Root of David, has triumphed. He is able to open the scroll and its seven seals." Then I saw a Lamb, looking as if it had been slain, standing at the center of the throne, encircled by the four living creatures and the elders. The Lamb had seven horns and seven eyes, which are the seven spirits of God sent out into all the Earth. He went and took the scroll from the right hand of him who sat on the throne. (Revelation 5:1-7)

Jesus, though called the Lion of Judah, and the covenantal Root of David, appears as the Lamb, which has been slain. It was His death that gave Him the authority to open this scroll. His death is what made Israel a widow:

A prophecy concerning Israel rejecting her "widowhood":

Now then, listen, you lover of pleasure, lounging in your security and saying to yourself, 'I am, and there is none besides me. I will never be a widow or suffer the loss of children.' (Isaiah 47:8)

Give her as much torment and grief as the glory and luxury she gave herself. In her heart she boasts, 'I sit enthroned as queen. I am not a widow; I will never mourn.' (Revelation 18:7)

To deny being a widow is to deny the death of her Husband. Jesus was God in the flesh, the Husband to Israel. The death of the husband was the legal way to break the covenant of marriage under the Law. This was the attitude of unfaithful Israel who

219

rejected the Cross and death of Jesus. They rejected Him being the Perfect Passover Lamb that brings deliverance from death. They rejected Him as the atoning sacrifice for the sins of the world, and the end of the Old Covenant law system.

It was Jesus, the Lamb who was slain from the foundation of the world, who was worthy to open the scroll of judgment. This was His coronation as King of Kings, Lord of Lords, and it was because of His appearance in the midst of the throne that the 24 elders cast their crowns.

There was a change in leadership, authority, priesthood and covenant occurring, as Jesus was bringing His blood, as that slain Lamb, to the ark of Heaven to ratify the New Covenant. Jesus was now the Husband, High Priest, Lamb of God, and King to the new Israel, the Bride. In Christ, we are joint heirs, and we have a crown or crowns. We are never to cast our crowns at the feet of Jesus. It would be disrespectful for us to do that, but they did that because of a covenantal change taking place in God's Kingdom. We reign with Christ, and we need not remove our crown.

Jesus came to offer believing Israel a new marriage in the New Covenant, e.g. to be married to the resurrected Lord after His Cross. Unbelieving Israel rejected this offer, and thus the divorce judgments fit for a harlot were implemented through the Revelation of Jesus Christ.

For the woman (Old Covenant Israel) which has a husband (Jesus, God in the flesh) is bound by the law (the previous covenant, the Old Covenant) to her husband (God) so long as he (Jesus, God in the flesh) lives; but if the husband be dead (Jesus dies on the Cross), she is loosed from the law of her husband (Israel became legally loosed from the previous covenant, the Old Covenant). (Romans 7:2)

So then if, while her husband lives (while Jesus was alive), she be married to another man, she shall be called an adulteress (she was legally bound to the marriage, the Old Covenant): but if her husband be dead (Jesus died on the Cross), she is free from that law (Old Covenant Israel became free from the previous covenant, the Old Covenant);

so that she is no adulteress, though she be married to another man. (Romans 7:3)

Wherefore, my brethren, you also are become dead to the law by the body of Christ (through His death on the Cross); that you should be married to another (a new marriage in the New Covenant), even to Him who is raised from the dead (the resurrected Christ), that we should bring forth fruit unto God (the fruit of the Spirit in the New Covenant, whereby many come to glory). (Romans 7:4)

Jesus came to Israel as their God in the flesh. Though Jeremiah had warned of a coming divorce, and Malachi spoke of a coming curse, Jesus came to give them a chance to come to Him, to make things right, in a New Covenant. Rather than a divorce, God was offering a new marriage, a new relationship, but the previous one had to be dealt with. According to the Law, the wife could only be free from the marriage if the husband died. Therefore, God came to die as their Husband, to legally break the marriage covenant. His rising from the dead would be their opportunity to marry anew, to marry their resurrected Husband, Jesus the King! Believing Israel embraced her new Husband, but unbelieving Israel said, "*I am no widow*"... Unbelieving Israel's refusal to accept that her Husband has come and died caused her to say, "*I am no widow, and my children will not die.*"

The story of Revelation is the judgment upon this harlot wife who refused to embrace her resurrected Husband.

Give her as much torment and grief as the glory and luxury she gave herself. In her heart she boasts, 'I sit enthroned as queen. I am not a widow; I will never mourn.' Therefore in one day her plagues will overtake her: death, mourning and famine. She will be consumed by fire, for mighty is the Lord God who judges her. (Revelation 18:7-8)

The Hebrew term "*widow*" can also mean "*a desolate house*". Jesus warned them that their house was being left to them desolate. This was the covenantal language of divorce.

Look, your house is left to you desolate. (Matthew 23:38)

The wonderful part of the story is that Jesus had many from Israel who embraced Him. They were "believing Israel", the remnant, the 144,000 (a symbolic number), the true Israel of God. When Jesus came, He divided Israel into 2 groups of people: Unbelievers and Believers. The glory of Israel is that they believed, the ones who did indeed believe, and they carried the message of the gospel and the Kingdom as a light to the world. We have been grafted into the Lord with them as one new man in Christ Jesus. This is the True Israel of God.

The Revelation of Jesus Christ is about Him being revealed to Old Covenant Israel and to the Roman Empire as King and Almighty God. The key players in the story line are:

- A harlot (old Jerusalem)

- An individual beast (Caesar Nero)

- 2 corporate beasts (the Romans Empire and the Temple rulership)

- A Bride (the new believers in Christ)

- An old city (Jerusalem which had become Babylon, Egypt and Sodom)

- A new city (the New Jerusalem, the Kingdom in the Spirit)

It's about a harlot who refuses to be faithful to her husband. The husband dies, and rises again to release her from the old marriage covenant in order to marry Him anew in a new marriage covenant. She refuses.

The Kingly husband courts a new bride, whom the harlot persecutes. This harlot comes into league with a beast, and they persecute this new bride together. A war breaks out, and the beast turns on the harlot and destroys her. The bride is now free to marry her husband. The marriage happens, and a new city emerges, which is the holy of holies, the New Jerusalem, the New Covenant. This is the story of the book of Revelation.

Revelation ultimately depicts a war taking place, described in fantastic, prophetic, covenantal language, concerning a judgment which was taking place through this war. The war was when

Roman armies sieged the city of Jerusalem in 66 AD, and it also covers the beginning of the Christian persecution around 64 AD. John uses the language of the Old Covenant prophets as He writes this through the revelation of the Spirit.

Babylon is Jerusalem, not Rome. The beast with 7 heads and 10 crowns is first century Rome, and the beast turns on the harlot, which is Jerusalem. Rome destroyed Jerusalem (Matthew 22:1-7).

Babylon is the great city, which is Jerusalem, also called the whore or harlot. Old Testament prophets called Jerusalem, Judah and Israel a harlot committing adultery.

The 7 scrolls are the divorce decree, the judgments due a harlot under the Law, which is full of wrath (Romans 4:15), but the wrath was finished after the destruction of Jerusalem (Revelation 15:1). The purpose of the judgment against unbelieving Israel was for rejecting their Husband, Jesus the risen Lord, and to remove all physical and visible signs of that Old Covenant.

The Revelation of Jesus Christ is about Him being revealed as King and Lord over all, along with His spouse, the Church, the New Jerusalem, which is filling the whole Earth. It's about the new Heaven and new Earth being revealed, which is the New Covenant, a covenant of forgiveness without wrath.

The next big aspect to understanding what the book of Revelation is really about is the "Song of Moses". Let's first look at the purpose of the Song of Moses:

The Lord said to Moses, "Now the day of your death is near. Call Joshua and present yourselves at the tent of meeting, where I will commission him." So Moses and Joshua came and presented themselves at the tent of meeting. Then the Lord appeared at the tent in a pillar of cloud, and the cloud stood over the entrance to the tent. And the Lord said to Moses: "You are going to rest with your ancestors, and these people will soon prostitute themselves to the foreign gods of the land they are entering. They will forsake me and break the covenant I made with them. And in that day I will become angry with them and forsake them; I will hide my face from them, and they will be destroyed.

Many disasters and calamities will come on them, and in that day they will ask, 'Have not these disasters come on us because our God is not with us?' And I will certainly hide my face in that day because of all their wickedness in turning to other gods. "Now write down this song and teach it to the Israelites and have them sing it, so that it may be a witness for me against them. When I have brought them into the land flowing with milk and honey, the land I promised on oath to their ancestors, and when they eat their fill and thrive, they will turn to other gods and worship them, rejecting me and breaking my covenant. And when many disasters and calamities come on them, this song will testify against them, because it will not be forgotten by their descendants. I know what they are disposed to do, even before I bring them into the land I promised them on oath."

So Moses wrote down this song that day and taught it to the Israelites. The Lord gave this command to Joshua son of Nun: "Be strong and courageous, for you will bring the Israelites into the land I promised them on oath, and I myself will be with you." After Moses finished writing in a book the words of this law from beginning to end, he gave this command to the Levites who carried the ark of the covenant of the Lord: "Take this Book of the Law and place it beside the ark of the covenant of the Lord your God. There it will remain as a witness against you. For I know how rebellious and stiff-necked you are. If you have been rebellious against the Lord while I am still alive and with you, how much more will you rebel after I die! Assemble before me all the elders of your tribes and all your officials, so that I can speak these words in their hearing and call the Heavens and the Earth to testify against them. For I know that after my death you are sure to become utterly corrupt and to turn from the way I have commanded you. In days to come, disaster will fall on you because you will do evil in the sight of the Lord and arouse his anger by what your hands have made." And Moses recited the words of this song from beginning to end in the hearing of the whole assembly of Israel. (Deuteronomy 31:14-30)

The actual song of judgment appears in Deuteronomy 32, but it's very clear that in Deuteronomy 31, the purpose of the song was to pronounce judgment upon unbelieving Israel. This came when unbelieving Israel rejected Christ and their New Covenant. The song is finally sung in the book of Revelation, as this judgment is happening to unbelieving Israel:

> *I saw in Heaven another great and marvelous sign: seven angels with the seven last plagues - last, because with them God's wrath is completed. And I saw what looked like a sea of glass glowing with fire and, standing beside the sea, those who had been victorious over the beast and its image and over the number of its name. They held harps given them by God and sang the song of God's servant Moses and of the Lamb: "Great and marvelous are your deeds, Lord God Almighty. Just and true are your ways, King of the nations. Who will not fear you, Lord, and bring glory to your name? For you alone are holy. All nations will come and worship before you, for your righteous acts have been revealed." After this I looked, and I saw in Heaven the temple - that is, the tabernacle of the covenant law - and it was opened.*
> (Revelation 15:1-5)

This section in Revelation 15 is speaking about the end of God's wrath, which had been poured out on the Old Covenant system. It was poured out by angels, in the realm of the Spirit, but it translated into a war between Roman armies and Israel. Remember, angels dispense His judgments under the Law covenant. This Song of Moses is sung, as the judgment of the Old Covenant is finalizing, and they sang a new song of the Lamb, which is the victory of the Kingdom coming with power:

> *And he said to them, "Truly I tell you, some who are standing here will not taste death before they see that the kingdom of God has come with power."* (Mark 9:1)

This is all part of the key of David - to open and to shut. Jesus opened up the New Covenant through His death and Resurrection, and He closed up the Old Covenant through the destruction of the city and Temple. This was His "coming" in 70 AD, that He told His disciples and others would happen:

When you are persecuted in one place, flee to another. Truly I tell you, you will not finish going through the towns of Israel before the Son of Man comes. (Matthew 10:23)

They would have gone through the cities of Israel evangelizing as many Jewish people as they could, but overall, the gospel message was rejected. By 70 AD, the Christians fled, and the coming of Jesus through the Roman war was upon them. As King, Jesus destroyed the city and Temple using His armies, the Roman Gentiles. They literally plowed the city under.

As Jesus was sitting on the Mount of Olives, the disciples came to him privately. "Tell us," they said, "when will this happen, and what will be the sign of your coming and of the end of the age?" (Matthew 24:3)

The disciples were asking Him a relevant question applying to their generation, not ours. They were not asking when the end of planet Earth would be. They were asking when the age of Moses would be finished. Jesus then proceeds to tell them of many signs they will see over the next 40 years leading up to this event happening. A birthing of the Kingdom and New Covenant was taking place.

But Jesus remained silent. The high priest said to him, "I charge you under oath by the living God: Tell us if you are the Messiah, the Son of God." "You have said so," Jesus replied. "But I say to all of you: From now on you will see the Son of Man sitting at the right hand of the Mighty One and coming on the clouds of Heaven." (Matthew 26:63-64)

Jesus told the high priest and those standing around him that they would see the "*Son of Man sitting at the right hand of the Mighty One and coming on the clouds of Heaven.*" Jesus quotes from Daniel to them. They knew the Scripture in Daniel to speak of the Messiah. When Jesus quoted that, He was declaring to them that He is that Messiah. It was blasphemy to them.

The revelation from Jesus Christ, which God gave him to show his servants what must soon take place. He made it known by sending his angel to his servant John. (Revelation 1:1)

John was banished to Patmos by Nero around 64 AD. He is probably being given this prophecy from Jesus around 65 AD. In 5 years, *"what must soon take place"* was going to take place in 70 AD.

> *"Look, he is coming with the clouds," and "every eye will see him, even those who pierced him"; and all peoples on Earth "will mourn because of him." So shall it be! Amen.* (Revelation 1:7)

Jesus declares His coming, quoting from Zechariah 12:12. He is coming as the Messiah Daniel spoke of, and the fulfillment as the Seed of David and Abraham, the King and Blessing to the world.

The key of David brings about 2 songs: The Song of Moses to close up the Old Covenant, and the Song of the Lamb to declare the victory of the Kingdom of God.

As the Song foretold, in Israel's final generation, God would both avenge the blood of His saints, and bring judgment on their killers. The song of the Lamb speaks of Jesus as our refuge. It proclaims the grace of God that has been revealed to us by the perfect obedience of our Savior Jesus.

In Revelation 5:9,10 we see the song of the Lamb, a different song from that of Moses.

> *And they sung a new song, saying, Thou art worthy to take the book, and to open the seals thereof: for thou wast slain, and hast redeemed us to God by thy blood out of every kindred, and tongue, and people, and nation; And hast made us unto our God kings and priests: and we shall reign on the Earth.*

The song of the Lamb is the victory of Jesus for us that has given us the inheritance of life, position of royalty, justification and glorification, and redemption in the finished work. One song ended one age but the other began a new age. Praise God we have a new song.

The book of Revelation ends with the destruction of the city, Babylon, which was Old Covenant Jerusalem, and then the wedding feast and marriage of Jesus to His Bride. It follows the timeline of the parable that Jesus gave in Matthew 22:

Jesus spoke to them again in parables, saying: "The kingdom of Heaven is like a king who prepared a wedding banquet for his son. He sent his servants to those who had been invited to the banquet to tell them to come, but they refused to come. "Then he sent some more servants and said, 'Tell those who have been invited that I have prepared my dinner: My oxen and fattened cattle have been butchered, and everything is ready. Come to the wedding banquet.' "But they paid no attention and went off - one to his field, another to his business. The rest seized his servants, mistreated them and killed them.

The king was enraged. He sent his army and destroyed those murderers and burned their city. "Then he said to his servants, 'The wedding banquet is ready, but those I invited did not deserve to come. So go to the street corners and invite to the banquet anyone you find.' So the servants went out into the streets and gathered all the people they could find, the bad as well as the good, and the wedding hall was filled with guests.

"But when the king came in to see the guests, he noticed a man there who was not wearing wedding clothes. He asked, 'How did you get in here without wedding clothes, friend?' The man was speechless. "Then the king told the attendants, 'Tie him hand and foot, and throw him outside, into the darkness, where there will be weeping and gnashing of teeth.' "For many are invited, but few are chosen." (Matthew 22:1-14)

Ultimately, what we see is that a city was destroyed and then the wedding feast and marriage occurred, with only certain ones (those born again) were able to attend the party. This follows the same timeline as Revelation:

After this I saw another angel coming down from Heaven. He had great authority, and the Earth was illuminated by his splendor. With a mighty voice he shouted: "'Fallen!

Fallen is Babylon the Great!' She has become a dwelling for demons and a haunt for every impure spirit, a haunt for every unclean bird, a haunt for every unclean and detestable animal. (Revelation 18:1-2)

Revelation 18:1-2 is when Jerusalem (referred to as Babylon) and its Temple fell.

When they see the smoke of her burning, they will exclaim, 'Was there ever a city like this great city?' They will throw dust on their heads, and with weeping and mourning cry out: "'Woe! Woe to you, great city, where all who had ships on the sea became rich through her wealth! In one hour she has been brought to ruin!' "Rejoice over her, you Heavens! Rejoice, you people of God! Rejoice, apostles and prophets! For God has judged her with the judgment she imposed on you." Then a mighty angel picked up a boulder the size of a large millstone and threw it into the sea, and said: "With such violence the great city of Babylon will be thrown down, never to be found again. (Revelation 18:18-21)

After the city had fallen, the marriage celebration could happen:

Then a voice came from the throne, saying: "Praise our God, all you his servants, you who fear him, both great and small!" Then I heard what sounded like a great multitude, like the roar of rushing waters and like loud peals of thunder, shouting: "Hallelujah! For our Lord God Almighty reigns. Let us rejoice and be glad and give him glory! For the wedding of the Lamb has come, and his bride has made herself ready. Fine linen, bright and clean, was given her to wear."

(Fine linen stands for the righteous acts of God's holy people.) Then the angel said to me, "Write this: Blessed are those who are invited to the wedding supper of the Lamb!" And he added, "These are the true words of God." (Revelation 19:5-9)

Jesus then appears as the Victor with His angelic armies, to present themselves as the Conquerors. All they had to do was show up. The battle was already won, and Jerusalem was destroyed.

Josephus, the Jewish Historian of that time period, documented seeing angelic chariots in the clouds over Jerusalem. There were many signs that pointed to the Revelation of Jesus Christ and His Lordship over Heaven and Earth.

I saw Heaven standing open and there before me was a white horse, whose rider is called Faithful and True. With justice he judges and wages war. His eyes are like blazing fire, and on his head are many crowns. He has a name written on him that no one knows but he himself. He is dressed in a robe dipped in blood, and his name is the Word of God. The armies of Heaven were following him, riding on white horses and dressed in fine linen, white and clean. Coming out of his mouth is a sharp sword with which to strike down the nations.

"He will rule them with an iron scepter." He treads the winepress of the fury of the wrath of God Almighty. On his robe and on his thigh he has this name written: King of kings and Lord of Lords. And I saw an angel standing in the sun, who cried in a loud voice to all the birds flying in midair, "Come, gather together for the great supper of God. (Revelation 19:11-17)

As the marriage supper is about to ensue, an angel cries out to the fowls that fly in the midst of Heaven to come and gather themselves to the supper of the great God. As this marriage supper is taking place, the final attacks of the war which is bringing a final end to the Jewish, Old Covenant, Temple world:

The symbolic description of war torn Jerusalem

...so that you may eat the flesh of kings, generals, and the mighty, of horses and their riders, and the flesh of all people, free and slave, great and small." Then I saw the beast and the kings of the Earth and their armies gathered together to wage war against the rider on the horse and his army. But the beast was captured, and with it the false prophet who had performed the signs on its behalf. With these signs he had deluded those who had received the mark of the beast and worshiped its image. The two of them were

thrown alive into the fiery lake of burning sulfur. The rest were killed with the sword coming out of the mouth of the rider on the horse, and all the birds gorged themselves on their flesh. (Revelation 19:18-21)

This is using a type of symbolic and prophetic language to show it was Jesus who orchestrated the events using the Roman armies to accomplish His goals.

Before the Bride descends in marriage to her Husband, a scene of judgment takes place:

I saw thrones on which were seated those who had been given authority to judge. And I saw the souls of those who had been beheaded because of their testimony about Jesus and because of the word of God. They had not worshiped the beast or its image and had not received its mark on their foreheads or their hands. They came to life and reigned with Christ a thousand years.

(The rest of the dead did not come to life until the thousand years were ended.) This is the first resurrection. Blessed and holy are those who share in the first resurrection. The second death has no power over them, but they will be priests of God and of Christ and will reign with him for a thousand years. (Revelation 20:4-6)

This was the final judgment on the Old Covenant, and the promise that those who live now will live in the power of the Resurrection of Jesus and rule and reign with Him as His priests on the Earth, inside this New Covenant. This is the new Heaven and new Earth that the New Covenant brought, through its mountain, marriage and baptism:

Then I saw "a new Heaven and a new Earth," for the first Heaven and the first Earth had passed away, and there was no longer any sea. I saw the Holy City, the new Jerusalem, coming down out of Heaven from God, prepared as a bride beautifully dressed for her husband. And I heard a loud voice from the throne saying, "Look! God's dwelling place is now among the people, and he will dwell with them. They will be his people, and God himself will be with them and be their God. 'He will wipe every tear from their eyes. There will be no more death' or mourning or crying or pain, for the old order of things has passed away." (Revelation 21:1-4)

With the Old Covenant gone, a new Heaven and Earth system comes on the scene. We live inside this new Heaven and new Earth today, as the ambassadorial kings and priests in Christ. Now can the fullness of the expression *"I shall be their God and they shall be My people"* be realized because of the finished work of Jesus.

John describes, again with symbolic language, the Kingdom of God on the Earth, as it is today and advancing:

It shone with the glory of God, and its brilliance was like that of a very precious jewel, like a jasper, clear as crystal. (Revelation 21:11)

I did not see a temple in the city, because the Lord God Almighty and the Lamb are its temple. The city does not need the sun or the moon to shine on it, for the glory of God gives it light, and the Lamb is its lamp. The nations will walk by its light, and the kings of the Earth will bring their splendor into it. On no day will its gates ever be shut, for there will be no night there. The glory and honor of the nations will be brought into it. Nothing impure will ever enter it, nor will anyone who does what is shameful or deceitful, but only those whose names are written in the Lamb's book of life. (Revelation 21:22-27)

We need not think these things are about Heaven. John is describing the Kingdom of God, using Hebraic symbolism, which is also used in the Old Testament and by Jesus.

Then the angel showed me the river of the water of life, as clear as crystal, flowing from the throne of God and of the Lamb down the middle of the great street of the city. On each side of the river stood the tree of life, bearing twelve crops of fruit, yielding its fruit every month. And the leaves of the tree are for the healing of the nations. No longer will there be any curse. The throne of God and of the Lamb will be in the city, and his servants will serve him. They will see his face, and his name will be on their foreheads. There will be no more night. They will not need the light of a lamp or the light of the sun, for the Lord God will give them light. And they will reign for ever and ever. (Revelation 22:1-5)

I believe the Church needs great revelation and understanding of these things spoken of by John concerning the Kingdom and New Covenant. This is our reality, but much of the Church thinks these things are in the future, or in Heaven, or not real.

Blessed are those who wash their robes, that they may have the right to the tree of life and may go through the gates into the city. (Revelation 22:14)

How do we wash our robes? Through faith in Jesus and His cleansing blood. We have the right to eat from the tree of life, the life in the Spirit, the blessedness of the Kingdom on the Earth.

The above Scriptures from Revelation describe the Kingdom of God for the Church today. This is where we live and what we have the ability to experience. We are the light, or the authority in the Earth, and the nations of this world are led by our Light. It's time we press into the depth of what this means and stop waiting for this to happen when we all get to Heaven. We live in the realm of Spirit and Truth now, and the above Scriptures are our reality.

If we want to find where we are in the Scriptures today, then we can look in Revelation 21 and 22 and try to make sense of the glorious and spiritual language used by John to describe this new bride. The Church is the authority in the Earth today.

The Seven Feasts are fulfilled:

When we speak of fulfilled eschatology, people often wonder about the feasts. Are the feasts something we should celebrate today? Or, have all the feasts and their pictures been fulfilled, or do we await some later fulfillment picture in one of the feasts? Here is the answer:

The feasts pointed to episodes in the finished work of Jesus. They have all been fulfilled. Let me explain:

1. **Feast of Passover** - Christ is our Passover, and He ate the Passover meal with His disciples before going to the Cross. This was fulfilled when He became the Passover Lamb at the Cross.

2. **Feast of Unleavened Bread** - This was fulfilled, as His body was the bread, which was broken at the Cross.

3. **Feast of Firstfruits** - This was fulfilled in His Resurrection. He is the firstfruits of Resurrection.

4. **Feast of Weeks** (Harvest or Pentecost) - This was fulfilled on the day of Pentecost when the Holy Spirit was poured out.

5. **Feast of Trumpets** - This was fulfilled in the trumpet judgments of the harlot, Old Covenant system in 70 AD.

6. **Day of Atonement** - Jesus was the atoning sacrifice, but the scapegoat was also part of the Day of Atonement, as the sins of Israel were put on its head, and it was led into the wilderness to be destroyed by the beasts. When the Temple and city fell in 70 AD, this was the picture of the scapegoat being destroyed by "the beast" (the Roman Empire). This has been fulfilled.

7. **Feast of Tabernacles** - This was the celebration of when Israel was released from Egyptian slavery and bondage and lived in tabernacles in the wilderness. Old Covenant Jerusalem was also a picture of Egyptian bondage, and when the city fell, the freedom from that slave system came as well. This has been fulfilled.

As Jesus said in Luke 21:22 "*For these be the days of vengeance, that all things which are written may be fulfilled*". The days of vengeance were the events of the 70 AD destruction of the Temple and Jerusalem.

Chapter Nineteen
Where have we been?

The New Covenant was established at the Cross in the body and blood of our Lord Jesus, made between a Perfect Father and His Perfect Son, in 30 AD. Forty years later, a generation, the destruction of Jerusalem and the Temple occurred. Since then, Jesus says the Kingdom has now come to be present with power. The goal is for God's Heavenly Kingdom to expand and advance over all the Earth. How has the Church been doing with advancing this Kingdom since the first century until now? Let's look at some Church history:

Acts 3:19-21 – God has been recovering His creation since the Resurrection of Jesus occurred. What we can see throughout Church history is a recovery process so that the saints may truly possess the Kingdom and do something with it in this Earth. Restoration, Recovery, Restitution (to restore to the original state or position).

"The process of recovery throughout Church history"

30 AD is the Cross and Resurrection. By 70 AD, Christianity in the Roman Empire is under severe persecution from the Temple system and empire. The great tribulation for Israel occurrs, and removes the *"synagogue of Satan"*, with the Kingdom being present with power.

In 313 AD, Constantine, the Emperor of the Roman Empire, sees the sign of the Cross in the sky while preparing for battle and takes this as sign from God to wage war under the banner of the Cross. He has a cross placed on his armies' shields and he begins to win battles. This action by Constantine changes the image of Jesus in the hearts and minds of people from a Humble and Suffering Savior to a Conquering King. Through all of this, Constantine legalizes Christianity in Roman Empire with benefits given to Christians, tax benefits, political power, and the Church begins to spread with a greater freedom.

325 AD – The council of Nicea, Christian doctrine agreed upon, the Apostles' Creed.

397 AD – The canon of Scripture is established (367 years after Christianity is born). The Catholic Church grows, gets powerful and political. Kings are under the Pope in authority.

400 AD to 800 AD – The desert fathers retreat into seclusion to copy Scripture, write books, separate from the "evil world", and seek to live a holy life of meditation on the goodness of God.

Most people, during this time, are illiterate. Artwork is used in Churches to teach the gospel to those who could not read. This shows a basic truth of the great need for knowledge and education of the covenantal story of the Bible. An ignorant people cannot progress in anything.

1300'S – John Huss and John Wycliffe begin to translate the Bible into their language for the common man. Prior to that only the priests could own and read the Bible.

1517 – Martin Luther's 95 theses: The reformation of "salvation is by grace through faith" is born. Martin Luther was an Augustinian monk who saw doctrinal errors in the Catholic Church. He sought to correct the doctrines and remain catholic. His 95 theses were refuting false teachings of the Church, such as, indulgences.

During this time, the Ana Baptists restore baptism by immersion for those who profess faith in Jesus. They refute the false doctrine of infant baptism salvation.

The reformation spreads. Catholics begin to lose power. Throughout the 1600's, many religious wars spring up throughout Europe, between the newly formed Protestants and the Catholics.

1727 – The first great awakening – Jonathan Edwards, George Whitfield, John Wesley. This awakening impacts both Europe and America. During this time, missions are restored, and prayer movements arise with many revival fires breaking out revivals.

1830's – Charles Finney is the driving force behind this second great awakening, which brings many salvations and revivals in America. It's also note-worthy that during this time, Joseph Smith starts the Mormon Church, and the false doctrine, which cripples much of the Church today, called Dispensationalism, is brought forth by John Darby.

1880's – Healing revivals and the prophetic ministry restored. Generals, such as, John Alexander Dowie and Maria Woodworth-Etter bring healing and the prophetic into the mainstream of the Body of Christ. The "mega-Church" is born during this time.

During the late 1800's and early 1900's, Generals, such as, Evan Roberts, Charles Parham and William Seymour bring the Pentecostal gospel to the mainstream of Christianity. During this time, the baptism in the Holy Spirit, with the evidence of speaking in tongues becomes an important doctrine for the Pentecostal Church.

William Seymour brings the Azusa street revival in California in 1906, with a strong focus on the baptism in the Holy Spirit, tongues, and gifts of the Spirit.

John G. Lake, Smith Wigglesworth, Aimee Semple McPherson bring healing and miracles to the Body of Christ with acts of power leading many to salvation. Smith Wigglesworth is known as the Apostle of Faith and he raises many people from the dead, as well as does many strange things on the stage when ministering healing to the masses. Many people are getting healed of sickness and disease.

During the 1940's and 1950's, evangelism is restored, with healing meetings becoming a big part of these tent revivals.

Kathryn Kuhlman, William Branham, Jack Coe, A.A. Allen draw mass crowds and do many things for the Kingdom of God.

1960's – a restoration of the teacher to the Body, many books written

1970's – the pastor is restored to the Body

1980's – the prophet restored to the Body; many prophets arise

1990's – the apostle restored to the Body; many apostles arise

2000's – called "the day of the saints", with the saints being equipped for ministry.

There are movements of grace, movements of eschatology, movements of theology, movements of interpretation, movements of the Kingdom, and many, many things going in the Body today. Many have become tired of Church and retreated to no Church, yet maintaining a loving relationship with the Lord. Sometimes Church can become stressful and anyone who has been in Church can understand the temptation for one to stop going to Church.

I wanted to mention something else that happened in the 1960's in the US and UK. The Hippy Movement of Peace and Love (and drugs).

The hippies of the 60's really tapped in to something big: **Peace and Love**. It created a movement and a culture, birthing songs and revolution. Yet, this movement was rooted in rebellion against authority and used sex and drugs as tools of their craft.

The Kingdom of God in the New Covenant is a movement of peace and love. Yet, its not rooted in rebellion against authority. In fact, it establishes a true authority, and offers blessing and help to the secular authorities. It's a movement rooted in Heaven and flowing into the Earth through people who believe in Jesus.

This movement has existed since the day of Pentecost in 30 AD, was fully released in the year 70 AD, with power, but ran into some snags, bumps, and detours along the historical road of its journey.

Today, many of us are grabbing hold of this message of the New Covenant. It has the prophetic potential of truly taking over the whole Earth, in a good and blessed way. In fact, on the day Jesus, our King, was born, angels declared *"Peace on Earth!"*

We continue to stand with this angelic and prophetic message of Peace on Earth. Peace and love, peace and love, yet without drugs, without fornication, without rebellion. This is the movement that God has ordained and is flowing from His very heart.

I believe a lot has been restored to the Body of Christ, but now the Body of Christ needs to be at work to restore the Earth and humanity. The Kingdom of God brings peace, love and justice into the nations, where wars cease, and the light of Jesus shines brighter and brighter. Isaiah prophesied of this restored state of humanity:

Heaven must receive him until the time comes for God to restore everything, as he promised long ago through his holy prophets. (Acts 3:21)

A biblical view of "end times" is not rooted in "the rapture" or the coming "great tribulation". Historically, the great tribulation happened when the Temple and Jerusalem was destroyed. That was God's wrath, using the Roman armies, against the Temple and city, which rejected the Cross.

The biblical view we must all embrace is that of the Kingdom of God. Will Jesus return again? I believe that He will - Yes! When? When His Kingdom has covered the Earth. What Scriptures do we use to understand this? Here are a few:

This verse in Acts 3:19-21 speaks of the "restitution" or "recovery" of all things. These are the things lost in the fall, which Jesus, the last Adam and new Man has come to restore. This is about the Kingdom covering the Earth. It's a restoration of the Earth and humanity itself.

For the creation waits in eager expectation for the children of God to be revealed. For the creation was subjected to frustration, not by its own choice, but by the will of the one who subjected it, in hope. (Romans 8:19-20)

...to be put into effect when the times reach their fulfillment - to bring unity to all things in Heaven and on Earth under Christ. (Ephesians 1:10)

While you were watching, a rock was cut out, but not by human hands. It struck the statue on its feet of iron and clay and smashed them. Then the iron, the clay, the bronze, the silver and the gold were all broken to pieces and became like chaff on a threshing floor in the summer. The wind swept them away without leaving a trace. But the rock that struck the statue became a huge mountain and filled the whole Earth. (Daniel 2:34-35)

They will neither harm nor destroy on all my holy mountain, for the Earth will be filled with the knowledge of the Lord as the waters cover the sea. (Isaiah 11:9)

For the Earth will be filled with the knowledge of the glory of the Lord as the waters cover the sea. (Habakkuk 2:14)

He told them another parable: "The kingdom of Heaven is like a mustard seed, which a man took and planted in his field. Though it is the smallest of all seeds, yet when it grows, it is the largest of garden plants and becomes a tree, so that the birds come and perch in its branches."

He told them still another parable: "The kingdom of Heaven is like yeast that a woman took and mixed into about sixty pounds of flour until it worked all through the dough. (Matthew 13:31-33)

The above Scriptures embody the concept that the Kingdom of Jesus, the Kingdom of light, which dispels darkness, began to come into the Earth when Jesus was born and will continue to expand until He comes again.

So, again, my question is, "How has the Church been doing for the past 2000 years of developing and advancing the Kingdom of God in the Earth, and in the hearts and minds of humanity?" I would say it's been a slow process, but a process that is accelerating exponentially.

The heart cry of the Church and of every Christian should be:

"Your kingdom come, your will be done, on Earth as it is in Heaven". (Matthew 6:10)

The idea is to get Heaven fully into the Earth. The false view for too long has been to get Christians out of the Earth so that God can rain down His wrath.

That is not the biblical view, and is becoming as "old wife's tales" to hear it taught anymore. Let's mature in our theological knowing and understand the covenant and Kingdom that we are a part of.

Heaven is a temporary place to go for the believer at death. The body (and soul, I believe), both die, but the Spirit lives on in Heaven waiting for the day of Resurrection. Earth is the inheritance of the redeemed of the Lord, but it's an Earth with Heaven's touch. We are moving toward this "Heaven on Earth" reality day after day. Do not lose heart, but rise up to your kingly, priestly and ambassadorial calling in Christ!

Chapter Twenty
Where are we going?

I hope to be able to answer this question with some form of inspiration from God. When I think about where we are going, as Humanity together on this planet, I think of the Kingdom. Some teach a doctrine that things are getting worse and that God will one day destroy the Earth, and then make a new one. I believe the Earth was created to last forever and that God's Kingdom will restore the Earth and humanity.

Generations come and generations go, but the Earth remains forever. (Ecclesiastes 1:4)

He set the Earth on its foundations; it can never be moved. (Psalm 104:5)

Your faithfulness continues through all generations; you established the Earth, and it endures. (Psalm 119:90)

That should create a shift in your thinking, if you have been taught the popular Christian view. I believe the new Heaven and new Earth that is spoken about in our Bible is the New Covenant, the New Jerusalem, the Bride married to her King. We live in this new Heaven and new Earth now. The Kingdom has expanded from Heaven to a land called Israel to a planet called Earth, spreading as leaven working its way through the dough. The Kingdom is said to be like a rock that grows into a great mountain, which fills the whole Earth. It's said to be like a seed, which is planted, and grows up into a great tree where the birds of the air take refuge.

The goal of God is to bring back the vital connection of God to man as in the garden. This will be achieved when we receive resurrected bodies, which cannot die. Then our being will be whole, our flesh will have caught up to our spirit by entering into a new reality called bodily resurrection. We shall reign on the Earth forever. This will be an Earth infused with Heaven, as Heaven and Earth become one.

You have made them to be a kingdom and priests to serve our God, and they will reign on the Earth. (Revelation 5:10)

With these foundational truths implanted in our hearts and minds, lets look at the future. I want to explore seven areas:

1. Population growth
2. God's view of humanity and the nations
3. Hot Bed's of Spiritual Activity on the Earth
4. The testimony of a man named Howard Storm
5. Justice Ministries that God is raising up and protecting
6. The restoration of the 5 fold ministry
7. The apostolic Kingdom of God

For those of you new to the view of an optimistic eschatology, or Partial Preterism (historical context of Scriptures) let me briefly explain what most of us believe, biblically:

1. Most of us believe every Old Testament prophecy is fulfilled. After the Cross and Resurrection, if there were any lingering Old Testament prophecies that needed fulfillment, they found their fulfillment through the events of 70 AD, also called the days of vengeance for Old Covenant Israel, based on this Scripture - Luke 21:22

For these be the days of vengeance, that all things which are written may be fulfilled.

2. Most of us believe in an ever advancing and increasing Kingdom of God on the Earth, until it covers the whole Earth, at which time Jesus will return, Heaven and Earth uniting, and we shall receive a bodily resurrection like His.

3. Most of us believe Satan is bound, without authority, though forces of darkness operate through lies and intimidation, but the Body of Christ is the authority in the Earth. He will be loosed in the future, only to be thrown into the lake of fire.

4. Most of us believe in the future, final judgment, in which all things not of the new creation will be cast to the lake of fire: death, hell, sheol, hades, Satan, devils, demons, fallen angels, sickness, disease, unbelievers. I believe the lake of fire is the place where all things not of the new creation cease to exist.

The term "forever" in our New Testament, concerning lake of fire and punishment is translated wrong, and should be a term meaning, "age enduring", which alludes to a span of time, as long as that age endures. When resurrection comes, a new age will have begun.

5. Most of us believe Earth is our ultimate home, with Heaven's connection. To die and go to Heaven is a temporary place to go until the day of Resurrection.

Christian Population Growth from 100 AD to Now

At 100 AD, about 1/360th of the world population was Christian

At 1000 AD, about 1/220th of the world population was Christian

At 1500 AD, about 1/69th of the world population was Christian

At 1900 AD, about 1/27th of the world population was Christian

At 1990 AD, about 1/7th of the world population was Christian

At 2015 AD, approximately 1/3rd of the world population is Christian

There are now about 7 billion people on planet Earth, and about 1/3 or 2.2 billion are Christians. They may have odd beliefs, or misinterpret sections of Scripture, but they believe that Jesus is the Savior and Lord and that His blood has washed our sins away. That's the only requirement to be born again - to believe on Jesus.

The population of the United States of America is about 330 million, which is only 5% of the world's population. For the preachers who always preach judgment is coming to the world because of America's sins, it's amazing that 5% of the people on Earth have the ability to bring such destruction. In 1990, America's population was about 250 million, and it's predicted to grow to about 350 million by 2025.

In 1804, the world population reached 1 billion people for the first time. In 2050, the population of the world could be as high as 10 billion people.

There are those who want to abort more babies and control the population through wars and plagues, but God is not caught off guard by the population explosion on planet Earth.

Man carries the glory of God, made in His image and likeness. With more people on Earth, we have the potential to experience more of God's glory.

Because of the population explosion, more will be done for human rights. Countries that were once third world are rising out of their poverty. Technology and the intelligent people who create it and sell it is advancing all over the world. More cures are being found for many illnesses. Breakthroughs in science and medicine are constantly happening.

The Earth and humanity has so much potential for the days ahead. We need not be pessimistic and predict the downfall of America or of planet Earth. We must continue to arise to our identity in Christ as the ambassadors and representatives of Heaven's Kingdom.

God's View of Humanity and the Nations

How does God view humanity today, in this New Covenant? Is He angry at sin and rebellion? Is He judging the sins and rebellion that we think He is angry at?

A good study of the atonement helps us understand the heart of the Father.

Three major historical views of the atonement:

1. Christus Victor Theory (Christ the Victor) – early Church fathers (first 1000 years of the Church)
2. Satisfaction Theory – Anselm of Canterbury (1033 – 1109)
3. Penal Substitution Theory – John Calvin (1509 – 1564)

1. Christus Victor Theory

From the Cross until AD 1100, only one view of the atonement existed, termed **Christus Victor**, which is Latin for "Christ the Victor". Another name for this belief is the ransom view. Christus Victor is the official name, but the ransom view is also used in reference to this view.

According to Christus Victor, God gave authority over the Earth to Adam and Eve. However, the devil deceived Adam and Eve into sinning and giving their authority to him. As a result, the devil had authority over the Earth. To remedy this, King Jesus died, forgiving sin, took the keys back from the devil, rose again and then gave them back to humanity. This is the Christus Victor concept, that as a Human, as "another Adam" who is sinless, Jesus came to take back the authority over Earth that Adam and Eve had lost. He went through the temptations and trials and was put to death, but then He came out of the grave. When He came out, He brought with Him all the captives, with the keys (the authority), and emptied the grave. In other words, He took over, took back everything the enemy had stolen from Adam and Eve, and gave it back to humankind.

This is seen in Luke 22, at the Last Supper before the Cross, where Jesus said to His disciples, "*I confer on you a Kingdom just as My Father conferred one on Me*" (Luke 22:29). Likewise, when he said to Peter, "*I will give you the keys of the kingdom of Heaven*" (Matthew 16:19), He was proclaiming His intention to give the Kingdom back to them. This is the basic Christus Victor view held by the Church for the first 1,100 years of its history and believed by all of the early Church fathers.

2. Satisfaction Theory

In the AD 1100's, there was a man named Anselm who was the Bishop of Canterbury, which was a highly esteemed position in the Church. He derived a new theory about what happened at the Cross, which is known as the **Satisfaction Theory**. Rather than the focus being on getting back humanity's authority, the focus was on the fact that human sin had dishonored God, creating a big wall between people and God. In other words, according to this theory, sin was the focus of the atonement, not the need to regain humanity's authority and identity. Thus, Jesus came to die for sin, because human sin had dishonored God. This is taken from Romans 6:23, where it says, *"the wages of sin is death."* Thus, sin, as a wage, had become so piled up that someone (Jesus) needed to come and satisfy God's side of the justice. Someone had to come pay back the debt of sin, because God is a just God.

When Anselm presented this concept in AD 1100, he did not say someone needed to be punished. He said God had been dishonored and someone had to honor Him again, but because none of our works were good enough to honor Him, Jesus came to Earth and lived the human life perfectly in order to honor God.

3. Penal Substitution Theory

In the 1500's, John Calvin added a third theory on the atonement, leaning heavily on the Satisfaction Theory, but not so much on the Christus Victor Theory. He said sin dishonored God, and, he added, sin deserved punishment (based on an Old Covenant model). This theory, known as *Penal Substitution*, changed the understanding of what happened at the Cross quite a bit. According to John Calvin, when Jesus died, He stood in for humanity. Humans deserve to be punished because of sin, and God should be sending judgment and wrath toward us, but instead He sent it upon Jesus. Jesus stood in our place and took our punishment so that we could go free. In other words, the focus of this view is sin's demand for justice.

Although this theory did not exist during the first 1,500 years of Christianity, today it is widespread, and many Christians believe it is the "normal" view of the atonement - that Jesus needed to come and be punished in our place. Along with this, Calvin also taught the idea of limited atonement. Simply put, limited atonement says Jesus took the punishment for Christians (the elect) but not for the rest of humanity, which means they are receiving judgment. The Christian is protected from God's judgment by a "Jesus bubble", but the non-Christian is being punished for the sins they continue to commit. The elect are covered by Jesus, but those who are not among the elect are not protected from judgment.

It is easy to undermine this idea simply based on 1 John 2:2, which says, *"He is the atoning sacrifice (propitiation) for our sins, and not only for ours but also for the sins of the whole world."* Because of this verse, even a lot of Calvinists have rejected the idea of limited atonement. Even the type and shadow of the atonement doesn't fit with limited atonement. On the Day of Atonement, the lamb was killed for all of Israel, good Israelites and bad Israelites alike. Everyone in Israel received the benefit of the sacrifice. In like manner, based on 1 John 2:2, everyone in the world is forgiven by God, but everyone has not yet received this forgiveness. It must be received by faith in Jesus Christ. Yet, the benefit of God not holding people's sins against them is for everyone in the world, under this New Covenant.

This brings up a very important question that shows the difference between the original view (Chrisus Victor) and the newer views (Satisfaction Theory and Penal Substitution): Is sin forgiven or punished?

If your child breaks the lamp, do you forgive them or punish them?

Some want to say it is both, but it must be one or the other. If a person owes a mortgage to the bank, that person has two options for how to own the house. Either that person can pay off the mortgage, or the bank can forgive the debt. If the person pays it, then that is not the same as having it forgiven. The same is true related to the debate between punishment and forgiveness. Either our sins were paid for, by Jesus taking the punishment we deserved, or they were forgiven, with no punishment.

Since the 1100's, the emphasis has primarily switched from the earlier concept of forgiveness to the concept of punishment. This is especially true since the formalization of Calvinism in the 1500's. Thus, the Church has adopted the concept of a courtroom scene where an angry Father God is Judge and demands payment for the debt of sin, and Jesus steps in, as the perfect Man, and says, "I will die in their place to pay for their sins." This concept of the courtroom, which historians refer to as "the legalization of Christianity", was invented by John Calvin, who had a background in law. Because of his legal mindset, Calvin saw the Father as a judge instead of a father, and he perceived the gospel message through a legal lens instead of a relational lens. This was the origin of Penal Substitution.

Even Martin Luther, who began this Protestant Reformation before John Calvin, stated that he was afraid of the Father but He adored Jesus.

Closely connected to this theory is the idea of an angry God. The Greek word for propitiation, which is a word rooted in Greek pagan religion, carries with it the idea of "appeasing the wrath of the angry god through sacrifice or penance." Unfortunately, this definition has carried through to what Jesus did at the Cross. If sin has to be punished, it follows that God must be very angry that His holy Law was continually being violated, even by Gentiles who had no law or covenant with God. Thus, the years of humanity's sinful defiance of God had built up a great deal of wrath, which eventually culminated at the Cross, where Jesus suffered the wrath of God in our place. As those who benefit from Jesus' suffering, we should be sad he suffered the wrath of God but also thankful He took our place. He stood between the angry, judging Father and us and took the punishment we deserved.

This is especially easy for people to accept if they have an angry father in the natural, because it fits their experience of what a father is like. Even for those who have gentle Earthly fathers, the concept of an angry God causes them to emotionally distance themselves from God. Thus, they can read a story like the Prodigal Son (see Luke 15) and think: "That does not connect with me. I connect with the Son, but is that really what the Father is like?" In this way, the image of God as an angry judge serves as a lens that color the way people read and understand the Bible. They see relationship with Him as hinging on Jesus' suffering in our place. "Jesus paid the penalty so we can have relationship with the just and angry God", is the thought of many Christians.

In fact, this teaching is also very connected to the Grace Movement. Some of their teachers are so pro-grace that they teach the penal substitution perspective. In other words, God the Father poured out His entire wrath on Jesus on the Cross, which means God has no wrath toward us. He took it all out on Jesus, and therefore, He is never upset with us. This is the logical conclusion that is the foundation of the Grace Movement. The problem with it, of course, is that when we read the New Testament we discover that there is more wrath. The subject of God's wrath comes up repeatedly in the New Testament, which does not make sense if God took out His entire wrath on Jesus on the Cross. Therefore, a view is created that says we are in an age of grace for now, and the wrath spoken of in the New Testament is for days in the future. But I thought all His wrath was poured out on Jesus at the Cross? And, what happened during the destruction of the Temple and Jerusalem in 70 AD – was that God's wrath? As we look back at the gospel accounts, the question must be asked, "Where do we see God pouring out wrath on the Cross? The answer is, we don't. The New Testament does not connect wrath to the Cross. The wrath of God was not present or involved in the crucifixion of Jesus Christ in any way.

But what about Psalm 22 and Isaiah 53? Wasn't He forsaken by God? Didn't God turn His face from Him on the Cross because He is too holy to look at sin? Didn't God punish Jesus at the Cross because it was punishment that was really for us? Didn't we deserve to die because of our sin, but Jesus died in our place? But what about how the gospel teaches us that we died with Him?

The New Covenant vs. the Law covenant

The simple answer to "How can a God Who forgives sin without punishment be righteous?" is this:

Jesus was establishing a New Covenant of forgiveness at the Cross. He took the Law covenant to death, fulfilling its types and shadows, being the Perfect Passover Lamb at the Cross, and made the Law covenant obsolete by His Cross. God was creating a New Covenant by which new laws were in operation. He was creating a new system by which a new creation could come forth. This New Covenant system operates by grace and forgiveness.

What this means is that by forgiving God was not overlooking or disobeying the Law, because He created a new law in the New Covenant that allowed for forgiveness. What makes any ruler or judge righteous in any land is a commitment to following the Law of that land. The New Covenant operates by new laws.

"For I will forgive their wickedness and will remember their sins no more." By calling this covenant "new," he has made the first one obsolete; and what is obsolete and outdated will soon disappear. (Hebrews 8:12-13)

"This is the covenant I will make with them after that time, says the Lord. I will put my laws in their hearts, and I will write them on their minds." Then he adds: "Their sins and lawless acts I will remember no more." (Hebrews 10:16-17)

David says the same thing when he speaks of the blessedness of the one to whom God credits righteousness apart from works: "Blessed are those whose transgressions are forgiven, whose sins are covered. Blessed is the one whose sin the Lord will never count against them." (Romans 4:6-8)

When you were dead in your sins and in the uncircumcision of your flesh, God made you alive with Christ. He forgave us all our sins. (Colossians 2:13)

Be kind and compassionate to one another, forgiving each other, just as in Christ God forgave you. (Ephesians 4:32)

...that God was reconciling the world to himself in Christ, not counting people's sins against them. And he has committed to us the message of reconciliation. (2 Corinthians 5:19)

That is exactly what God has done in the New Covenant. He forgave sin by changing the Law and establishing a New Covenant. Hebrews 7:12 says, *"For when the priesthood is changed, the law must be changed also."* The old Law has changed, and the Law we are under is the New Covenant of forgiveness. The New Covenant is one of forgiveness, which operates by faith, which is fueled by His love to us and in us. This means, for God to be a righteous Judge, He must forgive. If He tried to apply the Old Covenant to us, He would be unrighteous, because we are not under the Old Covenant, and the Cross was not about the Old Covenant Law. He fulfilled it by becoming the reality of the type and shadow it pointed to, but the Cross made the Law obsolete by creating a new law of forgiveness. We must remember, God lives inside the covenant He establishes, and He will be faithful to it, because He is righteous and always operates within the covenant He is in. Operating in the New Covenant He has with us looks like forgiveness, blessing, prosperity, health, and glory.

There is no shame, no judgment, no condemnation, no angry God toward us or humanity in the New Covenant. We might think there is, but there is not. It's our thinking that needs to change. We can grieve and even quench the Holy Spirit, but God is not angry at humanity inside this New Covenant, because He forgave sin at the Cross; all sin! God is love, and He is at work to draw people to Himself because of the work of forgiveness at the Cross. The propitiation was the atoning sacrifice, the mercy seat, the covenant activity of God by which He reveals Himself as love and as good. God did not change, but the covenant did change. The rules or laws changed when Jesus died and rose again. A new creation has come forth.

So, now we can ask those questions again:

How does God view humanity today, in this New Covenant? Is He angry at sin and rebellion? Is He judging the sins and rebellion that we think He is angry at?

And another question: Does God favor Israel as a nation more than other nations, and does He favor a Jewish person more than He does a non-Jewish person?

God sees humanity in two ways: You are either His child in Christ, or you are a lost prodigal who needs to come home. We are saved by grace through faith in what Jesus did. He gives us His righteousness, and we cannot improve upon or diminish its power. We are perfectly righteous and accepted in Christ Jesus, by faith. He is the perfectly loved Son, and we are inside of Him. We inherit the blessings of God through our marriage relationship to Jesus the King. Those born of His Spirit are all of His Bride, which is described as a city called the New Jerusalem.

Jerusalem is built like a city that is closely compacted together. (Psalm 122:3)

David wrote that to apply first to the shadow system of old Jerusalem, but then to be spiritually understood in the New Covenant as we are that city, closely compacted together, members one of another.

God is not angry or wrathful toward sin. He has forgiven sin at the Cross, for everyone and forever. He is grieved as a Father at the sin of humanity, so let's not think He doesn't care. He cares, and that is why He is always at work to bring people out of darkness and into His glorious light. Under the New Covenant, God encourages us to come out of sin. He does not punish us because of sin. Jesus forgave it at the Cross! You do not punish a forgiven sin.

Hebrews gives us some insight into this relationship. He uses an Old Testament Scripture in Proverbs about the relationship between a father and his son:

And have you completely forgotten this word of encouragement that addresses you as a father addresses his son? It says, "My son, do not make light of the Lord's discipline, and do not lose heart when he rebukes you, because the Lord disciplines the one he loves, and he chastens everyone he accepts as his son." Endure hardship as discipline; God is treating you as his children. For what children are not disciplined by their father? If you are not disciplined-and everyone undergoes discipline-then you are not legitimate, not true sons and daughters at all. (Hebrews 12:5-8)

The writer of Hebrews uses an Old Testament Scripture to make his point. The biggest point to be made here is that the true children of God undergo His discipline, and those outside of Christ do not. But, what is His discipline and chastisement in the New Covenant? To understand this correctly, we must learn what chastisement means to God. Chastisement is the covenant activity of God in one's life by which He reveals His glory. He brings this chastisement into the life of His children by training them in His ways, by His Spirit, through His Word, through fellowship with others, and through circumstances, as He continues giving us wisdom to walk through difficult situations. It's His covenant activity in our lives that only those who belong to Him in Christ will experience. The fruit is peace. Those who remain prodigals, He waits for them to come home. They are without chastisement, or without His covenant activity, yet also, without peace. That doesn't mean He is not reaching out, but they are simply not experiencing the covenantal blessings and leading of His Spirit.

In order to answer the question about Israel, and are they God's favored nation, we must understand the covenant story and their history:

(Most of what is in this article came from truth I gleaned from David Chilton and Jonathan Welton).

Dispensationalists have wrongly assigned the 7 Churches to represent "ages" of Church history, but the language of the 7 Churches actually relates to Israel's history, from the garden to 70 AD. David Chilton discovered this, and Jonathan Welton documents it in his book "The Art of Revelation". Let me briefly explain:

1. The Church at Ephesus relates to the Garden of Eden. This was the time of leaving the first love as Adam and Eve did, of Christ walking among the lampstands as God walked in the garden, the judgment of removing the lampstand as compared to the judgment of banishing Adam and Eve from the Garden, but then the promise of the tree of life to him who overcomes.

2. The Church at Smyrna relates to Israel's time during the 10 plagues of Egypt compared to the "tribulation of 10 days" mentioned to those in Smyrna.

3. The Church at Pergamum relates to Israel's time in the wilderness as compared to the enemies of the Church being as Balaam and Balak tempting them into idolatry, as Israel experienced in the wilderness.

4. The Church at Thyatira relates to Israel's monarchy, which had glory in David's day, the foundational covenant of Jesus announcing Himself as the Son of God to that Church, and the comparison to Jezebel as the enemies of the Church seducing

them into sin. It ends with the promise of having authority over the nations, a true Kingdom/monarchy promise.

5. The Church at Sardis relates to the captivity period in Israel's history. The call was to strengthen the things that remain, which is an acknowledgement that there are a few people who have remained faithful, all are reminiscent of prophetic language about the remnant in a time of apostasy.

6. The Church at Philadelphia relates to their return to the land after captivity and the rebuilding of the Temple and city of Jerusalem. This was done during a time of testing, as the Church is also warned, with the encouragement language eluding to the Temple and city, as "pillars in the Temple" and the blessings of the New Jerusalem.

7. The Church at Laodicea relates to the last day's period of unbelieving Israel where they rejected Christ, (vomiting out of His mouth), and were lukewarm and in apostasy, yet boasting of great wealth. Israel and the Church alike are urged to repent and return to Christ, and in doing this will receive the dominion of His throne, being seated with Him.

We must follow the covenantal change that took place in the Bible, and specifically in the New Testament. A new Israel organized in Christ took over the old Israel. This new Israel was comprised of believing Jews, the physical seed of Abraham who had become children of God through faith in Jesus, their Messiah. The new Israel then took the gospel of the Kingdom to the rest of the world. Today, the true Israel of God is in the Spirit, and it's made up of people all over the world. There is no favored nation today. The holy nation is the Church, the Body of Christ, the royal priesthood. It's about faith, not bloodline, and it's about Jesus and His Kingdom, not a physical nation called Israel with land. The New Jerusalem is taking over the Earth. Everything mentioned in the Bible before the New Jerusalem were as types and shadows of something greater.

Why is there so much turmoil in the Middle East today? Because the nation of Israel exists again. God had dispersed the Jews to inhabit the whole Earth. This was His will, I believe. Similar to the Tower of Babel, where God confused the languages to disperse the people. In the New Covenant, God gave tongues on Pentecost, and they were on one accord, but the goal, again, was to disperse into the world, and get out of Jerusalem. The dispersion was His plan, so that the Jews could be people of influence and resources all over the world. Jewish people today are heavily involved in the creative arts in Hollywood, in banking and business in New York, and other places in the world. God wants them saved, but He wanted them dispersed as well. This is why we have so much turmoil, not just in Israel, but throughout the Middle East, because of this recreation of national Israel, which was not the will or plan of God. In reality, many Arab people do not agree with Israel being able to take land in 1948. It created problems that exist today. And, the demonically inspired teachings of Islam, which all surrounding countries practice, teach the Muslim people to hate Jews. Arab families that had lived in that land for generations were uprooted in 1948.

Who has ever heard of such things? Who has ever seen things like this? Can a country be born in a day or a nation be brought forth in a moment? Yet no sooner is Zion in labor than she gives birth to her children (Isaiah 66:8).

This is the Scripture that Christian Zionists have used to prove the birth of Israel in 1948 was the fulfillment of prophecy. Nothing could be farther from the truth. The Scripture in Isaiah 66:8 pointed forward, as Isaiah wrote it, to the Church in the New Covenant. The Body of Christ is the holy nation that was born in one day, on the day of Pentecost, and continues to grow daily. The covenant transition period of 30 AD to 70 AD was the birthing period, to pass from darkness into light, from death into life. There is no double-fulfillment. Covenant-transitional Scriptures do not operate by a double-fulfillment.

God forgave sin at the Cross. That is a foundational truth to get into our hearts and minds. He is not judging sin today. He is training His children to be like Jesus, and drawing the lost to Himself. His Kingdom is expanding and advancing into all the Earth, and things are getting better, with minor setbacks here and there.

Hot Beds of Spiritual Activity on the Earth

Christianity has been spreading since the day of Pentecost, when the Spirit was poured out. Throughout the history of Christianity, there have been "hot beds" of Holy Spirit activity, where people were saved, healed, delivered, set free, communities were changed, crops grew better, kids acted right, bars shut down, and the animals plowed the field without a fight. A friend of mine and minster of the gospel, J.D. King, wrote a great blog where he captured so many of these historic details and current activity, which is what I would like to share.

The following information was taken from a blog that J.D. King wrote called "Why You've Been Duped Into Believing The Myth That The World Is Getting Worse and Worse", dated August 2015. (His article goes on to document how life and the world is getting progressively better, and not worse, because of the reality of the advancing Kingdom)

Spread of Christianity

People keep suggesting that things are growing worse and worse, but I'm convinced that they are greatly mistaken, which brings me to the underlying point of this article. The Earth is constantly improving because the gospel of Jesus Christ is taking root in every corner of the globe. The Kingdom of God is advancing and things are truly reflecting the Lord's great kindness and love.

Many aren't ready to acknowledge this, but the number of those who claim to be Christians around the world has nearly quadrupled in the last century, from about 600 million in 1910 to more than 2.3 billion as of 2011 (Some are suggesting the number may be as high as 3.2 billion). So, conservatively, over one-third of the world currently identifies with Christianity. This represents a significant shift over time.

Extrapolating relevant data from the 1990 report of the Statistics Task Force of the Lausanne Committee for World Evangelism, Jonathan Welton and Jim Wies asserted the following:

At AD 100, 1/360th of the world population was Christian. By AD 1000, 1/220th of the world population was Christian. By 1500, the percentage of Christians rose to 1/69th of the worldwide population. By 1900, with a world population of slightly over one billion, Christianity had risen to 1/27th of the population. By 1990, the percentage of Christians rose to 1/7th of the worldwide population. As was stated previously, it is now estimated that there are seven billion people on planet Earth and that a full one third of them (one out of every three people worldwide) are followers of Jesus!

Also evaluating statistical data that's currently being tabulated, Roman Catholic researcher George Weigel recounted the following:

There will be, by mid-2011, 2,306,609,000 Christians of all kinds in the world, representing 33 percent of world population...As of mid-2011, there will be an average of 80,000 new Christians per day.

Weigel's figures are significant for many different reasons. One should not overlook the fact that the bulk of global population growth over the last century has been in traditionally "non-Christian" regions such as India, China, Africa, and the Middle East. Births in the "Christian West" are actually declining at a considerable rate. So, Christianity's vast numerical growth during this period is quite astounding.

To the surprise of many, Christian conversions are actually outpacing the violent expansion of Islam. Reflecting on this ignored truth, Sociologist Rodney Stark recently noted, *"As recently as April 2015, the Pew Research Center declared that Muslims will soon overtake Christians by way of superior fertility. They won't...Islam generates very little growth through conversions, while Christianity enjoys a substantial conversion rate, especially in nations located in what my colleague Philip Jenkins describes as the 'global south' - Asia, Sub-Saharan Africa, and Latin America. And these conversions do not include the millions of converts being gained in China. Thus, current growth trends project an increasingly Christian world."*

Muslim growth is taking place through childbirth or bloodshed. In contrast, Christianity's growth is fueled by healing, deliverance, and interpersonal engagement.

In fact, the vast majority of Church growth is currently taking place in difficult environments that have been historically opposed to the gospel. Locales in Africa, Asia, Latin America, and even the Middle East are now experiencing unprecedented advancement. Ironically, this kind of expansion has defined Christianity from the very beginning.

Let's consider some of the encouraging statistics about what's happening around the world. I must admit that I get incredibly excited when I hear these accounts.

Africa

What has been transpiring throughout the continent of Africa has been utterly amazing. It is increasingly becoming a "Christian land." Reflecting on the reality of Christianity's unparalleled growth over the last century, Catholic researcher George Weigel declared,

Africa has been the most stunning area of Christian growth over the past century. There were 8.7 million African Christians in 1900 (primarily in Egypt, Ethiopia, and South Africa); there are 475 million African Christians today, and their numbers are projected to reach 670 million by 2025. Another astonishing growth spurt, measured typologically, has been among Pentecostals and Charismatics: 981,000 in 1900; 612,472,000 in 2011, with an average of 37,000 new adherents every day – the fastest growth in two millennia of Christian history.

Weigel's observations are backed up by the research of the Pew Research Forum. Their data also points to the amazing changes that have been transpiring in Africa. They report that,

The share of the population that is Christian in sub-Saharan Africa climbed from 9 percent in 1910 to 63 percent in 2010, or from 8.5 million to 516 million during that time.

In less than one century, Christianity has moved from margins to the center of sub-Saharan Africa life.

There are evidences all over the continent of these monumental shifts. For example, missionaries Heidi and Roland Baker, with 2,700 Church plants, have made a significant impact in the nation of Mozambique. The province they operate in was 99% Muslim before their arrival, but a little over ten years later those figures are remarkably different. Kelly Head writes,

The Bakers are now based full-time in Pemba, Mozambique, in an area where Heidi says was once called a 'graveyard to missionaries.' But recently the government announced publicly that it's no longer a Muslim providence; now it's a Christian providence.

The continent of Africa has been utterly transformed by the goodness and grace of the gospel.

Latin America

It's not just "darkest Africa" experiencing this unprecedented advancement, but a similar impact is being felt throughout Latin America. According to the Pew Forum, since 1900 the number of Latin American Christians has grown by an incredible 877%. This growth is evidenced in a number of diverse South American nations. For example, over 40% of Guatemala now identifies with Pentecostal-Charismatic Christianity. The numbers are even more significant in Brazil. A majority of that nation is currently part of the same global "Spirit-filled movement." Paul Strand observes that, *"Christianity is increasing in Brazil. If the trend continues, it is predicted that more than half of all Brazilians (109 million Christians out of 209 million citizens) will be evangelical Christians by 2020....Brazil is a land in revival... It's a place where belief in miracles and healings are high."*

What is taking place in Brazil is even more astounding when, prior to 1970, less than 3% of the Brazilian population was "Evangelical." To go from 2.5% to over 50% of the population in a rigidly Roman Catholic nation in less than 50 years is unprecedented.

Latin America is literally exploding with the flames of revival.

Asia

Perhaps the growth of Christianity is most astounding in the vast continent of Asia. The People's Republic of China only had about one million Protestants in 1949. Now there are conservatively more than 58 million Protestants in China. Prof Yang, a leading expert on religion in China, believes that number will swell to around 160 million by 2025. He declares, *"By 2030, China's total Christian population would exceed 247 million, placing it above Mexico, Brazil and the United States as the largest Christian congregation in the world."*

Other journalists and unbiased observers are also acknowledging this incredible expansion of Christianity in China. One noted English newspaper published the following, *"Estimates of the number of Christians in China today vary between 60 million and 120 million, which would suggest as many as one in 10 of the population are already believers. It has been predicted that by 2030 there could be almost a quarter of a billion Christians in China making it the biggest Christian population in the world."*

If the house Church participants, and those dispersed throughout the rural stretches of China are considered, perhaps as many as 30% of the Chinese are now associated with Pentecostal-Charismatic Christianity. Those numbers may be high, but there is little doubt about Christianity's significant inroads into this once closed-off nation.

A land that was once opposed to the gospel will likely be the center of it within a few decades.

The Middle East

This final report may surprise many, but Spirit-filled Christianity is also beginning to make advances throughout the violent Arab world.

In fact, it appears that more Muslims became Christians over the last 20 years than in the previous 1,500 years combined. Based on the observations of missiologists, journalist Audrey Lee suggests, *"More Muslims have committed to follow Christ in the last 10 years than in the last 15 centuries of Islam."*

In spite of the intense persecution, assassinations, and widespread Church bombings, revival is exploding throughout North Africa and other parts of the Middle East. It has been conservatively estimated that at least 2 to 7 million people from a Muslim background worldwide now follow Christ. Other reliable reports suggest that there may be as many as 10 to 15 million undocumented Christians in Muslim countries. Perhaps there's even more. Journalist George Thomas notes that, "*A Christian revival is touching the northernmost reaches of Africa. In a region once hostile to the gospel, now tens of thousands of Muslims are following Jesus. As the sun sets over the Mediterranean Sea, Muslims across Northern Africa are converting to faith in Jesus Christ in record numbers... What experts say is that there is a profound move of God in the predominantly Muslim nations of Mauritania, Western Sahara, Morocco, Algeria, Libya and Tunisia.*"

Tino Qahoush, a researcher and filmmaker, has been traveling to various parts of the Arab region to document the Christian revival that has been taking place. Reflecting on what he observed, he noted the following,

What God is doing in North Africa, all the way from actually Mauritanian to Libya is unprecedented in the history of missions. I have the privilege of recording testimonies and listening to firsthand stories of men and women, of all ages.

These abrupt changes are something that even the Muslim clerics are starting to recognize. In December 2001, Sheikh Ahmad al Qataani, the president of The Companions Lighthouse for the Science of Islamic Law in Libya, appeared on a live interview on Al-Jazeera satellite television. He declared the following: "*Islam used to represent, as you previously mentioned, Africa's main religion and there were 30 African languages that used to be written in Arabic script. The number of Muslims in Africa has diminished to 316 million, half of whom are Arabs in North Africa.*

So in the section of Africa that we are talking about, the non-Arab section, the number of Muslims does not exceed 150 million people. When we realize that the entire population of Africa is one billion people, we see that the number of Muslims has diminished greatly from what it was in the beginning of the last century. On the other hand, the number of Catholics [He means Christians in general] has increased from one million in 1902 to 329 million 882 thousand (329,882,000). Let us round off that number to 330 million in the year 2000. As to how that happened, well, there are now 1.5 million Churches whose congregations account for 46 million people. In every hour, 667 Muslims convert to Christianity. Everyday, 16,000 Muslims convert to Christianity. Ever year, 6 million Muslims convert to Christianity. These numbers are very large indeed."

Stunned, the interviewer interrupted the cleric. *"Hold on! Let me clarify. Do we have six million converting from Islam to Christianity?"* Al Qataani repeated his assertion. *"Every year,"* the cleric confirmed, adding, *"a tragedy has happened."*

While the expansion of Christianity in Islamic countries is modest compared to its growth in other regions, the Church is still making significant headway in a realm of deep opposition. Even the "10-40 window" is encountering the light of the gospel in an unparalleled manner.

There is little doubt that the Church is rapidly advancing around the globe. With the unfortunate exceptions of the United States, Canada, Europe, Japan, and a few other isolated places, Christianity is actually outpacing population growth everywhere.

The testimony of a man named Howard Storm

From Howard Storm's near death experience testimony, that angels showed him about the future:

The future that they showed me was almost no technology at all. What everybody, absolutely everybody, in this euphoric future spent most of their time doing was raising children. The chief concern of people was children, and everybody considered children to be the most precious commodity in the world.

And when a person became an adult, there was no sense of anxiety, or hatred, or competition.

There was this enormous sense of trust and mutual respect. If a person, in this view of the future, became disturbed, then the community of people all cared about the disturbed person falling away from the harmony of the group. Spiritually, through prayer and love, the others would elevate the afflicted person.

What people did with the rest of their time was that they gardened, with almost no physical effort. They showed me that plants, with prayer, would produce huge fruits and vegetables.

People, in unison, could control the climate of the planet through prayer. Everybody would work with mutual trust and the people would call the rain, when needed, and the sun to shine.

Animals lived with people, in harmony.

People, in this best of all worlds, weren't interested in knowledge; they were interested in wisdom. This was because they were in a position where anything they needed to know, in the knowledge category, they could receive simply through prayer. Everything, to them, was solvable. They could do anything they wanted to do.

In this future, people had no wanderlust, because they could, spiritually, communicate with everyone else in the world. There was no need to go elsewhere. They were so engrossed with where they were and the people around them that they didn't have to go on vacation. Vacation from what? They were completely fulfilled and happy.

Death, in this world, was a time when the individual had experienced everything that he or she needed to experience. To die meant to lie down and let go; then the spirit would rise up, and the community would gather around. There would be a great rejoicing, because they all had insight into the Heavenly realm, and the spirit would join with the angels that came down to meet it. They could see the spirit leave and knew that it was time for the spirit to move on; it had outgrown the need for growth in this world. Individuals who died had achieved all they were capable of in this world in terms of love, appreciation, understanding, and working in harmony with others.

The sense I got of this beautiful view of the world's future was as a garden, God's garden. And in this garden of the world, full of all beauty, were people. The people were born into this world to grow in their understanding of the Creator. Then to shed this skin, this shell, in the physical world, and to graduate and move up into Heaven there, to have a more intimate and growing relationship with God.

When you understand the ages, and how they tie into the message of the Kingdom, we are currently in the age of Pisces, of the fish being caught for the Kingdom, and we are heading into the cusp of the ages as the transition into Aquarius is maybe 100 years away.

The Mazzeroth age of Aries began with Abraham and Isaac on the mountain, and the ram was sacrificed in exchange for the life of Isaac. This began an age of the sacrificial system established firmly in the Law of Moses. When Moses went up to get the commandments from God on the mountain, the children of Israel were below making a gold idol of a calf, which represented the previous age, the age of Taurus. They had rejected the offer to be a Kingdom of priests, and were attempting to retreat in their hearts to the age before them, one where they had no responsibility to represent God in the Earth.

Jesus inaugurated the age of Pisces, represented by the fish, He being the Great Fisherman of the age. The early Church understood this. It's been an age of being fishers of men, but this age is coming to a close. The coming age is that of Aquarius. It's a time of great outpouring of love, faith, peace, freedom, great technology advances, more space travel, a unified people on the

Earth (which is a good thing, unified in Christ). Isaiah prophesied these things as the fullness of the New Covenant, and Joel spoke of the outpouring of the Spirit on all flesh. The picture of the Aquarian age is that of a man pouring out a large pitcher of water over all the Earth. This is the picture of the Kingdom of God, the glory of God, covering the Earth as the waters cover the seas.

The temptation is for many to be like Israel, and resist by retreating to a previous age. Being satisfied with just being fishers of men rather than embracing a new age of Kingdom advancement. We are in the death throws of a dying age and the life throws of an emerging age. This is not voodoo or astrology, but rather, its the biblical understanding of the ages by which God has revealed His plans in the stars. The new agers have perverted this. It's the Church's job to recovery this ancient wisdom.

"Canst thou bring forth Mazzaroth in his season? or canst thou guide Arcturus with his sons? Knowest thou the ordinances of Heaven? canst thou set the dominion thereof in the Earth?" (Job 38:32-33)

"Do you know the laws of the universe? Can you use them to regulate the Earth?" (Job 38:33 NLT)

Aquarius has always been thought to be a time of spirituality, love, peace, joy, life, purpose, and all the good things that humanity longs for. This ties into the restored Earth that Isaiah prophesied about:

I believe the Earth and humanity are moving toward a restoration because of the New Covenant. It's because the Kingdom of God is spreading throughout the entire Earth, as leaven spreads in dough. Here are some prophecies from Isaiah concerning this restoration, and then a word from Peter in the book of Acts that confirms this:

And he shall judge among the nations, and shall rebuke many people: and they shall beat their swords into plowshares, and their spears into pruninghooks: nation shall not lift up sword against nation, neither shall they learn war any more. (Isaiah 2:4)

The wolf also shall dwell with the lamb, and the leopard shall lie down with the kid; and the calf and the young lion and the fatling together; and a little child shall lead them. And the cow and the bear shall feed; their young ones shall lie down together: and the lion shall eat straw like the ox. And the sucking child shall play on the hole of the asp, and the weaned child shall put his hand on the cockatrice' den. They shall not hurt nor destroy in all my holy mountain: for the Earth shall be full of the knowledge of the Lord, as the waters cover the sea. (Isaiah 11:6-9)

There shall be no more thence an infant of days, nor an old man that hath not filled his days: for the child shall die an hundred years old; but the sinner being an hundred years old shall be accursed. And they shall build houses, and inhabit them; and they shall plant vineyards, and eat the fruit of them. They shall not build, and another inhabit; they shall not plant, and another eat: for as the days of a tree are the days of my people, and mine elect shall long enjoy the work of their hands. They shall not labour in vain, nor bring forth for trouble; for they are the seed of the blessed of the Lord, and their offspring with them. And it shall come to pass, that before they call, I will answer; and while they are yet speaking, I will hear. The wolf and the lamb shall feed together, and the lion shall eat straw like the bullock: and dust shall be the serpent's meat. They shall not hurt nor destroy in all my holy mountain, saith the Lord. (Isaiah 65:20-25)

And he shall send Jesus Christ, which before was preached unto you: Whom the Heaven must receive until the times of restitution of all things, which God hath spoken by the mouth of all his holy prophets since the world began. (Acts 3:20-21)

Justice Ministries that God is raising up and protecting

The very meaning of righteousness is justice, which is the foundation of the throne of the Kingdom. God's heart is justice for His creation, which was wreaked by satanic darkness. He dealt with the sin problem at the Cross, and brought forth a new creation at the Resurrection of Jesus to reorganize the Earth under the Kingdom of God. This has been taking place since 30 AD and will continue to take place until the last enemy, death, is removed. The greatest justice is the forgiveness of sin, which the Cross wrought in Christ. To bring healing and forgiveness to every region of the Earth is God's justice.

This is the heart of one such ministry that God is raising up today: **Expression58.org**

As Cornel West said "*Justice is love in public. We believe that justice is the restoration of every violation of love, and setting the world right again is what Jesus came to do. As a community, we are committed to seeking God about the injustices of our day and courageously taking action to bring hope and healing. Life is precious, and justice is beautiful. Jesus modeled love, creativity, and justice so brilliantly and lived Isaiah 58 to the fullest. At Expression 58 our desire is that as we pursue Jesus, we become like him. May our lives be full of his love, expanded by his creativity, and empowered to bring His justice*".

Another justice ministry is **Justice Rising**. They literally go into war torn areas and seek to bring restoration and justice - **Justicerising.org**

Justice Rising targets areas with active conflict and unrest. We're drawn to the places that are often written off or deemed "impossible" due to ongoing instability. After years of sitting with people during war and hearing stories from refugees, victims of rape and child soldiers, our hearts were broken over the devastation. It was from that place of compassion that our projects were launched.

The vision of Justice Rising is to see every war affected nation restored to peace. Justice Rising brings peace to communities affected by war by educating children at risk, creating sustainable jobs, and developing community leaders.

The ministry of Justice Rising has a story of being in a war torn area of Africa, where the soldiers and war Lords are still bringing destruction to the land and people. One such soldier, hyped up on drugs, was running toward their gathering. A pastor and a few women around him were meeting, and the soldier charged into their room and said, *"Everybody will die, and I will make her my wife"*, as he pointed to one of the women. The pastor boldly spoke up and said, *"I have a better plan. You are going to drop to your knees and let us pray for you."* The soldier dropped to their knees and they took authority over the situation, bringing salvation to the man eventually. After that happened, many other of the soldiers were saved and transformed. This brought the beginnings of hope and change to that region.

God is with a ministry like that, to guide them and protect them in very supernatural ways. I believe the days ahead will bring an end to Islam and every false religion until only the religion of Christ remains.

Here is a quote from Origen (182 AD - 254 AD) – *"Every form of worship will be destroyed except the religion of Christ, which will alone prevail. And indeed it will one day triumph, as its principles take possession of the minds of men more and more every day."*

This is the ultimate hope of the advancing Kingdom, that the Kingdom of God will completely cover the Earth. Apostolic faith lives with this in mind, not expecting things to get worse, but to get better and better.

Here is another quote from David Chilton (1951 – 1997) – *"Instead of a message of defeat, the Bible gives us hope, both in this world and the next. The Bible gives us an eschatology of dominion, an eschatology of victory. This is not some blind "everything-will-work-out-somehow" kind of optimism. It is a solid, confident, Bible-based assurance that, before the Second Coming of Christ, the gospel will be victorious throughout the whole world."*

This was the thinking of the early Church, but throughout the history of the Church, doctrines became twisted, and hope for the future became dim. Better Covenant Theology restores the message of hope and victory for the days ahead, unlike any of the other systems of theology.

The Restoration of The 5-Fold Ministry

The term 5-fold ministry refers to the offices of Apostle, Prophet, Evangelist, Pastor and Teacher. This is found in Ephesians 4:11.

The model of the Church that I have seen most of my life in the U.S.A. is a dispensational Church led by a pastor, with a board of deacons or elders. Most of these Churches would teach that there are no apostles or prophets today, but the pastor-teacher (they group these 2 callings together). The evangelist is the one who travels from town to town, living on love offerings, and preaching convicting sermons about the wages of sin in order to get people a ticket to Heaven.

To understand the Kingdom correctly is to understand that God has not withdrawn any gift or any power available to His saints to accomplish the work of the ministry. The purpose of the 5-fold, as defined in Ephesians 4:

So Christ himself gave the apostles, the prophets, the evangelists, the pastors and teachers, to equip his people for works of service, so that the body of Christ may be built up until we all reach unity in the faith and in the knowledge of the Son of God and become mature, attaining to the whole measure of the fullness of Christ. Then we will no longer be infants, tossed back and forth by the waves, and blown here and there by every wind of teaching and by the cunning and craftiness of people in their deceitful scheming. Instead, speaking the truth in love, we will grow to become in every respect the mature body of him who is the head, that is, Christ. From him the whole body, joined and held together by every supporting ligament, grows and builds itself up in love, as each part does its work. (Ephesians 4:11-16)

The purpose of the 5-fold ministry is twelve-fold:

1. To perfect or mature the saints.
2. To teach the saints to do work of the ministry.
3. To build up the Body of Christ.

4. To bring the Body to the unity of faith.

5. To bring the Body the knowledge of the Son of God.

6. To help the Body become like Jesus, a perfect Man.

7. To bring the Body to the fullest measure of Christ.

8. To help children grow into mature adults in the Body of Christ.

9. To establish apostolic doctrine along with Kingdom eschatology, that we may not be deceived.

10. To grow the Body into the Head, Jesus, through love.

11. To cause the Body to be rightly fitted and aligned together, through love, sound doctrine, common faith and fellowship, to have the same baptism in the Spirit, as well as the same Lord and Kingdom.

12. To cause the Body to function and supply each part, by grace, that the Body may grow in love.

There were more than 12 apostles mentioned in the Bible. Actually, a total of 25 held the office.

The following was taken from an article written by B. Mark Anderson, dated May 20, 2013, titled, "How many apostles in the New Testament – 12 or 25?"

An investigation of the Scripture reveals several individuals in addition to the original twelve who are explicitly referred to as apostles. We might call them "apostles of the throne ", "apostles of the Lamb" or "ascension-gift apostles." A complete listing of New Testament apostles follows.

James, the half-brother of Jesus and leader of the Jerusalem Church - Galatians 1:19

Barnabas - Acts 14:14

Paul - Acts 14:14 and many other references

Apollos - Corinthians 4:6-9

Timothy and Silvanus - 1 Thessalonians 1:1 and 2:6

Epaphroditus - Philippians 2:25. While the King James Version translates the word as "messenger", the Greek word (apostolon) is actually "apostle".

Two unnamed apostles - Corinthians 8:23. A brother of fame among the Churches, and a brother tested - *"As for our brethren, they are messengers of the Churches, a glory to Christ."* Again, the Greek word is "apostoloi" but is translated here as "messengers".

These nine now make a total of 22 (13 + 9 = 22).

Andronicus and Junia - Romans 16:7 *"Salute Andronicus and Junia, my kinsmen, and my fellow prisoners, who are of note among the apostles, who also were in Christ before me."* Were these genuine apostles or were they, as some (Charles Ryrie and others) translate, "well-known to the apostles"? If we count Andronicus and Junia, the total jumps to 24.

How Many Apostles?

Finally, Hebrews 3:1 designates **Jesus Christ** the *"Apostle and High Priest of our profession."* That makes 25 apostles in the New Testament!

Here are a few instances of prophets in the New Testament who were operating as New Covenant prophets during a covenant transition period. We live in a fuller version of the New Covenant, which is why we must understand these things by way of revelation in the heart and mind:

During this time some prophets came down from Jerusalem to Antioch. (Acts 11:27)

Now in the Church at Antioch there were prophets and teachers: Barnabas, Simeon called Niger, Lucius of Cyrene, Manaen (who had been brought up with Herod the tetrarch) and Saul. (Acts 13:1)

Judas and Silas, who themselves were prophets, said much to encourage and strengthen the believers. (Acts 15:32)

And as we tarried there many days, there came down from Judaea a certain prophet, named Agabus. (Acts 21:10)

And God has placed in the Church first of all apostles, second prophets, third teachers, then miracles, then gifts of healing, of helping, of guidance, and of different kinds of tongues. Are all apostles? Are all prophets? Are all teachers? Do all work miracles? (1 Corinthians 12:28-29)

But the one who prophesies speaks to people for their strengthening, encouraging and comfort. (1 Corinthians 14:3)

If anyone thinks they are a prophet or otherwise gifted by the Spirit, let them acknowledge that what I am writing to you is the Lord's command. (1 Corinthians 14:37)

The next Scripture I give is one that I feel is misused today, in the modern apostolic movement. It's a Scripture from Ephesians about how the Church is built on the foundation of the apostles and prophets.

Consequently, you are no longer foreigners and strangers, but fellow citizens with God's people and also members of his household, built on the foundation of the apostles and prophets, with Christ Jesus himself as the chief cornerstone. (Ephesians 2:19-20)

I do not believe that verse is saying the current Church is built upon the foundation of current apostles and prophets. I believe Paul was teaching covenantally here and stating that the Church is built upon the foundation of the Kingdom teachings of the Lord's apostles (which we have in the Bible), and the Old Testament prophets who spoke of the end of the Old Covenant and the establishing of the New Covenant.

Therefore, we are forever connected to the story of the Bible, being built upon the foundation of what it teaches. The problem is, much of the Church has narrowed down what the Bible teaches and missed the reality of the Kingdom along with many other things.

Dispensationalism is such a crippling disease to the Church. Dispensationalism puts the Scriptures about the destruction of Jerusalem in 70 AD off into our future, which is where the ideas of pre-tribulation, mid-tribulation, or post-tribulation, in regards to when the rapture occurs, come from. My understanding of the Bible is that there is no rapture, and the great tribulation happened in 70 AD. Understanding those two facts helps to rebuild a new system of belief based on the Bible.

What remains to be done is to advance the Kingdom and colonize the Earth to be like Heaven, not seek to escape the Earth. We are the royalty, the ambassadorial priestly sons of God, who carry the authority of the name of their King, Jesus, in all we do. The Church needs to become free in its thinking again, and allow this seemingly new, yet not new, system of theology called Kingdom Eschatology or Better Covenant Theology to come in to what we believe. The purpose of God is to ultimately reveal His glorious Kingdom in all the Earth, with no separation between God and redeemed man.

When we come to the office of evangelist, this is one who declares the good news. Well, that sounds like something we all do, or we all could do, but the truth is, there are certain ones who do it so well. They are gifted as Kingdom evangelists, and they carry good news everywhere they go. I preach and teach good news, but I do not carry it everywhere I go. Most of the time, the preacher is preaching to himself as well, knowing his own struggles with trusting God fully.

There are those everywhere who are true evangelists. They may be schoolteachers, homemaker moms, dads coaching the baseball team, or police officers. This can never been confined to the four walls of the Church, because evangelism is a lifestyle. Christians are commonly called "evangelicals", meaning we work at getting people saved and spreading the word everywhere we go. A true evangelist makes it look so easy to win someone to the Lord, but many times we do it and stumble through a presentation of the gospel. We need evangelists in the Church and in the community, but we also need the office of the evangelist to model what it looks like to joyfully share Christ as a Kingdom evangelist.

During the 1940's and 1950's in America, "healing evangelists" were setting up their big tents and traveling all over the country declaring that Jesus saves and heals people to demonstrate the Kingdom. I don't know if they knew they were demonstrating the Kingdom or not, but God was at work doing something powerful in this country. Some caught it and others mocked it and disbelieved. Some of the healing evangelists fell from grace and put a black eye on the ministry of others. Jesus was the Healing Evangelist. He carried the good news of the Kingdom and demonstrated His Kingdom everywhere He went.

The pastor has come to be the top name of leadership in the Church today, in most circles. The term apostle is gaining momentum with greater understanding of the Kingdom and the 5-fold ministry. We all can see Jesus as a Shepherd, and Psalm 23 is so close to our hearts, about the Shepherd feeding and tending the sheep. Yet, the pastor is rarely mentioned in the Bible.

To the elders among you, I appeal as a fellow elder and a witness of Christ's sufferings who also will share in the glory to be revealed: Be shepherds of God's flock that is under your care, watching over them-not because you must, but because you are willing, as God wants you to be; not pursuing dishonest gain, but eager to serve; not Lording it over those entrusted to you, but being examples to the flock. And when the Chief Shepherd appears, you will receive the crown of glory that will never fade away. (1 Peter 5:1-4)

Peter gives the idea that all the elders should function as a pastor, feeding the sheep and taking care of the flock they have been entrusted with. I have noticed there are those in the Body of Christ who truly have a pastor's heart. They may not hold the position in the Church, but they function in it in daily life, in the work place, in the shopping center, wherever they go, because it's a part of who they are. As leaders in a Church, the role of pastoring is always there, because people are under your care. The pastor of a Church today, is functioning as a pastor, taking care of the people, feeding them, tending to them, praying for them, counseling them, but the person in that position as leader of the Church may actually be an apostle, or a teacher, or a prophet, or maybe an evangelist. For example, the evangelist/pastor leader of a

Church is the one who thinks everyone should be an evangelist. I was in a Church like that once. The pastor was an evangelist and he thought everyone should be one. I remember it put great pressure on some people who were not comfortable operating as an evangelist. When we don't understand our role and our identity in a Church, especially as leaders, then we can bring harm with the good we also try to bring.

I look forward to a day when we are not afraid to recognize that someone is an apostle or prophet or teacher in the Body of Christ. I am an apostolic teacher in the Body of Christ, meaning my gift is of the 5 fold, the apostolic group, who are leaders in the Church. Some travel as leaders, and others serve a local Body. With the Internet, Facebook, Blogs, and You Tube videos available today, we can speak to a larger audience and help bring unity around the world for the Body of Christ. I believe Better Covenant Theology and Kingdom Eschatology are still in the infancy state, but will grow more and more to help the Body come into a greater maturity with love. David Chilton, in the 1980's, carried this message of Kingdom Eschatology when no one else would. He died at the age of 46 in 1997. I have wondered if the great weight he was under brought about his untimely and early death as he seemingly alone carried that heavy and controversial message.

Each office of the 5 fold is to train others to do what they do. The apostle oversees all the others. The prophets train the Church to be prophetic. The evangelist trains the Church to be evangelistic and carry the good news. The pastor draws the Church together and trains the Church to care for one another. The teacher teaches the doctrines and deep things of the Word, bringing the topics of atonement or eschatology so that the Church would understand the Kingdom they are a part of. The Word of God is Jesus. The Bible is the written record of the covenant journey of God with humanity. Unless the teachers learn the depth of the Word, the Body of Christ will be crippled in their understanding of things like "the end times", or "the Cross", or "Israel", and so many topics we can find people debating about. Jonathan Welton is an apostle and a teacher, who carries the heart of learning the truth of Scripture. So much of what is taught in the Church today may sound good, and it may have pieces of truth in it, but overall, there is error being mixed with the truth. It's like mixing the message in the Old Covenant with the message of the New Covenant. It creates a toxic brew that helps no one. Many things taught in the Church today about God create fear, not love. These are things the teachers in the Body of Christ need to continue to straighten out. Some think it's arrogant to think you can straighten out teaching in the Body, but that is what we are called to do as teachers, yet we do it with love and patience.

The Apostolic Kingdom of God

"Again Jesus said: Peace be with you! As the Father has sent me, I am sending you" (John 20:21). This is the heart of the apostolic, which means, "sent". It's the idea of dispersing the message and glory of the New Covenant Kingdom of God throughout all the Earth. The idea of an apostle was taken from the Roman Empire's government.

Whenever Roman armies conquered a land and a people, the next step was for the government to send an "apostolic delegation" into the newly conquered land and begin to teach the people how to be good citizens of Rome. They would show them the clothes to wear, the food to eat, the things to drink, the customs, the rituals, the pagan religions, their gods (Zeus, Jupiter, etc.), and most of all, the cult of Emperor worship. The Emperor was a god, a king, and worthy of worship and sacrifice.

The idea was to get that land, eventually, to look like the rest of the Roman Empire, so that when the king visits, he will feel at home.

God has always planned that planet Earth would be a reflection of His Heavenly Kingdom and that mankind would be a reflection of Him. This is the work of the apostolic Kingdom, to bring Heaven on Earth.

The Kingdom Advancing

There are those that believe that the Kingdom will arrive all at once in the future. They say that God's Kingdom will instantly triumph over all the powers of the devil when it finally appears.

This idea comes from thinking that we are currently in the "Church age."

Here are a few Scriptures that describe the advancing and ever increasing Kingdom:

The Kingdom of Heaven is like a mustard seed planted in a field. It is the smallest of all seeds, but it becomes the largest of garden plants; it grows into a tree, and birds come and make nests in its branches. (Matthew 13:31-32)

The Kingdom of Heaven is like the yeast a woman uses in making bread. Even though she puts only a little yeast in three measures of flour, it permeates every part of the dough. (Matthew 13:33)

As Daniel 2:44 says:

In the time of those kings, the God of Heaven will set up a kingdom that will never be destroyed, nor will it be left to another people. It will crush all those kingdoms and bring them to an end, but it will itself endure forever.

This verse is reminiscent of Isaiah 9:7, which says, "*Of the increase of His government and peace there shall be no end...*" (Isaiah 9:7; NKJV). The nature of the Kingdom of God is ever progressing - always expanding, never retreating, and continually growing. Take, for example, the following five progressive statements from Scripture. The Word says that we move from:

1. Brighter to Brighter

The path of the righteous is like the first gleam of dawn, shining ever brighter till the full light of day. (Proverbs 4:18 NIV)

2. Grace to Grace

And of His fullness we have all received, and grace for grace. (John 1:16 NKJV)

3. Strength to Strength

They go from strength to strength... (Psalm 84:7 NKJV)

4. Faith to Faith

For in it the righteousness of God is revealed from faith to faith; as it is written, "The just shall live by faith. (Romans 1:17 NKJV)

5. Glory to Glory

...For the Earth will be filled with the knowledge of the Lord as the waters cover the sea. (Isaiah 11:9 NKJV)

For the Earth will be filled with the knowledge of the glory of the Lord, as the waters cover the sea. (Habakkuk 2:14 NKJV)

But truly, as I live, all the Earth shall be filled with the glory of the Lord. (Numbers 14:21 NKJV)

It is important to understand that Jesus set up His Kingdom upon His first visit. The idea of God's Kingdom is one of continual growth and expansion. One-third of humanity belongs to Jesus, according to research. The population will continue to grow, and I believe, Christianity will continue to increase, with the decrease of Islam and all other religions.

Jesus said that All Authority both in Heaven and on Earth was now His. That means the Earth is not going down, but coming up. Heaven and Earth will one day fuse together again, and Resurrected people will live with God in a Heaven and Earth reality. You can see we have that today, but it's a faith relationship. In the age of Resurrection, we will not live by faith, but by reality.

I hope the content of this book has helped you understand the Bible in a new way.

THE END

Made in the USA
Lexington, KY
19 September 2016